DI

Advance Praise for
Digital Transformation

"Tom Siebel's *Digital Transformation* should alarm every CEO and government leader about the simultaneous arrival of an existential technological threat—and an historic opportunity. A must-read for every leader in business and government."

—Robert M. Gates,
Former U.S. Secretary of Defense

"Siebel explains why business evolution is speeding up, ushering in a new era of real-time data analysis and prediction. *Digital Transformation* is a top-priority read for CEOs and boards."

—Rich Karlgaard,
Publisher and Futurist, *Forbes*

"Digital technology is changing the world with breath-taking speed. In a clearly written book that combines market-tested experience and piercing insight, Tom Siebel provides leaders with the advice they need to guide organizations."

—Christopher L. Eisgruber,
President, Princeton University

"With great panache, Tom Siebel provides readers with an insightful insider's guide to the risks and opportunities posed by the confluence of four technologies: cloud computing, big data, the internet of things, and artificial intelligence. It should be essential reading for decision-makers within any public or private organization that hopes to navigate the challenges posed by digital transformation with clarity and vision."

—Anantha P. Chandrakasan,
Dean of the School of Engineering, MIT

"In *Digital Transformation*, Tom Siebel describes how the disruptive technologies of artificial intelligence, cloud computing, big data, and the internet of things are propelling massive changes in how nations, industries, and corporations function. Throughout the book, he offers valuable advice to corporations and individuals working in this transforming landscape."

—Robert J. Zimmer,
President, University of Chicago

"Tom Siebel describes the monumental importance of the ongoing digital transformation in historical context by way of compelling examples, at a level that can be easily understood by anyone broadly familiar with business or the tech industry. *Digital Transformation* is an excellent introduction to an important topic."

—Zico Kolter,
Assistant Professor, Computer Science, Carnegie Mellon University

"Tom Siebel provides a cogent and accessible explanation of this new generation of information technologies, and he gives a clear account of the specific nature of its disruptive effect upon commerce and government. This book is an essential roadmap for leaders in business and government."

—Richard Levin,
22nd President of Yale University

"Bracingly written and vigorously argued, his book is essential reading for anyone seeking to understand the revolutionary technological changes transforming our world."

—Carol Christ,
Chancellor, University of California, Berkeley

"Tom Siebel, long-time IT visionary, has demonstrated via his pioneering company C3.ai that AI can positively transform a breathtaking array of sectors. He convincingly explains how AI, if we ensure security, privacy, and ethical implementation, will improve the security and health of the planet and all its inhabitants."

—Emily A. Carter,
Dean, School of Engineering, Princeton University

"Siebel more than makes the case for why transformation is imperative—presenting the world-changing opportunities and challenges jointly brought about by cloud computing, big data, IoT, and AI."

—Ian A. Waitz,
Vice Chancellor, MIT

"Tom Siebel chose a deceiving title for his latest work. This book is really about our ability to predict the future. We are all mesmerized by our future and this explains why it is such a fascinating read."

—Francesco Starace,
CEO, Enel

"After four decades as a thought leader as well as a very successful entrepreneur, Tom Siebel has gathered in this fascinating book the knowledge that every executive should have on all critical digital technologies: big data, IoT, the cloud, and of course, AI."

—Isabelle Kocher,
CEO, ENGIE

"A must-read for any CEO trying to navigate the digital age maze. Tom's personal digital success and clear explanations about how it works and how to do it as a CEO make this a compelling study for CEOs."

—Dave Cote,
Chairman and CEO, Honeywell (Retired)

"*Digital Transformation* is an essential read for those in charge of today's economic, political, and social systems, and a call to action for those who will look after our world's safe and prosperous future."

—Andreas Cangellaris,
Vice Chancellor and Provost, University of Illinois at Urbana-Champaign

"This book is a compelling read for those of us who may not be deep into the technology but are trying to reshape businesses and industries. Tom is one of those unique individuals who has the credibility and experience to speak to both."

—Tilak Subrahmanian,
Vice President, Energy Efficiency, Eversource Energy

"Tom Siebel is, simply said, one of Silicon Valley's most outstanding entrepreneurs and leaders. His new book offers a seminal description of the profound technologies that are colliding today, and that offer remarkable opportunities for those entrepreneurs and leaders who act passionately and swiftly."

—Jim Breyer,
Founder and CEO, Breyer Capital

"Following Tom Siebel's journey into the amazing digital world is both fascinating and threatening. He helps you see the coming challenges and offers a way to manage them as opportunities."

—Fabio Veronese,
Head of ICT Infrastructure & Networks Solution Center, Enel

"In this remarkable book, Tom Siebel is taking us through the dynamics of high tech from the Cambrian explosion to the latest developments of machine learning and AI. This deliberate long-term historical perspective is giving us the keys to understand in depth the industry that propels the world into the 21st century."

—Yves Le Gélard,
Chief Digital Officer and Group CIO, ENGIE

"This is a brilliant, rigorous, and visionary analysis of the dramatic and disruptive impact of digital transformation on our post-industrial society. With his unique talent and experience, Tom Siebel has captured and clearly outlined the main challenges of the technology transition that we are facing."

—Marco Gilli,
Rector (Ret.) and Professor of Electrical Engineering at Politecnico di Torino;
"Scientific Attaché" at the Embassy of Italy in the USA

"Tom Siebel's *Digital Transformation* is a marvelous and timely book. The author's historical placement of the subject and his thorough grasp of the capabilities of next generation digital technology make for an excellent read."

—Tim Killeen,
President, University of Illinois

"This book will force you to think about the effects of digital transformation on your business and will change your perspective."

—Cristina M. Morgan,
Vice Chairman, Technology Investment Banking, J.P. Morgan

"Tom brilliantly surveys the tectonic forces at work and persuasively expresses the urgency with which industry CEOs and policymakers must adapt to this new reality or become extinct."

—Brien J. Sheahan,
Chairman and CEO, Illinois Commerce Commission

"Everyone talks about digital transformation, and here is our chance to actually understand and execute it well."

—Jay Crotts,
Chief Information Officer, Royal Dutch Shell

"Tom Siebel envisions a world in which the risks are as great as the rewards, a world transformed by technologies equipped with the freedom and force of mind. His book is both an inspiration and a warning. To ignore it is to make a serious mistake."

—Lewis H. Lapham,
Editor, *Lapham's Quarterly*; Former Editor, *Harper's Magazine*

"Few people are as well-suited to bring together the business, technical, and historical perspective that Tom so cogently weaves together. I recommend this book to any business leader who wants to cut through the buzzwords and understand how we got to where we are today."

—Judson Althoff,
Executive Vice President, Worldwide Commercial Business, Microsoft

"With *Digital Transformation*, Tom Siebel has brilliantly provided much more than an essential survival guide for organizations in the Information Age. He charts a true course for both civilian and military leaders and their teams to successfully navigate the turbulent waters of dynamic change towards much greater security and human value for global society."

—Vice Admiral Dennis McGinn,
U.S. Navy, Retired; Former Assistant Secretary of the Navy

"The book is a must-read for any executive who needs to understand both the challenges and also the opportunities of where the world is headed during this time of frame-breaking change."

—Robert E. Siegel,
Lecturer, Stanford Graduate School of Business

"Business is fundamentally different in the 21st century, and digital transformation is more urgent than ever. The difference between thriving or becoming the next Blockbuster or Kodak is how far businesses are willing to go in setting their organization up to compete digitally. *Digital Transformation* provides the clearest blueprint yet for leaders looking to reinvent their businesses across information technology, operations, culture, and business models."

—Aaron Levie,
Co-founder and CEO, Box

Digital Transformation

Survive and Thrive in an Era of Mass Extinction

Thomas M. Siebel

Foreword by
The Hon. Condoleezza Rice

RosettaBooks

NEW YORK 2019

First edition published 2019 by RosettaBooks

Cover design by Regan McCamey
Interior design by Scribe Inc. and Jay McNair
Illustrations by Alberto Mena

ISBN-13 (print): 978-1-9481-2248-1
ISBN-13 (ebook): 978-0-7953-5264-5

Library of Congress Cataloging-in-Publication Data

Names: Siebel, Thomas M., author.
Title: Digital transformation : survive and thrive in an era of mass
   extinction / by Thomas M. Siebel.
Description: New York : RosettaBooks, 2019. | Includes bibliographical
   references.
Identifiers: LCCN 2019012706 (print) | LCCN 2019017316 (ebook) |
   ISBN 9780795352645 (ebook) | ISBN 9781948122481 (print)
Subjects: LCSH: Digital electronics--Social aspects. | Technological
   innovations--Social aspects. | Information society. | Success in business.
Classification: LCC HM851 (ebook) | LCC HM851 .S5483 2019 (print) | DDC
   303.48/33--dc23

www.RosettaBooks.com
Printed in Canada

RosettaBooks

CONTENTS

A Call to Action

Over the years as an advisor to business leaders and in my own roles in government, I have learned firsthand the importance of identifying risks and opportunities—their sources, their scope, and their potential impact on the achievement of key goals. In his new book, Tom Siebel takes on what is simultaneously one of the largest risks and greatest opportunities facing both public- and private-sector organizations globally: digital transformation. Tom's book brings much-needed clarity to a critical subject that, while widely discussed, remains poorly understood.

As Tom lays out in the pages of this book, the confluence of four major technological forces—cloud computing, big data, artificial intelligence, and the internet of things—is causing a mass extinction event in industry after industry, leaving in its wake a growing number of organizations that have either ceased to exist or have become irrelevant. At the same time, new species of organizations are rapidly emerging, with a different kind of DNA born of this new digital age.

Thus far we have seen the most prominent effects of this tsunami-like wave of digital transformation in industries like retail, advertising, media, and music at the hands of digital-age companies such as Amazon, Google, Netflix, and Spotify. Digital transformation has created whole new industries and business models—on-demand transportation services like Uber and Didi Chuxing; lodging services like Airbnb and Tujia; and digital marketplaces such as OpenTable in the restaurant industry and Zillow in real estate. In the not-too-distant future, digital transformation is poised to reinvent the automotive sector with the arrival of self-driving technologies powered by artificial intelligence like Waymo.

We are beginning to see signs of digital transformation in financial services, as hundreds of fintech startups—backed by billions of dollars in venture capital—are eating away at every piece of the financial services value chain, from investment management and insurance to retail banking and payments.

In complex asset-intensive industries such as oil and gas, manufacturing, utilities, and logistics, digital transformation is taking hold through the deployment of applications powered by artificial intelligence, driving dramatic gains in productivity, efficiency, and cost savings. While not as widely publicized or visible as the digital transformation of consumer industries, these asset-intensive industries are undergoing massive change resulting in substantial economic and environmental benefits.

It is only a matter of time until digital transformation sweeps across every industry. No company or governmental agency will be immune to its impact. In my conversations with business executives and government leaders globally, digital transformation ranks at or near the top of their concerns and priorities.

At a nation-state level, the degree to which countries embrace and enable digital transformation today will determine their competitive stance and economic well-being for decades to come. History teaches that those who take the lead in technological revolution—which today's digital transformation most certainly is—reap the greatest rewards. The imperative to act, and to act swiftly, is clear and present.

No discussion of digital transformation would be complete without an account of its impact on national and global security. As Tom makes clear, artificial intelligence will have a profound role in determining national military capabilities and relations among the world's leading powers. Tom's realistic assessment of the global competition for AI leadership, and what it implies for the future, will surely capture the attention of business and government leaders.

Few people are as well qualified as Tom Siebel to help organizations understand and successfully navigate the challenges of digital transformation. For nearly a decade, I have had the privilege of working closely with Tom in my role as an outside director on the board of C3.ai—the company Tom founded and leads as CEO, which provides a technology platform specifically designed to enable enterprise digital transformation. Informed by a career that spans four decades as a technologist, business executive, and entrepreneur, Tom brings a unique perspective to the subject of digital transformation. He has gained the trust and respect of business and government leaders around the world.

In this book, Tom explores specific examples and case studies based directly on the experiences of organizations C3.ai works with around the globe. These are real-world digital transformation initiatives—some of the largest of their kind ever undertaken—at organizations such as 3M, Caterpillar, Royal Dutch Shell, and the U.S. Air Force.

Successful digital transformations, Tom writes in these pages, require the mandate and leadership of an organization's top executives: Digital transformation must be driven from the top down. While the intended readers of this book are CEOs and other senior leaders in both the private and public sectors globally—leaders who today are grappling with the risks and opportunities presented by digital transformation—every reader will learn much from Tom's insightful examination.

Like all accomplished entrepreneurs, Tom is both a constitutional optimist, always seeing a world of half-full glasses, and a person of vision and action. His goal is not just to help readers understand what digital transformation is but to provide actionable advice—based on proven experience—to help them move forward and achieve meaningful results. The CEO Action Plan he lays out at the conclusion of his book gives readers concrete guidance on how to get started with their digital transformation initiatives.

My advice to business and government leaders everywhere: Read this book. Study its lessons. Take its advice to heart. There is no better guide than Tom Siebel to show the way to digital transformation success.

Condoleezza Rice
Denning Professor in Global Business and the Economy,
Stanford University Graduate School of Business
Former U.S. Secretary of State
Former National Security Advisor
Former Provost, Stanford University

Post-Industrial Society

In 1980, as a graduate student at the University of Illinois at Urbana–Champaign, I happened upon an anthology at the Illini Union Bookstore, entitled *The Microelectronics Revolution: The Complete Guide to the New Technology and Its Impact on Society*, freshly published by the MIT Press.[1] The penultimate chapter, entitled "The Social Framework of the Information Society," was written by Daniel Bell.

My interest in this subject had been piqued by my classes in Operations Research and Information Systems—classes that led me to the computer lab to explore information technology in the early days of mainframe computing: CDC Cyber computers, FORTRAN, keypunch machines, and batch computing. I found it all quite fascinating. I wanted to know more.

I was particularly intrigued by Daniel Bell's big idea, first published in his book *The Coming Post-Industrial Society*, in 1973.[2]

Bell began his career as a journalist. He received his PhD from Columbia University in 1960 for the body of his published work and became a professor there in 1962.[3] In 1969, he was recruited to the faculty at Harvard, where he spent the balance of his career. He was a prolific writer, having published 14 books and hundreds of scholarly articles, and is perhaps most renowned for having coined the term "Post-Industrial Society."

Bell was a highly influential 20th-century American intellectual. In a 1974 study of the top 70 U.S. intellectuals who contributed most to widely circulated magazines and journals, Bell was ranked in the top 10.[4]

Professor Bell explored the developmental history of the structure of human economies and the evolution of the underlying philosophical thought behind those structures, in the context of economic trends and ongoing developments in information and communication technology.

Bell introduced the concept of the Post-Industrial Society and went on to predict a fundamental change in the structure of human economic and social interaction—a change with impact on the order of the Industrial Revolution—a change that he called "The Information Age."

Professor Bell theorized the emergence of a new social order—driven by and centered around information technology—dramatically altering the manner in which social and economic interactions are conducted. The way in which knowledge is promulgated and retrieved. The way in which we communicate. The way in which we are entertained. The manner in which goods and services are produced, delivered, and consumed. And the very nature of the livelihood and employment of humankind.

The Post-Industrial Society

Bell conceived of this idea before the advent of the personal computer, before the internet as we know it, before email, before the graphical user interface. He predicted that in the coming century, a new social framework would emerge based upon telecommunications that would change social and economic commerce; change the way that knowledge is created and distributed; and change the nature and structure of the workforce.[5]

The concept resonated. It was intuitively comfortable. It was consistent with my view of the world.

The term *post-industrial society* was used to describe a series of macroeconomic and social changes in the global economic structure on the order of magnitude of the Industrial Revolution. Bell developed his theory in the context of the history of economic civilization, positing three constructs: Pre-Industrial; Industrial; and Post-Industrial.

Pre-Industrial Societies

Bell described pre-industrial society as a game against nature. In a pre-industrial society, raw muscle power is applied against nature, primarily in extractive industries: fishing, mining, farming, forestry. The transformative energy is human. Muscle power is moderated by the vicissitudes of nature. There is a high dependence on natural forces: rain, sun, wind. The main social unit is the extended household. Pre-industrial societies are primarily agrarian structures in traditional manners of rhythm and authority. Productivity is low.[6]

In pre-industrial societies, power is held by those who control the scarcest resources, in this case land. The dominant figures are the landowners and the military. The economic unit is the farm or plantation. The means of power is direct control of force. Access to power is primarily determined by either inheritance or military invasion and seizure.[7]

Industrial Societies

Bell described goods-producing industrial societies as a game against fabricated nature. "The machine predominates," he wrote, "and the rhythms of life are mechanically paced: time is chronological, methodical, evenly spaced...it is a world of coordination in which men, materials, and markets are dovetailed for the production and distribution of goods."[8]

The game is about the aggregation of capital to establish manufacturing enterprises and apply energy to transform the natural into the technical.[9]

In industrial societies, the scarcest resource is access to various forms of capital, especially machinery. The essential economic unit is the company. The dominant figure is the business leader. The transformative energy is mechanical. The means of power is the indirect influence of the company. Bell argues that the function of organizations is to deal with the requirements of roles, not individuals. Power is determined by ownership of property, political stature, and technical skill. Access to power is through inheritance, patronage, and education.[10]

Post-Industrial Societies

A post-industrial society is about the delivery of services. It is a game between people. It is powered by information, not muscle power, not mechanical energy: "If an industrial society is defined by the quantity of goods as marking a standard of living, the post-industrial society is defined by the quality of life as measured by the services and amenities—health, education, recreation, and the arts—that are now available for everyone."[11] The core element is the professional, as he or she is equipped with the education and training to provide the skills necessary to enable the post-industrial society.[12] This portends the rise of the intellectual elite—the knowledge worker. Universities become preeminent. A nation's strength is determined by its scientific capacity.[13]

In a post-industrial society the primary resource is knowledge. Data becomes the currency of the realm. The most data—the greatest volume, the more accurate, the timelier—yields the most power. The central focus is the university. Researchers and scientists, including computer scientists, become the most powerful players. The class structure is determined by technical skills and levels of education. Access to power is provided by education.[14]

Bell traced the evolution of the U.S. economy from a pre-industrial agrarian society as recently as 1900, to an industrial society in the mid-century, to a post-industrial society by 1970. He supported his argument with an analysis of the U.S. workforce, showing the steady decline of farm workers and laborers from 50 percent of the workforce in 1900 to 9.3 percent in 1970. He showed the increase of white-collar service workers growing from 17.6 percent of the U.S. workforce in 1900 to 46.7 percent in 1970.[15] He provided the data showing the increase in "information workers" from 7 percent of the U.S. workforce in 1860 to 51.3 percent in 1980.[16]

Bell identified knowledge and data as the crucial values in the post-industrial era. He wrote:

> By information, I mean data processing in the broadest sense; the storage, retrieval, and processing of data become the essential resource for all economic and social exchanges. These include:
>
> (1) Data processing of records: payrolls, government benefits (e.g., social security), bank clearances, and the like. Data processing for scheduling: airline reservations, production scheduling, inventory analysis, product-mix information, and the like.
>
> (2) Data-bases: characteristics of populations as shown by census data, market research, opinion surveys, election data, and the like.[17]

The Information Age

In later writings, Bell introduced the idea of the emerging Information Age, an age that would be dominated by a new elite class of professional technocrats. He foretold of the day when scientists and engineers would replace the propertied bourgeoisie as the new ruling class.

It's hard to overstate the scale of Bell's vision for the Information Age. "If tool technology was an extension of man's physical powers," he wrote, "communication technology, as the extension of perception and knowledge, was the enlargement of human consciousness."[18]

Bell envisioned the confluence of technologies to create the Information Age. In the 19th and first half of the 20th century, the primary means of communication of information was through books, newspapers, journals, and libraries. In the second half of the 20th century, these were supplanted by the radio, television, and cable—encoded communications transmitted by radio wave or wire. The confluence of these technologies with the advent of the computer in the second half of the 20th century was the spark that initiated the Information Age.[19]

Bell identified five structural changes that would transpire to shape the Information Age:[20]

1. The confluence of telephone and computer communications into a single medium.

2. The replacement of printed media by electronic communications enabling electronic banking, electronic mail, electronic document delivery, and remote electronic news.

3. The dramatic expansion of television enhanced by cable communications, allowing for a panoply of specialized channels and services, linked to home terminals for immediate and convenient access.

4. The advent of the computer database as the primary centralized aggregator of the world's knowledge and information enabling interactive, remote group research and immediate personal access to homes, libraries, and offices.

5. A dramatic expansion of the education system through computer-aided education on virtually any subject immediately and remotely accessible at global scale.

Looking at the future from the perspective of 1970, Bell didn't miss much. The internet, email, cable and satellite TV, search engines, database technology—he even predicted the emergence of the enterprise application software industry. He clearly saw this development. By example he explicitly hypothesized the creation of a new, Information Age reservation industry: "This 'industry' sells its services to airlines, trains, hotels, theater box offices, and automobile rental companies through computerized data networks....If a single company created an efficient reservation network...it could sell to all these industries."[21]

As we look back on these predictions from the first quarter of the 21st century, it may all seem quite obvious. It is amazing that a man could predict this future a half century ago during a decade of stagflation and war, when the economy was dominated by General Motors, Exxon, Ford Motor Company, and General Electric. Exxon's revenues were one-tenth of what they are today. The Intel 4004 processor had just been invented. Its primary use was to enable electronic calculators that automated addition, subtraction, and other relatively simple mathematical calculations. The Home Brew Computer Club, the genesis that later sparked the invention of the personal computer, first convened two years after Bell published his book. The big names in computing were Control Data, Data General, Sperry—all irrelevant today. Information technology was a nascent industry. This man had great vision.

Much of the balance of my educational, professional, and community activity has been about pursuing this idea. Understanding this idea. Developing this idea. And attempting to contribute to the realization of this idea. It proved a point of inflection in my life. This idea drove me to enroll in the graduate school of engineering at the University of Illinois to pursue and complete a graduate degree in computer science.

Motivated to develop a fluency in the languages of engineering and information technology, I pursued a graduate education in those fields. This, in turn, brought me to Silicon Valley where I founded, managed, and financed companies. Served on corporate and university boards.

Engineering college boards. Business school boards. Published. Spoke. Built businesses.

My goal was to have a seat at the table as this vision to which I strongly subscribed played itself out. The years from 1980 to today in fact unfolded pretty much as Bell predicted. Information technology has grown from roughly a $50 billion industry in 1980 to a $3.8 trillion industry in 2018.[22] It is expected to reach $4.5 trillion by 2022.[23]

This is my fourth decade in the game. I have had the opportunity to have a seat at the table with the many giants who made this happen: Gordon Moore, Steve Jobs, Bill Gates, Larry Ellison, Lou Gerstner, Satya Nadella, Andy Jassy, and many others.

I have had the great privilege to be an innovator and active participant in the development of the database industry, enterprise application software industry, and internet computing.

As we power into the 21st century, it is clear to me that the trends identified by Daniel Bell are accelerating. We are seeing a new convergence of technology vectors including elastic cloud computing, big data, artificial intelligence, and the internet of things, the confluence of which enables us to address classes of applications that were inconceivable even 25 years ago. We can now develop prediction engines. This is what digital transformation is all about. This is when the fun starts.

Chapter 1

Punctuated Equilibrium

I am not sure history repeats itself, but it does seem to rhyme.[1] In management, I find one of the most important skills is pattern recognition: the ability to sort through complexity to find basic truths you recognize from other situations. As I approach my pursuits in information technology, my decisions and choices are made in historical context.

I recently addressed an investment conference in New York. There, I was intrigued by a discussion at lunch with Jim Coulter, a founder of Texas Pacific Group. Jim was thoughtfully wrestling with the similarities he saw between the dynamics of evolutionary biology and societal change. His talk highlighted the idea of evolution by "punctuated equilibrium"—a relatively new take on how and why evolution occurs. It piqued my curiosity, and I began to research the topic.

In his pioneering book *On the Origin of Species*,[2] Charles Darwin proposed that natural selection was the driving force of speciation and evolution. Darwinian evolution is a force of continuous change—a slow and unceasing accumulation of the fittest traits over vast periods of time. By contrast, punctuated equilibrium suggests that evolution occurs as a series of bursts of evolutionary change. These bursts often occur in response to an environmental trigger and are separated by periods of evolutionary equilibrium.

The reason this idea is so compelling is its parallel in the business world: Today we are seeing a burst of evolutionary change—a mass extinction among corporations and a mass speciation of new kinds of companies. The scope and impact of this change, and the evolution required for organizations to survive, are the focus of this book.

According to Darwinian natural selection, organisms morph gradually from one species into another. Species go through intermediate forms between ancestor and descendant. Thus all forms should persist

Discontinuity, Driven by Disruption, Is the Rule

Evolutionary development is marked by isolated episodes of rapid speciation between long periods of little or no change.

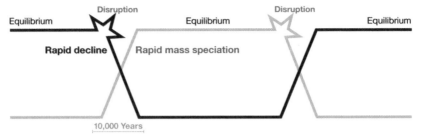

FIGURE 1.1

in the fossil record. Evolutionary biologists like Darwin relied heavily on fossils to understand the history of life. Our planet's fossil record, however, does not show the same continuity of form assumed by natural selection. Darwin attributed this discontinuity to an incomplete fossil record: dead organisms must be buried quickly to fossilize, and even then, fossils can be destroyed by geological processes or weathering.[3] This core assumption of *Origin* has been hotly debated and widely criticized since its publication in 1859. But no critic provided a viable alternative that could explain the scattered fossil record.

In geologic time, the fossil record shows discontinuity as the rule, not the exception. Evidence for the first forms of life dates back to about 3.5 billion years ago, as microscopic, single-celled organisms. These bacteria-like cells ruled the planet in evolutionary stability for almost 1.5 billion years—about a third of our planet's history. Fossils then show an explosion of diversity resulting in the three cell types that founded the three domains of life. One of those cell types was the first ancestor of everything that is commonly considered life today: animals, plants, fungi, and algae.

According to the fossil record, another 1.5 billion years passed in relative equilibrium before life on Earth experienced another evolutionary burst approximately 541 million years ago. This rapid diversification of multicellular life, known as the Cambrian Explosion, was vital to transforming simple organisms into the rich spectrum of life as we know it today. Over a time span of 20–25 million years—less than 1 percent of Earth's history—life evolved from prehistoric sea sponges to land-dwelling plants and animals. The basic body shape of every plant and animal species alive on the planet today can be traced back to organisms born of the Cambrian Explosion.[4]

The known fossil record indicates that species suddenly appear, persist, and more often than not, disappear millions or billions of years later.

In 1972, Darwin's foundational work in evolutionary theory was successfully reinterpreted in the context of such a punctuated fossil record. Evolutionary biologist and paleontologist Stephen Jay Gould published his new theory of evolution in *Punctuated Equilibrium*,[5] "hoping to validate our profession's primary data as signal rather than void."[6] *Punctuated Equilibrium* suggests that the absence of fossils is itself data, signaling abrupt bursts of evolutionary change rather than continuous, gradual transformations. According to Gould, change is the exception. Species stay in equilibrium for thousands of generations, changing very little in the grand scheme of things. This equilibrium is punctuated by rapid explosions of diversity, creating countless new species that then settle into the new standard.

An essential piece of this evolutionary theory is *scale*. In punctuated equilibrium, Gould focuses on species-wide patterns of evolution, whereas Darwinian evolution draws insight from the traits, survival, and reproduction of individual organisms through generations. A finch and its direct descendants, for example, will certainly show small changes in form as they are passed down through the generations. Much like agricultural corn has become plump and juicy from generations of breeding and interbreeding only the plumpest and juiciest kernels, finches with beaks that enable them to access and eat their main food source most easily will pass their beak structure on to future generations. Some finches have a longer beak to reach insects in small cracks; others have a thicker, stouter beak to crack open seeds. But the crucial point Gould makes is that a beak is still a beak—this is not a revolutionary innovation. It is the difference between graphite and ink, not pen and printing press.

Mass Extinction, Mass Diversification

When science and technology meet social and economic systems, you tend to see something like punctuated equilibrium. Something that has been stable for a long period suddenly disrupts radically—and then finds a new stability. Examples include the discovery of fire, the domestication of dogs, agriculture, gunpowder, the chronograph, transoceanic transportation, the Gutenberg Press, the steam engine, the Jacquard loom, the locomotive, urban electrification, the automobile, the airplane, the transistor, television, the microprocessor, and the internet. Each of these innovations collided with stable society, and then a little hell broke loose.

Sometimes hell literally does break loose on Earth. Natural disasters like volcanic eruptions, asteroid impacts, and climate change send life into an evolutionary tizzy. This does not just mean a burst of new species. Historically, evolutionary punctuations have been intimately linked with the widespread death of species. Especially the dominant ones. Over and over again.

Since the Cambrian Explosion, the cycle of evolutionary stasis and rapid diversification has become more frequent and more destructive with each repetition. Roughly 440 million years ago, 86 percent of species on Earth were eliminated in the Ordovician-Silurian extinction from mass glaciation and falling sea levels. Life on our planet nearly came to an end roughly 250 million years ago in what is often called "the Great Dying."[7] In this Permian-Triassic extinction, a whopping 96 percent of species became extinct due to enormous volcanic eruptions and subsequent global warming and ocean acidification. Perhaps most well known, 65 million years ago the combination of an asteroid impact in the Yucatán, volcanic activity, and the resultant climate change eliminated 76 percent of species on Earth—including the dinosaurs, a group of animals that had sustained itself successfully for over 150 million years of relative stasis.[8]

Evolutionary punctuations are responsible for the cyclic nature of species: inception, diversification, extinction, repeat.

In the past 500 million years, there have been five global mass extinction events. A minority of species survived. The voids in the ecosystem were then rapidly filled by massive speciation of the survivors. After the Cretaceous-Tertiary event, for example, the dinosaurs were replaced largely by mammals. And thank goodness. But for that, I would not be here to write, nor you to read.

Evolutionary Mass Extinction Events

Earth has witnessed five mass extinction events where as much as 96 percent of species disappeared because of environmental disruption.

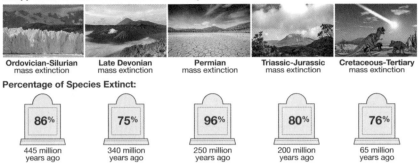

Ordovician-Silurian mass extinction	Late Devonian mass extinction	Permian mass extinction	Triassic-Jurassic mass extinction	Cretaceous-Tertiary mass extinction

Percentage of Species Extinct:

86%	75%	96%	80%	76%
445 million years ago	340 million years ago	250 million years ago	200 million years ago	65 million years ago

FIGURE 1.2

Evolutionary punctuations are not a matter of competitive advantage like beak size is; they are *existential*. This is the case in technology and society as much as in biology. Think horse-drawn carriages disappearing at the advent of automobiles. But it's not all doom and gloom. From mass extinction springs astonishing mass diversification.

The first known mass extinction in Earth's history was the Great Oxidation Event, about 2.45 billion years ago. Also known as the Oxygen Holocaust,[9] this was a global apocalypse. For the first half of our planet's history, there was no oxygen in the atmosphere. In fact, oxygen was poisonous to all life, and nearly all life that did exist resided in the oceans. The dominant species at the time were cyanobacteria, also known as blue-green algae. They were photosynthetic: using sunlight to produce fuel and releasing oxygen as a waste product. As the cyanobacteria flourished, the oceans, rocks, and ultimately the atmosphere were filled with oxygen. The cyanobacteria were literally poisoning themselves and became threatened as a species. Their populations plummeted, along with almost all other life on Earth.[10]

The anaerobic species—those that could not metabolize oxygen—died off or were relegated to the depths of the ocean where oxygen was minimal. Organisms that survived the Great Oxidation Event used oxygen to produce energy remarkably efficiently—16 times more so than anaerobic metabolism. Life had reinvented itself. Anaerobic life remained microscopic, concealed, and slow, while aerobic life bred faster, grew faster, and lived faster. Unsurprisingly, these survivors exploded into a dizzying array of pioneering new species that thrived on oxygen and finally ventured out of the ocean.[11] It was the first—and possibly greatest—mass extinction our planet has ever seen. But without it, the dinosaurs never would have existed in the first place for our mammal ancestors to replace them.

Every mass extinction is a new beginning.

Punctuated Equilibrium and Economic Disruption

I find the construct of punctuated equilibrium useful as a framework for thinking about disruption in today's economy. In the technology world, we often think about Moore's Law[12] providing the foundation for constantly increasing change, much like Darwinian evolution's constant accumulation of change. But that's not the way revolutionary evolution works.

The exponential trend described by Moore's Law—that the number of transistors on an integrated circuit doubles every two years at half the cost—is appropriate. But its application underestimates evolution. Just as profound biological evolution is not a measure of how quickly a finch's beak elongates, profound technological evolution is not a measure of how quickly the number of transistors on a circuit increases. Measures of evolutionary growth should not revolve around rates of change of innovations. Instead, they should focus on what brings about those revolutionary changes. History shows that punctuations themselves are occurring more and more frequently, causing more and more rapid upheavals of species and industries alike.

In the past million years alone, the world has experienced disruptive evolutionary punctuations on the average of every 100,000 years.[13] That's 10 punctuations in 1 million years. Compare that to five mass extinctions in 400 million years, and the singular Great Oxidation Event in the previous 3.3 billion years. Disruptive punctuations are clearly on the rise, and the periods of stasis in between punctuations are dwindling. This same pattern is evident in the industrial, technological, and social realms.

We see this in telecommunications. The telegraph revolutionized long-distance communication in the 1830s thanks to Samuel Morse.

Forty-five years later, Alexander Graham Bell disrupted telegraph communication with the first telephone. It took 40 years to place the first transcontinental call from New York City to San Francisco. Add another 40 years for the first wireless telecommunication with pagers. Only 25 years later, pagers and landline operators were massively disrupted by the first cell phones. The arrival of high-speed wireless, increased processing power, and touch screens led to the first "web phones" and then billions of smartphones starting in 2000.[14] We saw economic "speciation" from Motorola, Nokia, and RIM (maker of BlackBerry), each at one time dominating the market. The mobile phone industry was in turn upended with Apple's introduction of the iPhone in 2007. In the following decade, that has settled into a new stasis with Samsung, Huawei, and Oppo offering a set of products that look similar to the iPhone. Today the telecommunications industry is dominated by over 2.5 billion smartphone users.[15] And it hasn't even been 20 years!

The digital entertainment industry has seen similar accelerating punctuations driven by technology and social trends. The world's first movie theater, the Nickelodeon, opened its doors in 1905, exclusively showing motion pictures for the price of a nickel (hence its name). Fifty years later, in-home television decimated the theater industry. VHS tapes ruled the market for about 20 years until DVDs made them a relic. Now, DVDs and their evolutionary replacement, Blu-ray discs, have all but vanished in the market. The convergence of mobile and personal computing and the internet—with over-the-top video streaming services like Netflix, Hulu, and Amazon—has led to an explosion of professional and amateur video content and binge watching that is reshaping the video entertainment world.[16] Sorting out this change in an established industry is every bit as interesting and complex as the invention of the new technology.

Punctuations in the personal transportation industry have resulted in largely internal evolution. After the first automobile replaced human- and animal-powered vehicles, the general form of automobiles has remained remarkably stable, although nearly everything under the hood has changed. Sound familiar? Just as the Cambrian Explosion laid the foundation for the underlying body structures of all life in existence today, so too did the first automobiles define the basic form of all those that followed. Whatever replacements occurred, under the flesh or under the hood, they provided the same or enhanced functionality with improved performance. The steam engine, for example, was replaced by the gasoline engine in the early 20th century because it was lighter and more efficient, and gas was cheap, abundant, and readily available at the time.[17] Gas was risky—flammable and toxic—but the risk paid off. Sound familiar again? As the Great Oxidation Event did for life, this energy revolution allowed automobiles to go faster, longer, and stronger. After a period of relative equilibrium, the synchronous arrival of electric cars like Tesla; ride-sharing services like Uber and Lyft; and autonomous vehicle technologies like Waymo is now creating chaos in the industry. It will eventually settle into a new stasis.

The evidence suggests that we are in the midst of an evolutionary punctuation: We are witnessing a mass extinction in the corporate world in the early decades of the 21st century. Since 2000, 52 percent of the Fortune 500 companies have either been acquired, merged, or have declared bankruptcy. It is estimated that 40 percent of the companies in existence today will shutter their operations in the next 10 years. In the wake of these extinctions, we are seeing a mass speciation of innovative corporate entities with entirely new DNA like Lyft, Google, Zelle, Square, Airbnb, Amazon, Twilio, Shopify, Zappos, and Axios.

Merely following the trends of change is not enough. Just like organisms facing the Great Oxidation Event, organizations need to reinvent the way they interact with the changing world. They must recognize when an existing model has run its course, and evolve. They must create new, innovative processes that take advantage of the most abundant and available resources. They must prepare for future upheavals by developing systems with interchangeable parts: produce faster, scale faster, work faster. They must build something that will establish a clear existential advantage in order to survive into the new stasis and prosper.

Mass extinction and subsequent speciation don't just happen without reason. In the business world, I believe the causal factor is "digital transformation." Industries facing the wave of digital transformation are predicted to follow similar diversify-or-die trends as life during the Great Oxidation Event. While digitally transformed companies drive their industries to rise above the ocean, the rest are caught in the race to either learn to breathe again or go extinct.

This book attempts to describe the essence of digital transformation: what it is, where it comes from, and why it's essential to global industries. For now, suffice it to say that at the core of digital transformation is the confluence of four profoundly disruptive technologies—cloud computing, big data, the internet of things (IoT), and artificial intelligence (AI).

Enabled by cloud computing, a new generation of AI is being applied in an increasing number of use cases with stunning results. And we see IoT everywhere—connecting devices in value chains across industry and infrastructure and generating terabytes of data every day.

Yet few organizations today have the know-how to manage, let alone extract value from, so much data. Big data now pervade every aspect of business, leisure, and society. Businesses now face their own Oxygen Revolution: the Big Data Revolution. Like oxygen, big data are an important resource with the power to both suffocate and drive revolution. During the Great Oxidation Event, species began to create new channels of information flow, use resources more efficiently, and mediate connections previously unheard of, transforming oxygen from a lethal molecule into the source of life. Big data and AI, along with cloud computing and IoT, promise to transform the technoscape to a similar degree.

The history of life shows that established species whose survival depends on tried-and-true, perfectly functioning processes have no room for error, no room for innovation. Species that can only utilize a finite set of resources risk losing those resources as the world changes around them. Likewise, those who try to use new resources without the knowledge, instruments, or determination to process them will also fail. Companies that survive this punctuation will be truly digitally transformed. They will completely reinvent the way society, technology, and industry relate to one another. The resulting diversity of innovation is likely to be just as extraordinary as aerobic respiration, the Cambrian Explosion, and the human race.

It is nearly impossible to know what these innovations will look like at the end of an evolutionary punctuation like digital transformation. It is the dogged process of rapid innovation, constant learning through experience, and reiteration along the way that will make the difference between thriving existence and ultimate extinction. Companies that figure out how to breathe big data—how to harness the power of this new resource and extract its value by leveraging the cloud, AI, and IoT—will be the next to climb out of the data lake and master the new digital land.

Chapter 2

Digital Transformation

What is digital transformation? It arises from the intersection of cloud computing, big data, IoT, and AI, and it is vital to industries across the market today. Some describe it as the power of digital technology applied to every aspect of the organization.[1] Some refer to it as using digital technologies and advanced analytics for economic value, agility, and speed.[2]

I find it more valuable to describe digital transformation through examples. This is partly because we are in the midst of massive disruption and constant change. The scope of digital transformation and its implications are still evolving, and its impacts are still being understood. Each iteration—whether across companies or industries or even within a single organization—will bring new insights and layers to our understanding of digital transformation.

To be clear, digital transformation is not a series of generational changes in information technology or simply the migration of a company's processes, data, and information onto a digital platform. As industry analyst Brian Solis of Altimeter Group writes, "Investing in technology isn't the same as digital transformation."[3] I'll write more about this later.

This book will walk through the foundations of the current period of digital transformation and explain how companies can tackle digital transformation and avoid extinction. This is critical for companies of all sizes that risk extinction if they do not transform. It is particularly imperative for large incumbent organizations that face threats from smaller, nimbler players, that have the tools and data to potentially lead transformation.

To put digital transformation in context, let's take a step back and look at the previous waves of digital evolution. What we see is reminiscent of punctuated equilibrium—periods of stability followed by rapid change and disruption, resulting in new winners and losers. For those of us who've been in technology for several decades, we can retrace the waves of extraordinary productivity growth among organizations and governments. But we will see that the changes during past periods are vastly distinct from what we are experiencing today with digital transformation.

Something different and more profoundly disruptive is happening today. The first and second waves of innovation—digitalization and the internet—will be overwhelmed by the tsunami of digital transformation. Although digital transformation will bring about similar productivity benefits, these benefits will be achieved in a very different way.

The First Wave: Digitalization

Before workgroups started adopting personal computers in the 1980s, computing was entirely centralized. Mainframes were controlled by a small cadre of administrators, and you had to reserve time just to be able to use them. Mainframes and minicomputers were mostly used to perform calculations.

The arrival of the PC ushered in great flexibility. Workers could control their schedules and get work done more efficiently. Beyond just calculations, workers could perform tasks like word processing (with software applications such as WordStar, WordPerfect, and Microsoft Word) and graphic design (Corel Draw, PageMaker, Adobe Illustrator). With workgroup email systems, communications transformed. Digitalizing calculations, spreadsheets, and databases—previously created and maintained by hand—transformed hours, days, or months of human work into seconds of automated logic available by keyboard.

Soon, competing suites of desktop applications, email, operating systems with graphical user interfaces, lower-cost computers, modems, and laptops brought new worker productivity. Then several generations of desktop suites gave us sophisticated applications that replaced specialized systems—desktop publishing, graphics design systems (Apollo workstations, computer-aided design, or CAD, applications like Autodesk), and complicated multi-tab spreadsheets with formulas and algorithms that started to hint at what we can do with AI today.

All those improvements unlocked a huge wave of economic growth. Annual global GDP growth shot up from 2.5 percent between 1989 and 1995, to 3.5 percent between 1995 and 2003—a 38 percent increase in the rate of growth.[4] Digitalization made work easier, more accurate, and more automated.[5]

The Second Wave: The Internet

The Advanced Research Project Agency (ARPA, now known as the Defense Advanced Research Project Agency, or DARPA) was created in 1958, during the height of the Cold War. The U.S. was increasingly concerned about a potential Soviet Union attack to destroy the U.S. long-distance communications network. In 1962, ARPA and MIT scientist J.C.R. Licklider suggested connecting computers to keep communications alive in the event of a nuclear attack. This network came to be known as ARPANET. In 1986, the public network (National Science Foundation Network, or NSFNET) was separated from the military network, and connected university computer science departments. NSFNET became the internet backbone, linking emerging internet service providers (ISPs). Then came the hypertext transfer protocol (HTTP), the World Wide Web, the Mosaic web browser, and the broadening of the NSFNET for commercial use.[6] The internet was born.

The early instances of the web—such as the home pages of Yahoo! and Netscape—consisted of mostly static pages and a read-only, passive user experience. In the early 2000s, the emergence of Web 2.0 brought usability improvements, user-generated data, web applications, and interaction through virtual communities, blogs, social networking, Wikipedia, YouTube, and other collaborative platforms.

The first years of the internet caused disruption in business, government, education—every aspect of our lives. Innovative companies streamlined processes, making them faster and more robust than their analog counterparts. Automated human resources and accounting systems meant employee services and payroll operated faster and with fewer errors. Companies interacted with customers according to rule-based insights from customer relationship management (CRM) systems.

Before the internet, booking a vacation required human travel agents and potentially days-long planning spent poring over itineraries. And travel itself involved the hassle of paper itineraries, tickets, and maps. Consider pre-internet retail: physical stores, paper coupons, mail-order catalogs, and 800 numbers. Or pre-internet banking: trips to the branch office, paper checks, and jars of change. Investors scanned newspaper stock columns, spent time at the local library, or contacted a company directly to have a copy of the latest financial report sent to them by mail.

With the internet, these industries reaped enormous productivity boosts, and winners and losers emerged. Travel can now be booked via an app, providing instant mobile passes and tickets. Hotels can be compared on social sites. And a new "gig economy" emerged with apps for hiring cars, renting rooms, taking tours, and more. Retail became virtually frictionless: a global marketplace for mass merchandise and artisan handcrafts, one-click purchasing, scan and buy, almost anything delivered, faster supply chains for faster trend-to-stores, customer service via Twitter. Many new brands have emerged, and many (both old and new) have disappeared, as companies experimented with e-commerce and digital transactions.

In all these cases, processes were streamlined, but not revolutionized: they were the same analog processes, duplicated in digital form. But these market disruptions nonetheless caused shifts among companies, organizations, and individual behavior.

The Impact of Two Waves

Most of these productivity advancements typically fell under the control of an organization's traditional information technology (IT) function. They spurred productivity by using digital technologies to work more effectively and efficiently. They replaced human hours with computing seconds and dramatically streamlined the user experience across many industries. The 1990s through early 2000s saw the rise of the CIO as an important driver of innovation. Examples like Cisco's quarterly Virtual Close[7]—where the company could close its books and provide performance results in near-real-time—meant significant agility and business intelligence.

Most organizations started by digitizing non-real-time ("carpeted office") departments, where productivity gains were relatively low risk. Employee services such as HR were a relatively easy lift. Accounting was another early adopter, where decades of data processing underpinned the successive adoption of client-server applications, data center capabilities, and ultimately cloud solutions. Automation of customer-facing functions with CRM was another large step for organizations: internet sites enabled customers to research, buy, and access service via the web.

Some industries that rely heavily on information systems, such as finance, digitized core parts of their business early and rapidly, because the competitive advantages were extremely clear. For example, banks moved to high-speed trading where milliseconds could mean real money. They invested aggressively in data centers early on to provide speed and scale for bankers, along with flexibility and service for customers.

More recently, the chief marketing officer (CMO) has been frequently seen as the locus of digital transformation in many larger companies. A 2016 survey found that at 34 percent of large enterprises, ownership of digital transformation resided with the CMO.[8] This is likely because other business operations, such as sales, HR, and finance, have already digitalized with tools like CRM and enterprise resource planning (ERP). Marketing was one of the last support functions to digitalize.

The productivity gains from each of these transitions were significant and measurable. Faster internal communications and improved decision-making, smoother supply chain operations, increased revenue, better customer service, and higher customer satisfaction were just some of the benefits companies reaped from the rise of Web 2.0 technologies.

The impact of both the internet and the wave of digitalization that preceded it was primarily to digitize *existing competencies*. They were simply outsourced to a new worker: computers. But neither wave fundamentally changed the processes being replaced. They were just that—*replacements*. Think of airlines digitizing reservations and tickets, banks providing electronic account information and services, and Walmart digitizing its supply chain.

Similar to Darwin's finches, the first two waves of digital change gave industries new adaptations with which they could use existing resources more easily and effectively.

"Digitization was using digital tools to automate and improve the existing way of working without really altering it fundamentally or playing the new rules of the game," says technology strategist and veteran industry analyst Dion Hinchcliffe. Digital transformation "is a more caterpillar-to-butterfly process, moving gracefully from one way of working to an entirely new one, replacing corporate body parts and ways of functioning completely in some cases to capture far more value than was possible using low-scale, low-leverage legacy business."

Simply investing in technology to digitize existing functions and processes is not enough to truly transform a company or industry. It's a necessary ingredient, but not sufficient. Digital transformation demands revolutionary changes to key competitive corporate processes.

Pharmacies are a good example: Walgreen's and CVS have innovated with conveniences for customers to refill or check a prescription's status using an app, or to order medications by email. But they could be disrupted by newcomers, as we saw in early 2018 when Amazon, Berkshire Hathaway, and JP Morgan announced their intent to enter the market. Stocks of existing health care companies dropped in response to the news.

Banks invest heavily in IT and have dramatically improved customer service with flexible capabilities and tailored offerings. But they too face competition from upstarts like Rocket Mortgage and LendingTree in the U.S. and companies like Ant Financial and Tencent in China.

The way to maintain leadership is to innovate. Charles Schwab president and CEO Walt Bettinger notes that "successful firms disrupt themselves."[9] One notable example is the e-payment system Zelle, from Early Warning Services, that is owned jointly by a group of banks including Bank of America, BB&T, Capital One, JPMorgan Chase, PNC Bank, US Bank, and Wells Fargo, among others. Zelle is an industry response to a surge of offerings from non-traditional entrants—including Venmo (owned by PayPal), Apple Pay, and Google Pay—into the $2 trillion global digital payments market. Since its launch in 2017, Zelle has surpassed Venmo as the leading U.S. digital payments processor by volume.[10]

Evolutionary Adaptation

Digital transformation is a disruptive evolution into an entirely new way of working and thinking. And this process could require a full transformation of corporate body parts for new ways of functioning. It is for this reason that we see so many legacy businesses failing and already becoming extinct. They find it difficult to engineer radical new processes because they rely so heavily on current ones.

And it is why digital transformation can be so frightening: Companies must shift their focus from what they know works and invest instead in alternatives they view as risky and unproven. Many companies simply refuse to believe they are facing a life-or-death situation. This is Clayton Christensen's aptly named "Innovator's Dilemma": Companies fail to innovate, because it means changing the focus from what's working to something unproven and risky.

The threats emerge with the rise of companies using the newest tools, technologies, and processes, without the burdens of previous generations. Threats can also arrive via competitors with a clear vision and focus. Often this comes with founder-led organizations—Jeff Bezos at Amazon, Elon Musk at Tesla, Reed Hastings at Netflix, Jack Ma at Alibaba, and Brian Chesky at Airbnb, to name just a few. But a potential threat could also come from a CEO at a large, existing company, with the vision and support to make needed changes.

Larger, established companies tend to become risk-averse—why innovate when the current operations are doing so well? When Apple introduced the iPhone, it was dismissed by Nokia and RIM, among others.[11] Apple was performing poorly at the time, spurring it to take chances. Nokia and RIM did not feel the need to innovate. Which company is thriving today? Think of Henry Ford's horseless carriage. Think of Walmart eating Main Street. And now, Amazon is eating Walmart.

Recall how the Great Oxidation Event's cyanobacteria and oxygen resulted in new processes of oxygenic respiration. Today, cloud computing, big data, IoT, and AI are coming together to form new processes, too. Every mass extinction is a new beginning. Changing a core competency means removing and revolutionizing key corporate body parts. That's what digital transformation demands.

Companies that will survive through the era of digital transformation are those that recognize that survival is survival, regardless of how it happens; that environments change and resources fluctuate rapidly. If a company is reliant on a single resource, then it will not survive because it cannot see the great opportunity to revolutionize and breathe new life into its core abilities.

Digital Transformation Today

Today, digital transformation is everywhere. It's one of the biggest buzzwords of the past few years. Google "digital transformation" and see how many results you get. (I just got 253 million.) "Top Ten Digital Transformation Trends" lists are abundant. In 2017 alone, over 20 digital transformation conferences were held, not including countless digital transformation roundtables, forums, and expos. Digital transformation is being talked about by everyone, including the C-suite, governments, policymakers, and academia.

Digital transformation goes by many different names. Perhaps the most familiar is "the fourth Industrial Revolution." Past revolutions occurred when innovative technologies—the steam engine, electricity, computers, the internet—were adopted at scale and diffused throughout the ecosystem. We are approaching a similar tipping point—where cloud computing, big data, IoT, and AI are converging to drive network effects and create exponential change.[12]

Others refer to digital transformation as "the Second Machine Age." MIT professors Erik Brynjolfsson and Andrew McAfee argue that the crux of this machine age is that computers—long good at following instructions—are now able to learn. Extensively predicted, this capability is going to have dramatic effects on the world. Computers will diagnose diseases, drive cars, anticipate disruptions in supply chains, take care of our elderly, speak to us—the list goes on and on, to things we haven't even thought of yet. The first Industrial Revolution allowed humans to master mechanical power. In the last one, we harnessed electronic power. In the era of digital transformation, we will master *mental power*.[13]

This brings us back to punctuated equilibrium. As in evolutionary theory, periods of economic stability are suddenly disrupted with little forewarning, fundamentally changing the landscape. A significant difference with this wave is the speed with which it is happening. In 1958, the average tenure of companies in the S&P 500 was over 60 years. By 2012, it had fallen to under 20 years.[14] Once iconic companies like Kodak, Radio Shack, GM, Toys R Us, Sears, and GE have been rapidly disrupted and pushed out of the S&P 500. Digital transformation will further accelerate the pace of disruption.

As a result of its disruptive force, digital transformation is rapidly becoming a focus in the corporate world—from the boardroom, to industry conferences, to annual reports. The Economist Intelligence Unit recently found that 40 percent of CEOs place digital transformation at the top of the boardroom agenda.[15] But there is no uniform way in which CEOs are thinking about this.

Leaders who focus on digital transformation understand that to survive, their companies will have to go through a fundamental change. And they are being proactive about that change.

Take Ford's CEO Jim Hackett, who recently announced, "Ford will prepare for disruption by becoming fit. There's no doubt that we've entered this period of disruption, you all know that.... Disruption is often referred to, but is not easily understood. It's like the thief in the night that you didn't expect, but it can steal your livelihood. And it doesn't wait for businesses to be in the best shape to deal with it either."[16]

Or listen to Nike CEO Mark Parker: "Fueled by a transformation of our business, we are attacking growth opportunities through innovation, speed and digital to accelerate long-term, sustainable and profitable growth."[17]

Revolutionaries exist in the public sector, too. The U.S. Department of Defense has invested tens of millions of dollars in its Defense Innovation Unit (DIU), an organization established under President Barack Obama to build ties with Silicon Valley and the commercial tech sector. DIU is set up to fund innovative startups with proprietary technologies: It funds transformation projects, like launching micro-satellites to provide real-time imagery of U.S. troops on the ground; developing self-healing software that uses AI to identify and fix code vulnerabilities; testing aircraft with AI-based simulations; using AI to manage inventory and supply chains; and applying AI to perform predictive maintenance on military aircraft, identifying failures before they happen.[18]

In Europe, ENGIE, a French electric utility company, has made digital transformation a key strategic priority, "convinced that a new industrial revolution driven by the worlds of energy and digital technology is now under way."[19] Under the bold leadership of CEO Isabelle Kocher, ENGIE has embarked on this effort across virtually every aspect of its operations and services: digitizing billing services and customer energy use self-management; analyzing energy efficiency savings through the use of smart sensors; optimizing energy generation from renewable sources; and establishing its Digital Factory to unite data scientists, developers, and business analysts to propagate digital transformation techniques across the enterprise.[20] I'll discuss ENGIE's efforts in more detail in later chapters of this book.

But others take a narrower view—simply treating digital transformation as their company's next IT investment, or the next wave of digitalization. For example, some senior executives view it only as a necessary shift in customer interaction. An IBM Research survey in early 2018 found that "68 percent of C-suite executives expect organizations to emphasize customer experience over products." Asked which external forces will most impact them, C-suite executives listed changing customer preferences at the top.[21] This narrow view is insufficient and dangerous.

Even more perilous, some CEOs simply don't get it. While they may recognize what digital transformation is, they show no sense of urgency. One 2018 study noted that fully one-third of C-suite executives reported little or no impact from digital transformation in their industries, and almost half felt no urgency to evolve.[22] They either don't see the massive change hurtling toward them or don't understand how quickly and overwhelmingly it will show up.

Some CEOs understandably see digital transformation as a fundamental risk to their companies. Size is not a guarantee of stability or longevity. If large companies don't evolve, they can be replaced by smaller, nimbler upstarts. JP Morgan Chase CEO Jamie Dimon sounded an alarm in the company's 2014 annual report: "Silicon Valley is coming. There are hundreds of startups with a lot of brains and money working on various alternatives to traditional banking. The ones you read about most are in the lending business, whereby the firms can lend to individuals and small businesses very quickly and—these entities believe—effectively by using Big Data to enhance credit underwriting."[23] He is now breaking ground on a 1,000-employee Palo Alto campus to digitally transform fintech.

John Chambers, as he left his two-decades-long role as Cisco CEO and Chairman, delivered a keynote in which he presciently foretold: "Forty percent of businesses in this room, unfortunately, will not exist in a meaningful way in 10 years. If I'm not making you sweat, I should be."[24]

The focus of this book is on established companies—industry incumbents that risk outright extinction if they do not transform. My purpose is to discuss how leading enterprises across industries can successfully understand the opportunity ahead and take advantage of the underpinning technologies—cloud computing, big data, IoT, and AI—to digitally transform at their *core*.

Geoffrey Moore's model of "context" versus "core" in business helps illustrate why transformation at the core is important.[25] Moore's model describes the cycle of innovation as it relates to both vital and support processes of a company. "Core" is what creates differentiation in the marketplace and wins customers. "Context" consists of everything else—things like finance, sales, and marketing. No matter how well you do it or how many resources you put into context, it does not create a competitive advantage. Every company does it. According to Moore:

> Core is what companies invest their time and resources in that their competitors do not. Core is what allows a business to make more money and/or more margin, and make people more attracted to a business than to its competitors. Core gives a business bargaining power: it is what customers want and cannot get from anyone else.[26]

In his book *Dealing with Darwin*,[27] Moore uses the example of Tiger Woods to clarify core and context. There is no debate that Tiger Woods's core business is his golfing, and his context business is marketing. While marketing generates a large amount of money for Woods, there could not even be marketing (the context) without his golfing (the core). Context helps to support and keep the core running, while core is a company's competitive advantage. The general rule of thumb: Context means outsourcing, while core means intellectual property.

Overwhelmingly, today's companies and industries have already replaced most if not all of their context competencies with digital counterparts. But their core remains to be digitalized. Core cannot simply be replaced with something that works the same but has a shinier finish or faster engine. Digitalizing core is a true transformation. This digital transformation demands a complete overhaul of core processes and capabilities. It demands a removal of corporate body parts with the promise not to replace them but to instead create something faster, stronger, and more efficient that can do the same job in a totally different way—or do entirely new things.

Because digital transformation goes to the core of corporate capabilities, it can only happen when change is empowered to pervade the entire organization—not just at the IT, marketing, or any other business-line level. It can't be dealt with just as a technology investment, or as a problem with a particular business process or department. It requires fundamentally transforming business models and business opportunities, and the CEO needs to drive it. The mandate must come from the top.

I have witnessed many tech-adoption cycles over the past four decades. With the promise of performance improvements and productivity increases, such innovations were introduced to industry through the IT organization. Over months or years, and after multiple trials and evaluations, each gained the attention of the chief information officer, who was responsible for technology adoption. The CEO was periodically briefed on the cost and result.

With 21st-century digital transformation, the adoption cycle has inverted. What I'm seeing now is that, almost invariably, corporate digital transformations are initiated and propelled by the CEO. Visionary CEOs, individually, are the engines of massive change. This is unprecedented in the history of information technology—possibly unprecedented in the history of commerce. Today, CEO-mandated digital transformation drives the company's roadmap and goals.

For such change to happen, the entire organization needs to be committed—from the CEO to the board to each function and line of business. This change needs to proceed in a unified, holistic manner.

That's why the companies that will succeed are those that not only transform a business process, or a department, but also look at wholesale digital reinvention. They take it so seriously that they create Centers of Excellence to bring together data scientists, business analysts, developers, and line managers from across the organization. These Centers of Excellence can align the organization around digital transformation efforts, unify disparate departments, and grant employees the skills necessary to be successful in this effort. For example, ENGIE CEO Isabelle Kocher has assembled a C-suite team to drive the transformation of the company. Together they have updated ENGIE's strategy with new business targets that include specific expectations for digital value creation.

Other CEOs I work with are thinking through scenarios to anticipate future disruption, asking questions like, "What are our customers really buying? Do they really need us, or could a digital competitor provide a better insight or product at a lower cost?" They're using these "what if" scenarios to break out of cloistered mindsets and reallocate investments for future digital efforts.

One health care CEO used scenarios to craft a roadmap for hundreds of next-generation application improvements across its lines of business. Where new talent is required to bolster C-level efforts, CEOs now recruit for roles such as chief digital officer with the authority and budget to make things happen.

Get Ready, or You'll Miss the Boat

Digital transformation indices are cropping up everywhere to capture how prepared (or unprepared) CEOs and their companies are. The Dell Digital Transformation Index ranks 4,600 business leaders on their digital journey.[28] The McKinsey Global Institute (MGI) Industry Digitization Index ranks U.S. sectors based on their degree of digitization/digital transformation.[29] Germany's Industrie 4.0 Maturity Index focuses on companies in manufacturing. The most compelling lesson from these indices confirms what we already know: The gap between the companies and sectors that have digitally transformed and those that have not is already wide and will increase exponentially.

In an extensive 2015 report, MGI quantified the gap between the most digitized sectors and the rest of the economy over time. It found that "despite a massive rush of adoption, most sectors have barely closed that gap over the past decade":

> The lagging sectors are less than 15 percent as digitized as the leading sectors. The companies leading the charge are winning the battle for market share and profit growth; some are reshaping entire industries to their own advantage. But many businesses are struggling to evolve quickly enough. Workers in the most digitized industries enjoy wage

growth that is twice the national average, while the majority of US workers face stagnant incomes and uncertain prospects.[30]

The stakes are high. Europe may either add €1.25 trillion of gross industrial value, or lose €605 billion of value by 2025, according to Roland
Berger Strategy Consultants.[31]

Once you miss the boat, it gets harder to catch up.

More optimistically, and to repeat a theme of this book, these indices
show the massive size of the opportunity ahead. Sectors in the earliest
stages of digital transformation—like health care and construction—
could be huge drivers of economic growth. As McKinsey argues, "Looking at just three big areas of potential—online talent platforms, big data
analytics, and the internet of things—we estimate that digitization could
add up to $2.2 trillion to annual GDP by 2025, although the possibilities
are much wider."[32]

As we will cover in the following chapters, a variety of tools and
resources have emerged to propel organizations on the digital transformation path. Companies can now take advantage of robust cloud
computing platforms like Amazon Web Services, Microsoft Azure, IBM
Watson, and Google Cloud, to enable transformation initiatives.

Digital transformation consultancies are booming as CEOs start to
understand that disruption is coming, and scramble to position themselves against the coming tsunami. The market for digital transformation consulting alone is worth an estimated $23 billion. McKinsey, BCG,
and Bain have all built new digital consulting divisions, and many are
acquiring digital and design firms to bolster their capabilities. New,
niche consulting firms are being created entirely to focus on digital
transformation.[33]

Since the emergence of the internet, the digital consultancy market
has evolved with the successive waves of digitalization. In the first wave,
consulting firms began helping customers build their digital presence.
Then with Web 2.0, consulting firms focused on interactive design and
customer experience. Today, in the current wave of digital transformation, consultancies are helping clients use data to reinvent their business
models. We'll continue to see this shift in how firms engage with customers, collaborate with technology partners, and jump on this disruption wave.

Digital Transformation Will Create Trillions of Dollars of Value

While estimates vary regarding the global economic impact of digital transformation, leading studies forecast on the order of trillions of dollars annually.

Potential Economic Impact

Increase in Global Business and Social Value	Timeframe	Source
$100 Trillion	**2016–2030**	World Economic Forum, 2016

Increase in Annual Global GDP		
$15.7 Trillion (driven by AI)	**By 2030**	PwC, 2017
$13.0 Trillion (driven by AI)	**By 2030**	McKinsey, 2018
$11.1 Trillion (driven by IoT)	**By 2025**	McKinsey, 2015
$3.9 Trillion (driven by AI)	**By 2022**	Gartner, 2018

FIGURE 2.1

Governments, too, are focused on the need to evolve and stay competitive. Nations have long competed—for skilled workers, jobs, companies, new technologies, and ultimately, economic growth. This competition will only intensify, particularly as urbanization grows as a driving force in the public sphere. As more people move to cities (68 percent of the world will live in cities by 2050), public infrastructure and resources—water and energy in particular—are being strained.[34] Digital transformation will be essential to government efforts to keep up with this rapid change, through more efficient delivery of services and the eventual creation of "digital cities"—cities designed around integrated infrastructure addressing traffic, energy, maintenance, services, public safety, and education with services such as e-transport, e-health care, and e-government.[35]

Governments that understand this are striving to ensure the next wave of digital transformation happens in their own countries. They are spurring investment in research and development, encouraging higher education in digital technologies, and implementing policies favorable to digitally transformed companies. Examples abound:

- Singapore's latest 10-year master plan relies heavily on digital technology. "AI Singapore" (AISG) is an entire national program devoted to catalyzing Singapore's AI capabilities through research institutions, AI startups, and larger companies developing AI products.[36]

- The U.A.E.'s Vision 2021 National Innovation Strategy targets core sectors including AI, software, and smart cities, and strives to encourage adoption of technologies across sectors.[37]

- Amsterdam's smart city initiative spans mobility, infrastructure, and big data, with initiatives such as using GPS data to manage traffic flows in real time, optimizing trash and recycling pickups, and replacing parking meters with pay-by-phone apps.[38]

- China's 13th Five-Year Plan calls for massive investment in next-generation artificial intelligence and the internet to establish international hegemony.[39]

Just as in the corporate world, governments that adopt AI, big data, cloud computing, and IoT across all levels will prosper; countries that don't will struggle to keep up.

The academic world is also taking notice. As the scope of digital transformation expands and accelerates, universities are beginning to dig in. MIT launched the MIT Intelligence Quest in early 2018, "an initiative to discover the foundations of human intelligence and drive the development of technological tools that can positively influence virtually every aspect of society." Recognizing the sweeping impact digital transformation will have across society, MIT announced that the outcomes of this initiative may yield "practical tools for use in a wide array of research endeavors, such as disease diagnosis, drug discovery, materials and manufacturing design, automated systems, synthetic biology, and finance." In October 2018, MIT announced a $1 billion investment in its new college of computing focused on advancing the rise of artificial intelligence.

Executive education classes, master's degrees, and MBA programs focused on digital transformation have sprung up. Columbia Business School's Digital Business Leadership Program, for instance, aims to "develop leadership abilities to lead digital transformation."[40] Harvard Business School has an entire executive education course on "Driving Digital Strategies."[41] And MIT Sloan's "Initiative on the Digital Economy" offers a variety of research, executive education, and MBA-level classes examining the impact of digital technology on businesses, the economy, and society.[42]

The open-ended nature of what these classes teach conveys a critical point about digital transformation: its inherent nature of constant change. "[Digital transformation] is not a process that will ever be complete, at least not in the near future," writes Boston College professor Gerald Kane. Rather, he writes, "new classes of technologies—artificial intelligence, blockchain, autonomous vehicles, augmented and virtual reality—will likely become widely adopted over the coming decade or two, fundamentally changing expectations yet again. By the time you adapt to today's digital environment, that environment will have likely already changed significantly."[43]

Digital transformation requires companies to continuously monitor current trends, experiment, and adapt—and academic institutions are developing curricula to teach these new capabilities to future and current business leaders.

The Future of Digital Transformation

What does the future of digital transformation hold? From where I sit, it's clear the benefits for business and society will be enormous—on the order of the Industrial Revolution. These new technologies will boost economic growth, promote inclusiveness, improve the environment, and extend the length and quality of human life. According to a 2016 World Economic Forum study, digital transformation will have far-reaching impact across industries—not only in terms of economic and job growth, but in environmental benefits as well—that "could deliver around $100 trillion in value to business and society over the next decade."[44]

Think about the many ways digital transformation will improve human life:

- In medicine, expect very early disease detection and diagnosis, genome-specific preventative care, extremely precise surgeries performed with the help of robots, on-demand and digital health care, AI-assisted diagnoses, and dramatically reduced costs of care.

- In the automotive industry, expect self-driving cars, reduced crashes and casualties, fewer drunk drivers, lower insurance premiums, and decreased carbon emissions.

- In manufacturing, 3D printing and manufacturing-as-a-service will allow for mass, inexpensive customization with low or no distribution costs.

- In resource management and sustainability, resources will be matched with need, waste minimized, and constraints alleviated. Digital transformation even has the potential to completely decouple emissions and resource use from economic growth.

The list goes on and on. Many of these benefits cannot even be conceived of today.[45]

Consider the likely impact on productivity growth. Total U.S. economic output per worker has been stagnant since the Great Recession of 2008. Digital transformation allows companies to use machine learning, AI, IoT, and cloud computing so even smaller firms can increase employee productivity and reverse this trend.[46] Digital progress adds value to the national economy in ways we don't yet measure accurately. "At first glance, free services like Wikipedia, Skype and Google don't seem to add anything to gross domestic product. But when you look closer, you see that they certainly do add value," said MIT's Brynjolfsson, who developed a method to measure the value innovative IT companies generate. Using this method, he has found that disruptive business models such as online networks and digital services create $300 billion in value each year—value that isn't captured by the statistics or by the critics.[47]

We have to acknowledge that such tremendous change will also have potentially negative effects. While Brynjolfsson emphasizes the benefits to overall productivity from digitization, he also points to a trend he calls the "great decoupling" of economic growth and job creation: Despite the last 15-20 years of economic and productivity growth, median income and job growth have stagnated. What's to blame? Technology's role in productivity: machines replacing humans.

Some argue that this is a temporary shock that has been repeated throughout history, and that jobs will rebound once workers adjust their skills and learn how to work with new technologies. Harvard economist Lawrence Katz observes there is no historical precedent for the permanent reduction of jobs. While it can take decades for workers to acquire the expertise needed for new types of employment, Katz claims "we never have run out of jobs. There is no long-term trend of eliminating work for people. Over the long term, employment rates are fairly stable. People have always been able to create new jobs. People come up with new things to do."[48]

But this doesn't mean that we can just stand by and expect jobs to come. As a society, we need to understand how to reconceptualize education and provide more flexible and agile workforce training programs that match the skills of the digital economy. Five years from now, 35 percent of the important workforce skills will have changed. We need to invest in education and basic research and admit more skilled immigrants. And we need to address the mismatch between supply and demand for digital skills. This means training people not only in technical skills, like coding, but also in skills that will increasingly be needed in the digital age to complement the work of machines—creativity, teamwork, and problem-solving.

As the World Economic Forum wrote in an influential 2016 white paper on digital transformation:

> Robotics and artificial intelligence systems will not only be used to replace human tasks, but to augment their skills (for example, surgeons working with advanced robotics systems to perform operations). This, too, will provide challenges for businesses, which will need to reskill employees so they can work effectively with new technology. Reskilling will be critical to realizing the full potential of technological augmentation, both through boosting productivity and mitigating job losses from automation.[49]

Regulations and public policy also need to keep up, to promote entrepreneurship and encourage the founding of new companies. Antitrust laws and tax policies need to be reconceptualized. Skilled immigration needs to be encouraged.

We cannot predict exactly how and where the impacts of digital transformation will fall, but we can recognize the scale of change will be enormous. In some cases, it can threaten products, companies, or entire industries with outright extinction: encyclopedias, phone books, travel agencies, local newspapers, book stores. Film and photography companies were wiped out by digital cameras. Today the taxi industry is being threatened by ride-sharing services like Lyft and Uber, while malls and retail stores are being upended by e-commerce.

In other cases, the disruption could create new, ancillary markets. Take Airbnb, for example. When it was first launched, many predicted that Airbnb would completely disrupt the hotel industry as travelers would increasingly choose to stay in private apartments and houses over hotels. But the hotel industry has not crumbled—in fact, it is still thriving. So is Airbnb. Airbnb's actual impact has been in other areas: reducing the number of homes available in a neighborhood for people to live, potentially driving up the price of rent. Instead of competing with hotels, Airbnb is competing with renters. "Was that Airbnb's intent? Almost certainly not," writes journalist Derek Thompson. "But that is the outcome, anyway, and it is a meaningful—even, yes, disruptive—one. Airbnb is a transformative travel business. But most people failed to predict the thing it would transform—for good and bad."[50]

Other industries like banking are informative. With each new wave of innovation, banks invest in capturing that value. Brokerages became services of retail banks; online payments were integrated; and credit card, bill payment, and financial planning offers are now standard.

Hotels and airlines initially offered excess inventory through sites like Expedia, Hotels.com, Orbitz, Kayak, and Trivago. But they soon captured value—and strengthened customer relationships—with their own apps that offered the best pricing and options.

The point here is that digital transformation will have profound effects, but not necessarily the effects we can predict or even measure now. Clearly, the building blocks to enable digital transformation are available, robust, and accessible: cloud computing, big data, AI, and IoT.

Chapter 3

The Information Age Accelerates

CEOs and other senior leaders need to understand the technologies driving today's digital transformation in far more detail than was required of them in the past. Why is that? In contrast to previous waves of technology adoption, we've seen that digital transformation goes to the very core of how organizations operate and what they do. If you are an auto manufacturer, for example, is your business fundamentally about making cars—or is it about delivering *transportation and mobility* to your customers? And what is more valuable: Your IP around powertrain design, or your AI-based self-driving algorithms fed by real-time telemetry and usage data generated by the vehicles you make? Leaders in every industry need to ask such questions and thoroughly examine how these technologies will profoundly change their market and how they do business.

And the stakes have never been higher—in terms of both the risk of extinction and the potential rewards. In my experience, for any large enterprise, the annual economic value of deploying AI and IoT applications ranges from hundreds of millions to billions of dollars. At Royal Dutch Shell, for example, deploying an AI-based predictive maintenance application for more than 500,000 refinery valves globally is estimated to yield several hundred million dollars a year in reduced maintenance costs and increased operating efficiency. Shell plans to roll out many more AI applications across its upstream, downstream, and midstream operations globally. The expected benefit is on the order of *billions of dollars annually.*

Implementing a digital transformation agenda means your organization will build, deploy, and operate dozens, perhaps hundreds or even thousands, of AI and IoT applications across all aspects of your organization—from human resources and customer relationships to financial processes, product design, maintenance, and supply chain operations. No operation will be untouched. It is therefore incumbent on senior leaders to firmly understand these technologies.

My advice is to learn enough about these technologies to have well-informed discussions with your internal technical staff and to choose the right technology partners who will be critical to your success. The investment will pay valuable dividends, in terms of avoiding unqualified partners and drawn-out internal projects that never deliver value.

This chapter provides an overview of the four key technologies that both drive and enable digital transformation—elastic cloud computing, big data, AI, and IoT. Readers who want to extend their understanding to a deeper level—particularly executives with direct responsibility for driving digital transformation initiatives—will benefit from reading the subsequent four chapters that delve further into each technology.

The Challenges Are Daunting—But Proven Solutions Are Available

The technologies that propel digital transformation are clearly game changing, but we are in the very early stages of this new era. And while the potential is enormous, the challenges in developing and scaling AI and IoT applications across an enterprise can be daunting.

The baseline capability required is the aggregation and processing of rapidly growing petabyte-scale data sets—that's *1 million gigabytes*—continuously harvested from thousands of disparate legacy IT systems, internet sources, and multimillion-sensor networks. In the case of one Fortune 500 manufacturer, the magnitude of the data aggregation problem is 50 petabytes fragmented across 5,000 systems representing customer, dealer, claims, ordering, pricing, product design, engineering, planning, manufacturing, control systems, accounting, human resources, logistics, and supplier systems, fragmented by mergers and acquisitions, product lines, geographies, and customer engagement channels (i.e., online, stores, call center, field). With hundreds of millions of sensors embedded in products generating high-frequency readings of 1 Hz (1 per second) or greater, these data sets grow by trillions of readings daily.

The technologies required to aggregate, correlate, and extract the value from these data for business transformation did not exist a decade ago. But today, the availability of inexpensive sensors (under $1) and credit card–sized AI supercomputers interconnected by fast networks provide the infrastructure to dramatically transform organizations into real-time adaptive enterprises. Cloud computing, big data, AI, and IoT converge to unlock business value estimated by McKinsey of up to *$23 trillion annually* by 2030.[1]

A key challenge for organizations is how to bring together and leverage these technologies to create meaningful value and positive return on investment. For now, let me just say there is much good news for organizations embarking on digital transformation—robust tools and expert knowledge are now available to dramatically accelerate digital transformation efforts and ensure successful outcomes. I will return to this topic in more depth in chapter 10, "A New Technology Stack."

Cloud Computing

Cloud computing is the first of the four technologies that drive digital transformation. Without cloud computing, digital transformation would not be possible. Cloud computing is a model of accessing shared pools of configurable hardware and software resources—computer networks, servers, data storage, applications, and other services—that can be rapidly provisioned with minimal management effort, typically via the internet. Those resources may be privately owned by an organization for its exclusive use ("private cloud") or owned by a third party for use by anyone on a pay-for-what-you-use basis ("public cloud").

In its manifestation as the on-demand rental of compute and storage resources from a third-party provider, cloud computing was pioneered by Amazon through its Amazon Web Services unit. What began as an internal service for Amazon developers in 2002 became a public offering in 2006 with the introduction of Elastic Compute Cloud (EC2) and Simple Storage Service (S3). The public cloud computing market is estimated to reach a staggering $162 billion by 2020, just a decade and a half after its inception.[2] Amazon Web Services alone is forecasted to grow to $43 billion in annual revenue by 2022.[3] Competition from Microsoft and

Google is acute, which guarantees rapidly falling compute and storage prices converging toward zero.

Recognizing that cloud providers can do a better and cheaper job of running a huge number of servers and storage devices across global networks of secure and reliable data centers, organizations are rapidly shifting legacy applications ("workloads") out of their corporate data centers into public clouds.

Chief information officers now acknowledge traditional IT data centers will be extinct within a decade.[4] Research supports that hypothesis. Cisco forecasts that by 2021, 94 percent of workloads will be processed by cloud data centers and 73 percent of cloud workloads will be in public cloud data centers.[5]

Examples of companies shuttering data centers are numerous. Rome-based utility Enel is shuttering 23 data centers with 10,000 servers supporting its operations in 30 countries, and they're consolidating 1,700 legacy applications to 1,200 applications and moving them to AWS. Netflix, Uber, Deutsche Bank, and countless others now have all or a significant percentage of their information technology operating on public clouds.[6]

Virtualization and Containers

A key enabler of cloud computing's superior economies of scale is a technology innovation known as "virtualization." Previously, in traditional data centers, hardware was sized and provisioned to handle peak demand. Organizations installed enough servers and storage to support the highest level of computing requirements they anticipated, which typically occurred only for relatively brief periods (e.g., end-of-quarter order processing). This resulted in largely idle data centers with very low hardware utilization rates averaging in single-digit percentages. Virtualization allows the creation of multiple simulated environments and dedicated resources from a single, physical hardware system. "Containers" are another innovation enabling efficient sharing of physical resources. A container is a lightweight, stand-alone, executable software package that includes everything needed to run it—code, runtime, system tools and libraries, and settings. The use of virtualization and containers to share hardware across applications results in significantly

Virtualization Dramatically Increases Hardware Utilization

Virtualization enables infrastructure resources to be shared across multiple applications, resulting in a dramatic increase in hardware utilization.

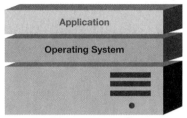 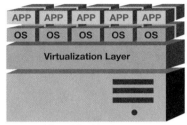

Traditional Architecture   **Virtual Architecture**

FIGURE 3.1

higher and vastly more cost-effective utilization rates. This translates into the highly compelling economic value proposition that is driving widespread adoption of public cloud computing platforms like AWS, Microsoft Azure, IBM Cloud, and Google Cloud.

X-as-a-Service: IaaS, PaaS, and SaaS

Cloud computing was initially driven by both independent and corporate software developers looking to save the upfront time, cost, and effort of acquiring, building, and managing scalable and reliable hardware infrastructures. Developers were attracted to the cloud model because it allowed them to focus on developing software, while the cloud provider handled the infrastructure (Infrastructure-as-a-Service, or IaaS), scalability, and reliability.

Today's cloud platforms are "elastic"—that is, they dynamically determine the amount of resources an application requires and then automatically provision and de-provision the computing infrastructure to support the application. This relieves developers and IT teams from many operational tasks, such as hardware and software setup and configuration, software patching, operating a distributed database cluster, and partitioning data over multiple instances as required to scale. The cloud customer pays only for resources actually used.

Cloud offerings now extend beyond IaaS to include application development platforms (Platform-as-a-Service, or PaaS) and software

Cloud Services Models

X-as-a-Service (XaaS): Today's cloud computing providers enable organizations to access a range of resources "as a service," from infrastructure to software.

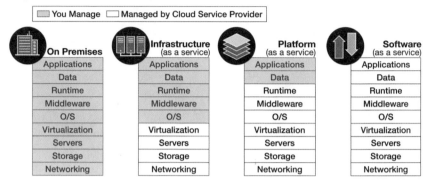

You Manage	Managed by Cloud Service Provider		
On Premises	**Infrastructure** (as a service)	**Platform** (as a service)	**Software** (as a service)
Applications	Applications	Applications	Applications
Data	Data	Data	Data
Runtime	Runtime	Runtime	Runtime
Middleware	Middleware	Middleware	Middleware
O/S	O/S	O/S	O/S
Virtualization	Virtualization	Virtualization	Virtualization
Servers	Servers	Servers	Servers
Storage	Storage	Storage	Storage
Networking	Networking	Networking	Networking

FIGURE 3.2

applications (Software-as-a-Service, or SaaS). PaaS offerings provide software development tools and services specifically for building, deploying, operating, and managing software applications. In addition to managing the underlying infrastructure (servers, storage, networking, virtualization), PaaS offerings manage additional technical components required by the application, including the runtime environment, operating system, and middleware.

SaaS offerings are complete, prebuilt software applications delivered via the internet. The SaaS provider hosts and manages the entire application, including the underlying infrastructure, security, operating environment, and updates. SaaS offerings relieve customers from having to provision hardware or install, maintain, and update software. SaaS offerings generally allow the customer to configure various application settings (for example, customize data fields, workflow, and user access privileges) to fit their needs.

Multi-Cloud and Hybrid Cloud

CIOs now recognize the importance of operating across multiple cloud vendors to reduce reliance on any one provider (so-called "vendor lock-in") and to take advantage of differentiation in public cloud provider services. Multi-cloud refers to the use of multiple cloud computing

Multi-Cloud and Hybrid Cloud

To avoid vendor lock-in and to take advantage of differentiation among public cloud service providers, organizations are adopting multi-cloud and hybrid cloud approaches.

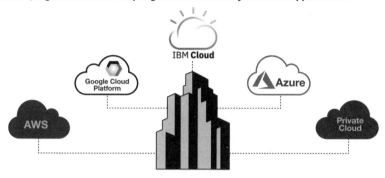

FIGURE 3.3

services in a single heterogeneous architecture.[7] For example, an application may use Microsoft Azure for storage, AWS for compute, IBM Watson for deep learning, and Google Cloud for image recognition.

It's also important to be able to operate an application across private and public clouds (i.e., a "hybrid cloud" environment). Ultra-sensitive customer data might be stored in a private cloud, while public cloud infrastructure might be used for on-demand "burst capacity"—excess capacity to handle spikes in transaction processing—or other analytic processing.

More difficult to achieve is "cloud portability" while taking advantage of native cloud provider services—i.e., the ability to easily replace various underlying cloud services that an application uses with services from another cloud vendor. For example, replacing Google's image recognition service with Amazon's image recognition. While the use of "containers" (technology that isolates applications from infrastructure) enables cloud portability of *applications*, containers do not enable portability of *cloud provider services*.

Big Data

The second technology vector driving digital transformation is "big data." Data, of course, have always been important. But in the era of digital transformation, their value is greater than ever before. Many AI applications in particular require vast amounts of data in order to "train" the algorithm, and these applications improve as the amount of data they ingest grows.

The term "big data" was first used in fields such as astronomy and genomics in the early 2000s. These fields generated voluminous data sets that were impossible to process cost effectively and efficiently using traditional centralized processing computer architectures, commonly referred to as "scale-up" architectures. In contrast, "scale-out" architectures use thousands or tens of thousands of processors to process data sets in parallel. Over the last dozen years or so, software technologies have emerged that are designed to use scale-out architectures for parallel processing of big data. Notable examples include the MapReduce programming paradigm (originally developed at Google in 2004) and Hadoop (Yahoo!'s implementation of the MapReduce paradigm, released in 2006). Available today under open source software license from the Apache Software Foundation, the Hadoop MapReduce framework comprises numerous software components.

As we've seen, digital transformation initiatives require the capability to manage big data at petabyte scale. While the Apache Hadoop collection provides many powerful and often necessary components to help manage big data and build AI and IoT applications, organizations have found it exceedingly difficult to assemble these components into functioning applications. In chapter 10, I will discuss the need for a new technology stack, and I'll describe how this new stack addresses the complex requirements of digital transformation. But first, there is more to the story of big data than just volume.

Big Data Explosion

Historically, collecting data was time consuming and labor intensive. So organizations resorted to statistics based on small samples (hundreds to thousands of data points) to make inferences about the whole population. Due to these small sample sizes, statisticians expended significant effort and time curating data sets to remove outliers that could potentially skew the analysis.

But today, with the elastic cloud providing unlimited compute and storage capabilities, along with the emergence of software designed for

Global Growth of Connected Devices

Today there are three times as many devices connected to the internet as there are people in the world, increasing at 10 percent annually.

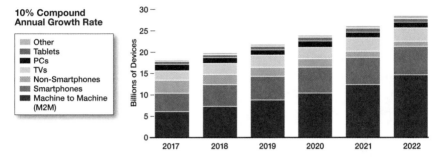

10% Compound Annual Growth Rate

Legend:
- Other
- Tablets
- PCs
- TVs
- Non-Smartphones
- Smartphones
- Machine to Machine (M2M)

Y-axis: Billions of Devices (0, 5, 10, 15, 20, 25, 30)
X-axis: 2017, 2018, 2019, 2020, 2021, 2022

FIGURE 3.4

parallel processing of data at massive scale, there is no longer the need for sampling nor the need to curate data. Instead, outliers or otherwise imperfect data are appropriately weighted through the analysis of large data sets. As a result, with over 20 billion internet-connected smartphones, devices, and sensors generating a stream of continuous data at a rate of zettabytes a year and rapidly growing—one zettabyte being equivalent to the data stored on about 250 billion DVDs—it is now possible for organizations to make near-real-time inferences based on all available data. As we shall see, this ability to process *all the data* captured is fundamental to recent advances in AI.

Another significant shift made possible by the ability to apply AI to all the data in a data set is that there is no longer the need for an expert hypothesis of an event's cause. Instead, the AI algorithm is able to learn the behavior of complex systems directly from data generated by those systems.

For example, rather than requiring an experienced loan officer to specify the causes of mortgage defaults, the system or machine can learn those causes and their relative importance more accurately, based on analyzing all available data for prior mortgage defaults.

The implications are significant. An experienced mechanical engineer is no longer required to predict engine failures. An experienced physician is no longer required to predict the onset of diabetes in a patient. A geological engineer is no longer required to predict oil well placement for optimal production. These can all be learned from data by the computer—more quickly and with much greater accuracy.

Artificial Intelligence

The third major technology driving digital transformation is artificial intelligence. AI is the science and engineering of making intelligent machines and computer programs capable of learning and problem solving in ways that normally require human intelligence.

The types of problems tackled by AI traditionally included natural language processing and translation; image and pattern recognition (for example, fraud detection, predicting failure, or predicting risk of chronic disease onset); and decision-making support (for example, autonomous vehicles and prescriptive analytics). The number and complexity of AI applications are rapidly expanding. For example, AI is being applied to highly complex supply chain problems, such as inventory optimization; production problems, such as optimizing the yield of manufacturing assets; fleet management problems, such as maximizing asset uptime and availability; and health care problems, such as predicting drug dependency risk, to name just a few. I will cover some of these in more detail later in the book.

Machine Learning

Machine learning—a very broad subset of AI—is the class of algorithms that learn from examples and experience (represented by input/output data sets) rather than relying on hard-coded and predefined rules that characterize traditional algorithms. An algorithm is the sequence of instructions a computer carries out to transform input data to output data. A simple example is an algorithm to sort a list of numbers from highest to lowest: The input is a list of numbers in any order, and the output is the properly sorted list. The instructions to sort such a list can be defined with a very precise set of rules—an example of a traditional algorithm.

Computer scientists have created algorithms since the earliest days of computing. However, using traditional approaches they had been unable to develop effective algorithms for solving a wide range of problems

Machine Learning and Deep Learning Drive the AI Renaissance

First conceived in the 1950s, artificial intelligence has rapidly evolved in recent years, demonstrating dramatic impact through the application of machine learning and deep learning methods.

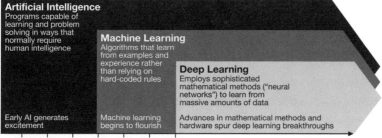

Artificial Intelligence
Programs capable of learning and problem solving in ways that normally require human intelligence

Machine Learning
Algorithms that learn from examples and experience rather than relying on hard-coded rules

Deep Learning
Employs sophisticated mathematical methods ("neural networks") to learn from massive amounts of data

Early AI generates excitement

Machine learning begins to flourish

Advances in mathematical methods and hardware spur deep learning breakthroughs

1950s 1960s 1970s 1980s 1990s 2000s 2010s

FIGURE 3.5

across health care, manufacturing, aerospace, logistics, supply chains, and financial services. In contrast to the precisely defined rules of traditional algorithms, machine learning algorithms mathematically analyze any variety of data (images, text, sounds, time series, etc.) and their interrelationships in order to make inferences.

An example of machine learning is an algorithm to analyze an image (input) and classify it as an "airplane" or "not airplane" (output)—potentially useful in air traffic control and aviation safety, for example. The algorithm is "trained" by giving it thousands or millions of images labeled as "airplane" or "not airplane." When sufficiently trained, the algorithm can then analyze an unlabeled image and infer with a high degree of precision whether it's an airplane. Another example is an algorithm in the health care field to predict the likelihood someone will have a heart attack, based on medical records and other data inputs—age, gender, occupation, geography, diet, exercise, ethnicity, family history, health history, and so on—for hundreds of thousands of patients who have suffered heart attacks and millions who have not.

The advent of machine learning combined with unlimited computational power has resulted in a whole new class of algorithms to solve previously unsolvable problems. Consider the case of assessing the risk of aircraft engine failure. By characterizing all relevant inputs (i.e., flight hours, flight conditions, maintenance records, engine temperature, oil pressure, etc.) and a sufficiently large number of engine failure cases (i.e., outputs), it is possible not only to predict whether an engine is likely to fail but also to diagnose the causes of failure. This can all be done without the need to understand material science or thermodynamics. What this does require is useful data, and lots of it.

Traditionally, machine learning has also required extensive "feature engineering." (Advances in "deep learning," discussed below, have reduced or in some cases eliminated this requirement.) Feature engineering relies on experienced data scientists working collaboratively with subject matter experts to identify the significant data and data representations or features (e.g., engine temperature differential, flight hours) that influence an outcome (in this case, engine failure). The complexity comes from choosing among the hundreds or thousands of potential features. The machine learning algorithm is trained by iterating over thousands (or millions) of historic cases while adjusting the relative importance (weights) of each of the features until it can infer the output (i.e., engine failure) as accurately as possible.[8] The result of a trained machine learning algorithm is a set of weights that can be used to infer the proper output for any input.[9] In this case, while the algorithm determines the weights, human analysts determined the features. We'll see in deep learning approaches that the algorithm can determine both the relevant features and the associated weights directly from the data.

The training process is computationally intensive and time consuming, while the inference is lightweight and fast. Advances in the design and use of computing hardware have helped improve the performance of machine learning applications. For example, graphics processing units (GPUs) are designed to process a training set in parallel, whereas field-programmable gate arrays (FPGAs) are optimized for processing lightweight inferences. The leading cloud computing platforms now provide resources optimized for AI computing that leverage these hardware innovations.

Machine learning can be divided into "supervised" and "unsupervised" approaches. In supervised learning, the algorithm is trained using labeled training data, as in the aircraft engine failure example. This approach requires the availability of large amounts of historical data to train a machine learning algorithm.

If there are a limited number of occurrences to train a machine learning model, unsupervised learning techniques can be applied where the learning algorithm searches for outlier data. Unsupervised learning algorithms are useful in finding meaningful patterns or clusters in a large data set. For example, a retailer could use unsupervised machine learning algorithms for cluster analysis of customer data to discover new meaningful customer segments for marketing or product development purposes.

Deep Learning

Deep learning is a subset of machine learning with vast potential. As noted earlier, most traditional machine learning approaches involve extensive feature engineering that requires significant expertise. This can become a bottleneck, as data scientists are needed to classify and label the data and train the model. In deep learning, however, the important features are not predefined by data scientists but instead learned by the algorithm.

This is an important advance, because while feature engineering can be used to solve certain artificial intelligence problems, it is not a viable approach for many other AI problems. For many tasks, it is exceedingly difficult or impossible for data scientists to determine the features that should be extracted. Consider, for instance, the problem of image recognition, such as creating an algorithm to recognize cars—a critical requirement for self-driving technology. The number of variants in how a car may appear is infinitely large—given all the possibilities of shape, size, color, lighting, distance, perspective, and so on. It would be impossible for a data scientist to extract all the relevant features to train an algorithm. For such problems, deep learning employs "neural network" technology—described below—an approach originally inspired by the human brain's network of neurons, but in reality having little in common with how our brains work.

Deep learning enables computers to build complex concepts out of a simpler hierarchy of nested concepts. You can think of this as a series of chained algorithms: Each layer of the hierarchy is an algorithm that performs a piece of the inference in succession, until the final layer provides the output. In the case of the car recognition task, for instance, the neural network is trained by feeding it a large number of images (with and without cars in them). Each layer of the neural network analyzes

How a Neural Network Recognizes a Car Image

Using multilayered neural networks, deep learning AI enables computers to build complex concepts out of a simple hierarchy of nested concepts.

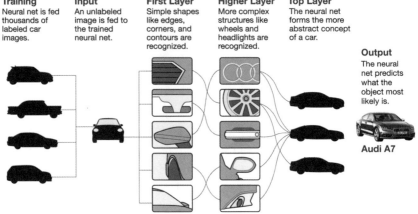

Training
Neural net is fed thousands of labeled car images.

Input
An unlabeled image is fed to the trained neural net.

First Layer
Simple shapes like edges, corners, and contours are recognized.

Higher Layer
More complex structures like wheels and headlights are recognized.

Top Layer
The neural net forms the more abstract concept of a car.

Output
The neural net predicts what the object most likely is.

Audi A7

FIGURE 3.6

the various components of the image data—progressively identifying abstract concepts such as edges, corners, contours, circles, and rectangles that represent a car's wheels, body, etc.—and eventually develops the concept of a car based on that hierarchy of nested concepts.[10] Once trained, the neural network can be given an image it has not seen before and determine with a high degree of precision whether it is a car.

As you can imagine, deep learning has vast potential for many applications in business and government. In addition to their use in computer vision problems presented by self-driving cars and factory robots, neural networks can also be applied to tasks like voice recognition in smart devices (e.g., Amazon Echo and Google Home), automated customer service, real-time language translation, medical diagnostics, prediction and optimization of oil field production, and many others. Deep learning is especially interesting because it can potentially be applied to any task—from predicting engine failure or diabetes to identifying fraud—with far less data scientist intervention compared to other machine learning methods, due to the greatly reduced or eliminated need for feature engineering.

AI is an enormously exciting area with endless possibilities, and the field is rapidly advancing. A number of catalysts are accelerating the use of AI, including the continuous decline in the cost of computing and storage as well as ongoing hardware improvements and innovations. As computing becomes both more powerful and less expensive, AI can be applied to ever larger and more diverse data sets to solve more problems and drive real-time decision-making.

It is no exaggeration to say that AI will profoundly change the way we work and live. While we remain in the early stages of using AI in business and government, the AI arms race has clearly begun. Forward-thinking organizations are already actively engaged in applying AI across their value chains. They are positioning themselves to preempt competitors and thrive, as digital transformation determines which organizations will lead and which will fall aside. Today's CEOs and other senior leaders should be actively thinking about how AI will impact the landscape in which they operate—and how to take advantage of the new opportunities it will open up.

Internet of Things (IoT)

The fourth technology driving digital transformation is the internet of things. The basic idea of IoT is to connect any device equipped with adequate processing and communication capabilities to the internet, so it can send and receive data. It's a very simple concept with the potential to create significant value—but the IoT story doesn't end there.

The real power and potential of IoT derives from the fact that computing is rapidly becoming ubiquitous and interconnected, as microprocessors are steadily getting cheaper and more energy efficient, and networks are getting faster. Today, inexpensive AI supercomputers the size of a credit card are being deployed in more devices—such as cars, drones, industrial machinery, and buildings. As a result, cloud computing is effectively being extended to the network edge—i.e., to the devices where data are produced, consumed, and now analyzed.

NVIDIA's TX2 is an example of such an edge AI supercomputer. The TX2 can process streaming video in real time and use AI-based image recognition to identify people or objects. For example, it can be embedded in self-driving delivery robots to power their computer vision system for navigating city streets and sidewalks. The 2-by-3-inch TX2 incorporates advanced components, including a powerful 256-core

GPU and 32 gigabytes of RAM local storage capable of recording about an hour of video. Power consumption, an important consideration in applications such as drones, is under 8 watts.

With such advances, we are seeing an important evolution in the form factor of computing (which I will cover in more depth in chapter 7). Cars, planes, commercial buildings, factories, homes, and other infrastructure such as power grids, cities, bridges, ports, and tunnels all increasingly have thousands of powerful computers and smart cameras installed to monitor, interpret, and react to conditions and observations. In essence, everything is becoming a computing device and AI capabilities are increasingly being built into these devices.

The technical name for IoT—*cyber-physical systems*—describes the convergence and control of physical infrastructure by computers. Deployed across physical systems, computers continuously monitor and effect change locally—for example, adjusting the setting of an industrial control—while communicating and coordinating across a wider area through cloud data centers.

An example of such a system is the smart grid in the electric utility industry, which uses locally generated power when available and draws from the power grid when necessary. The potential is to make the global power infrastructure 33 to 50 percent more efficient. Enabling such a system requires AI to be deployed on edge computers to continuously make real-time AI-based forecasts (or inferences) of energy demand and match that demand to the most cost-effective energy source, whether local solar, battery, wind, or from the power grid. The idea of a "transactive" grid, in which individual nodes on microgrids make instantaneous energy buying and selling decisions, is closer to becoming reality.

Other examples of local processing combined with cloud processing include the Amazon Echo, autonomous vehicles, camera-equipped drones for surveillance or other commercial and industrial uses (such as insurance damage assessments), and robotics in manufacturing systems. Soon, even humans will have tens or hundreds of ultra-low-power computer wearables and implants continuously monitoring and regulating blood chemistry, blood pressure, pulse, temperature, and other metabolic signals. Those devices will be able to connect via the internet to cloud-based services—such as medical diagnostic services—but will also have sufficient local computing and AI capabilities to collect and analyze data and make real-time decisions.

Today, even as we remain in the early stages of IoT, numerous IoT applications already deliver enormous value to business and government. In the energy sector, for example, utilities realize substantial value from predictive maintenance applications fed by telemetry data from sensors installed throughout the utility's distribution network. For instance, a large European utility runs an AI-based predictive maintenance application that consumes data from sensors and smart meters across its 1.2-million-kilometer distribution network to predict equipment failure and prescribe proactive maintenance before equipment fails. The potential economic benefit to the utility exceeds €600 *million per year.*

In the public sector, the U.S. Air Force deploys AI-based predictive maintenance applications to predict failure of aircraft systems and subsystems for a variety of aircraft models, enabling proactive maintenance and reducing the amount of unscheduled maintenance. The applications analyze data from numerous sensors on each aircraft, as well as other operational data, to predict when a system or subsystem will fail. Based on results of initial deployments of these applications, the USAF expects to increase aircraft availability by 40 percent across its entire fleet.

These are just a few examples of AI-powered IoT applications deployed today that deliver significant value as part of digital transformation initiatives at large enterprises. I will discuss additional IoT use cases and examples in chapter 7.

AI and IoT Applications Require a New Technology Stack

We have seen that each of the four technologies driving digital transformation—elastic cloud computing, big data, AI, and IoT—presents powerful new capabilities and possibilities. But they also create significant new challenges and complexities for organizations, particularly in pulling them together into a cohesive technology platform. In fact, many organizations struggle to develop and deploy AI and IoT applications at scale and consequently never progress beyond experiments and prototypes.

These organizations typically attempt to develop the application by stitching together numerous components from the Apache Hadoop open source software collection (and from commercial Hadoop distributors such as Cloudera and Hortonworks) on top of a public cloud platform (AWS, Microsoft Azure, IBM Cloud, or Google Cloud). This approach almost never succeeds—often after months, even years, of developers' time and effort. The corporate landscape is littered with such failed projects. Why is that?

Software components like those in the Hadoop collection are independently designed and developed by over 70 contributors. They use different programming languages and interface protocols with high programming-model switching costs, and they exhibit dramatically varying levels of maturity, stability, and scalability. Moreover, the number of permutations that developers must contend with—of infrastructure service calls, enterprise systems and data integrations, enterprise data objects, sensor interfaces, programming languages, and libraries to support application development—is almost infinite. Finally, most enterprises need to design, develop, and operate hundreds of enterprise applications that all require slightly different "plumbing" of the Hadoop components. The resulting complexity overwhelms even the best development teams. This stitch-it-together approach is rarely successful.

In reality, neither the Hadoop collection nor the public clouds by themselves provide a complete platform for developing AI and IoT applications at scale. The technical requirements to enable a complete, next-generation enterprise platform that brings together cloud computing, big data, AI, and IoT are extensive. They include 10 core requirements:

1. **Data Aggregation**: Ingest, integrate, and normalize any kind of data from numerous disparate sources, including internal and external systems as well as sensor networks

2. **Multi-Cloud Computing**: Enable cost-effective, elastic, scale-out compute and storage on any combination of private and public clouds

3. **Edge Computing**: Enable low-latency local processing and AI predictions and inferences on edge devices, enabling instantaneous decisions or actions in response to real-time data inputs (e.g., stopping a self-driving vehicle before it hits a pedestrian)

4. **Platform Services**: Provide comprehensive and requisite services for continuous data processing, temporal and spatial processing, security, data persistence, and so on

5. **Enterprise Semantic Model**: Provide a consistent object model across the business in order to simplify and speed application development

6. **Enterprise Microservices**: Provide a comprehensive catalog of AI-based software services enabling developers to rapidly build applications that leverage the best components

7. **Enterprise Data Security**: Provide robust encryption, user access authentication, and authorization controls

8. **System Simulation Using AI and Dynamic Optimization Algorithms**: Enable full application lifecycle support including development, testing, and deployment

9. **Open Platform**: Support multiple programming languages, standards-based interfaces (APIs), open source machine learning and deep learning libraries, and third-party data visualization tools

10. **Common Platform for Collaborative Development**: Enable software developers, data scientists, analysts and other team members to work in a common framework, with a common set of tools, to speed application development, deployment, and operation

Model-Driven Architecture

These requirements are uniquely addressed through a "model-driven architecture." Model-driven architectures define software systems by using platform-independent models—that is, the models are independent of the underlying infrastructure services provided by a particular cloud platform provider, whether AWS, Azure, IBM, Google, or any other. Models are then automatically translated to one or more cloud platform–specific implementations. This means the developer doesn't need to worry about which underlying components the application will use or which cloud platform the application will run on. As a result, with a model-driven architecture, AI and IoT applications can be configured and deployed much faster than alternative approaches, with small teams of between three and five software engineers and data scientists.

A model-driven architecture simplifies and accelerates development because it provides a "domain-specific model" that enables software engineers to encode the business logic of their AI and IoT applications with only a fraction of the code required by traditional programming approaches.

The resulting benefits are dramatic. Small teams of programmers and data scientists can develop production AI and IoT applications in as little as 10 weeks, with large-scale projects typically requiring 12 to 16 weeks from design and development to testing and live production deployment. I will return to this topic in greater depth in chapter 10, "A New Technology Stack."

The four technologies driving digital transformation—elastic cloud computing, big data, AI, and IoT—have finally come together in a unified and accessible way. With this convergence, I believe we are poised to see remarkable acceleration of digital transformation initiatives across industries globally. For readers who want to understand these technologies in more detail, the next four chapters examine each in more depth. Readers who want to jump ahead to see how these technologies are being harnessed today in real-world digital transformation initiatives can turn to chapter 9, "The Digital Enterprise."

Chapter 4

The Elastic Cloud

Now entering its second decade, elastic cloud computing is an essential foundation and driving force of digital transformation. By providing universal access to unlimited amounts of computing resources and storage capacity on a pay-for-what-you-use basis—removing the need for expensive upfront capital outlays—the cloud has democratized IT. It enables organizations of any size to apply AI to data sets of any size.

While an increasing number of existing organizations are rapidly shifting large parts of their IT to public cloud platforms, many still resist moving to the cloud. Such resistance is often based on outdated beliefs about inadequate cloud security, availability, and reliability. In fact, since the emergence of the first public cloud offerings more than a decade ago, the rapid evolution and extensive investments of the leading cloud providers have catapulted them to the forefront, outpacing traditional data centers in virtually every measure.

This chapter examines in greater detail the rise of cloud computing, its business value, benefits, and risks. It's important that business and governmental leaders understand this paradigm, which fundamentally changes the economics of computing and IT infrastructure. Organizations unable or unwilling to embrace cloud computing will be at a severe disadvantage compared to their competitors.

The "elastic cloud" gains its name from the ability to rapidly and dynamically expand and contract to satisfy compute and storage resource needs. This elasticity has transformed software deployment models, the costs of IT, and how capital is allocated. Cloud computing has even transformed entire industries and enabled new ones to emerge. Music, for example, is almost entirely delivered and accessed today through cloud-based services like Spotify and Apple Music, rather than on CDs. Cloud-based streaming media services like Netflix and Amazon Prime

Video are rapidly growing, luring viewers away from traditional cable TV and movie theaters. And ride-sharing services like Uber and Lyft would not exist without the cloud.

Developers no longer have to invest heavily in hardware to build and deploy a service. They no longer worry about overprovisioning—thus wasting costly resources—or underprovisioning for an application that becomes wildly popular and missing potential customers and revenue. Organizations with large computing operations that can be done in parallel rather than in a linear sequence—such as processing streams of credit card transactions—can get results as quickly as their programs can scale, since using 1,000 servers for one hour costs the same as using one server for 1,000 hours.

This elasticity of resources, with no premium for large-scale computation, is unprecedented in the history of IT.[1]

Evolution of the Elastic Cloud: From Mainframes to Virtualization

The evolution of the cloud began with the emergence of mainframe computers back in the 1950s. Mainframes subsequently became the bedrock of enterprise computing for several decades. Whether you booked an airline ticket or withdrew cash at an ATM, you indirectly interacted with a mainframe. Enterprises trusted mainframes to run critical operations because they were designed for "reliability, availability, and serviceability" (RAS), a term popularized by IBM.[2]

John McCarthy, then a professor at MIT, introduced the idea of time-sharing of computing resources on an air defense system in 1959.[3] In 1961, a working demonstration of time-sharing called the Compatible Time-Sharing System (CTSS) launched two decades of development across academia and industry. The Multiplexed Information and Computing Service (Multics) and subsequent Unix time-sharing operating systems propelled academia and businesses to widely adopt time-sharing as a way to access and share expensive, centralized computing resources.

Virtualization—the ability to create private partitions on computational, storage, and networking resources—is the technological innovation that makes today's cloud possible. This is what enables cloud providers like AWS, Azure, and Google Cloud to offer customers private, secure resources while maintaining large pools of servers and storage facilities in central locations, connected by high-speed networks. While the concept emerged in the 1970s, the term *virtualization* was popularized only in the 1990s. The first system that offered users a virtualized machine was IBM's CP40 operating system, released in the early 1970s.[4] With the CP40, users had their own operating system without having to work with other time-sharing users.

Application virtualization was first popularized in the early 1990s with Sun Microsystems' Java. The Java Runtime Environment (JRE) enabled applications to run on any computer that had JRE installed. Until Java, developers had to compile code for each platform their software ran on. This was slow and resource intensive, particularly across the many Unix platforms popular at the time. Java created the ability to run internet-ready applications without having to compile code for each platform. The success of Java ushered in an era of similar tools that supported multiplatform deployment, including Connectix's Virtual PC for Macintosh (1997)[5] and VMware's Workstation (1999).[6]

In the early 2000s, VMware transformed application virtualization by introducing software known as a "hypervisor," which didn't require a host operating system to run. Hypervisor software, along with virtual desktop interfaces (VDIs), made virtualization an easy move for many enterprises at the time. This separation of hardware from the operating system and applications led to the evolution of the enterprise data center, a more flexible version of shared compute and storage resources than mainframes. Major players like HP, VMware, Dell, Oracle, IBM, and others led this market for what we today call the "private cloud."

In parallel, several networking advances led to the development of the public cloud. From 1969, with the initial demonstration of ARPANET (from which the internet was born),[7] to the introduction of the Transmission Control Protocol (TCP), X.25 networks, Internet Protocol (IP), Packet Switching, Frame Relay, Multiprotocol Label Switching (MPLS), and Domain Name System (DNS), both public and private networks advanced quickly. Virtual private network (VPN) technology enabled businesses to use public networks as private networks, which freed them from expensive and slow, dedicated connections between facilities. Commercialized by major telecom giants in the late 1990s and 2000s, VPNs enabled organizations to conduct business online securely.

All these advances, plus better and cheaper networking hardware, set the stage for today's public cloud.

The Rise of the Public Cloud

In 2006, Amazon Web Services (AWS) introduced Simple Storage Service (S3) for storing data of any kind and size; Elastic Compute Cloud (EC2), an IaaS virtual machine for computation at any scale; and Simple Queue Service (SQS), for sending and receiving messages between software components of any volume. This marked the introduction of the public cloud, a commercial offering for companies needing to simply and securely collect, store, and analyze their data at any scale. The idea you could "rent" units of compute and storage resources that could be instantly provisioned and managed by a third party to support operations and users anywhere in the world was revolutionary.

The impact of the public cloud cannot be overstated. It freed enterprises from huge administrative burdens and insulated IT departments from the ongoing cycle of matching resources with demand. Equally important, the public cloud freed IT staff to work with lines of business to better understand requirements and business needs.

Amazon's three initial services effectively paved the way for other cloud service providers to follow. Google entered the cloud business with the launch of the Google App Engine in 2008.[8] Microsoft announced Azure later that year and released its first cloud products in stages from 2009 through early 2010.[9] IBM entered the fray with its acquisition of SoftLayer, the progenitor of IBM Cloud, in 2013.[10]

The range of capabilities available on the public cloud (and consequently, the range of use cases) has increased over the years. AWS, for example, has introduced major advances including the content delivery network CloudFront (2008), Virtual Private Cloud (2009), Relational Database Service (2009), and its serverless offering, Lambda (2014). All these advances, from AWS and others, have created an environment where companies can be born, built, and operated in the cloud. Cloud-born companies can move quickly and scale up or down as needed.

Cloud Computing Today

Cloud computing continues to evolve, being redefined and reimagined with new characteristics, deployment models, and service models. Since 2006, when Google's then-CEO Eric Schmidt popularized the term "cloud" to describe the business model of providing services across the internet, many varying definitions of cloud have led to confusion, skepticism, and market hype. In 2011, the U.S. National Institute of Standards and Technology (NIST) recognized the importance of cloud computing and standardized the definition. NIST defines cloud computing as a "model for enabling ubiquitous, convenient, on-demand network access to a shared pool of configurable computing resources (e.g., networks, servers, storage, applications, and services) that can be rapidly provisioned and released with minimal management effort or service provider interaction."[11]

Today, cloud computing critically underpins and helps drive digital transformation. The mass emergence of digital-native companies today would not be possible without easy, immediate, and affordable access to the scalable computing resources available through the elastic public cloud. Existing organizations are taking note of both the favorable economics and greater agility the cloud offers to enable their own digital transformation efforts, and they are leveraging the growing set of cloud computing features.

Cloud Features

Five core features of cloud computing make it essential to digital transformation:

1. **Infinite capacity**: Storage and compute resources are essentially unlimited.

2. **On-demand self-service**: Users can unilaterally provision computing resources without requiring human interaction from the cloud provider.

3. **Broad network access**: Users can operate on the cloud through traditional telecommunication services like Wi-Fi, internet, and

mobile (e.g., 3G, 4G, or LTE) on nearly any device, which means cloud computing is accessible anywhere.

4. **Resource pooling**: Cloud providers serve multiple users through a multitenant model, enabling a pool of physical and virtual resources to be dynamically assigned and reassigned according to each user's demand—thereby reducing resource costs for all users.

5. **Rapid elasticity**: Resources can be automatically, seamlessly, and rapidly provisioned and deprovisioned as a user's demand increases or decreases.

Cloud Deployment Models

Beyond its core technical features, two aspects of cloud computing—the deployment model (who owns the infrastructure) and the service model (what type of services are provided)—have significant impacts on business operations. There are three different deployment models, determined by ownership:

- **Public cloud** is infrastructure available for use by anyone. It is owned, managed, and operated by a business (e.g., AWS, Azure, IBM, or Google Cloud) or a government. The public cloud has gained significant traction with corporations due to its infinite capacity, near-real-time elasticity, strong security, and high reliability.

- **Private cloud** is infrastructure owned by and operated for the benefit of a single organization—effectively a data center, or collection of data centers, operated on a cloud model by an organization for its exclusive use. An organization's private cloud often has limited elasticity and finite capacity because it is gated by hardware.

- **Hybrid cloud** combines private and public cloud infrastructures. Hybrid cloud infrastructure is a dynamic space, where public cloud providers are offering up dynamic extensible private cloud environments (e.g., AWS GovCloud) within a public cloud, thereby offering the best of both worlds.

Cloud Deployment Models

Organizations have a range of choices in cloud deployment models, from a purely public cloud (owned, managed, and operated by a business for anyone's use) to hybrid cloud (a mix of public and private).

Public Cloud	**Private Cloud**	**Hybrid Cloud**
Cloud infrastructure is provisioned for open use by the general public.	Cloud infrastructure is provisioned for exclusive use by a single organization.	Cloud infrastructure is a combination of public and private clouds, which remain unique entities but are bound together by standardized or proprietary technology that enables data and application portability.
It may be owned, managed, and operated by a business, academic, or government organization, or some combination of them. It exists on the premises of the cloud provider.	It may be owned, managed, and operated by the organization, a third party, or some combination of them. It may exist on premises or off premises.	

FIGURE 4.1

As business executives define a cloud computing strategy, they must align their digital transformation approach with the pros and cons of the chosen deployment mode.

Cloud Service Models

The second aspect of cloud computing that significantly impacts how organizations leverage the cloud is the service model. The cloud industry has evolved three broad ways in which a business can harness the power of the cloud:

- **Infrastructure-as-a-Service** (IaaS) comprises the infrastructure building blocks (compute, storage, and networking resources) provisioned and offered on demand. The cloud service provider is responsible for the infrastructure and users have access to their own virtual machines, with control over the operating system, the virtual disk images, IP addresses, etc. AWS Elastic Compute Cloud (EC2), Azure Virtual Machines, IBM Cloud, and Google Compute Engine are the most prominent examples of IaaS.

- **Platform-as-a-Service** (PaaS) means ready-to-use development platforms that enable users to build, test, and deploy applications on the cloud. The platform manages the underlying infrastructure, operating system, environments, security, availability, scaling, backup, and any associated needs such as a database. AWS Elastic

Beanstalk, Azure Web Apps, and Google App Engine are examples of general-purpose cloud platforms.

- **Software-as-a-Service** (SaaS) refers to software applications hosted on cloud infrastructure (either public or private) and accessed by users through the internet via a web browser. Before the advent of SaaS, businesses typically had to install and run licensed software applications on their own infrastructure and they had to manage operations like server availability, security, disaster recovery, software patches, and upgrades. Most organizations did not specialize in these hardware and software maintenance capabilities. In the SaaS model, an organization's IT team does not need to worry about those infrastructure details. The SaaS vendor manages it all. In addition, organizations are typically billed annually, usually based on the number of users licensed to access the SaaS offering. SaaS has had a transformational effect on organizations—they can now focus completely on running their business with dramatically lower IT costs and demands. Over the last two decades, several large SaaS businesses such as Salesforce, Workday, ServiceNow, and Slack have emerged. In addition, all traditional software giants like Microsoft, Oracle, SAP, Adobe, and Autodesk now offer SaaS applications.

This rapid evolution of cloud deployment and service models over the last decade has been a major driver and enabler of digital transformation for both existing organizations and startups across industries. As part of their digital transformation initiatives, organizations are migrating their own private cloud or hybrid cloud environments to public clouds. At the same time, we see new businesses born on the elastic public cloud that readily incorporate these new resources as essential components of their digital DNA.

Global Public Cloud Infrastructure

The major cloud service providers—Amazon Web Services, Google Cloud Platform, and Microsoft Azure—compete fiercely for enterprise customers and their workloads. They invest heavily in state-of-the-art hardware (compute, storage, and networking) and software (hypervisors, operating systems, and a broad array of supporting microservices)—all in order to provide the best in connectivity, performance, availability, and scalability. For enterprises, this has helped reduce cloud costs substantially: Microsoft Azure's storage costs have dropped by 98 percent over the last 10 years.[12]

Similarly, the rise in demand and drop in costs have fueled the rapid addition of computing capacity. In 2015, Amazon added enough capacity every day to support a Fortune 500 enterprise. And the pace of cloud growth does not seem to be slowing. In 2018, worldwide public cloud services market revenue grew 21 percent to $175.8 billion, up from $145.3 billion in 2017. It will exceed $278 billion in 2021.[13]

The trend is clear. Intense competition among the public cloud vendors, for whom cloud computing represents a rapidly growing multibillion-dollar line of business, will continue to drive down costs for their customers while increasing the richness of these offerings. The business imperative to embrace cloud computing becomes more compelling each day.

Connectivity to the Cloud

Adoption of cloud services globally is also propelled by improved connectivity of the telecommunications industry. Network speeds around the world are increasing significantly thanks in part to fiber installations in cities and buildings. Average network speed throughout the U.S. is over 18 megabits per second (Mbps)—only tenth in the world. South Korea tops the list at almost 30 Mbps. Worldwide, the average speed is just over 7 Mbps, increasing 15 percent a year.[14,15]

Historically, fixed networks offered speeds and latencies superior to mobile networks. But continued innovation in mobile network technology—3G and 4G (third- and fourth-generation), and Long-Term Evolution (LTE)—has rapidly narrowed the performance gap between fixed and mobile networks. And worldwide demand for next-generation tablets and smartphones pushes carriers to invest in mobile networking infrastructure. Even higher speeds of 5G (fifth-generation) technology will further accelerate the adoption of cloud computing.

While 5G networks are only in the very early roll-out stages, and estimates about actual speeds abound, it's clear they will be significantly faster than 4G. At the 2018 Consumer Electronics Show in Las Vegas,

Qualcomm simulated what 5G speeds would be in San Francisco and Frankfurt. The Frankfurt demo showed download speeds greater than 490 Mbps for a typical user—compared with typical rates of just 20-35 Mbps over today's 4G LTE networks. San Francisco was even faster: 1.4 Gbps (gigabits per second).

The key point for business and governmental leaders is that cloud computing technology and the infrastructure it relies on continue to improve and evolve at a rapid pace. Performance and scalability are getting better all the time—all the more reason to move to the cloud without delay.

Converting CapEx to OpEx

Public cloud IaaS growth of 30-35 percent per year over the last three years[16] illustrates that businesses—particularly those undertaking digital transformations—are moving to the cloud for a variety of technical and financial reasons. As enterprises transition to elastic public clouds, they quickly realize the economic appeal of cloud computing, often described as "converting capital expenses to operating expenses" (CapEx to OpEx) through the pay-as-you-go SaaS, PaaS, and IaaS service models.[17] Rather than tie up capital to buy or license depreciating assets like servers and storage hardware, organizations can instantly access on-demand resources in the cloud of their choice, for which they are billed in a granular fashion based on usage.

Utility-based pricing allows an organization to purchase compute-hours distributed non-uniformly. For example, 100 compute-hours consumed within an eight-hour period, or 100 compute-hours consumed within a two-hour period using quadruple the resources, costs the same. While usage-based bandwidth pricing has long been available in networking, it is a revolutionary concept for compute resources.

The absence of upfront capital expenses, as well as savings in the cost of personnel required to manage and maintain diverse hardware platforms, allows organizations to redirect this freed-up money and invest in their digital transformation efforts, such as adding IoT devices to monitor their supply chain or deploying predictive analytics for better business intelligence.

Additional Benefits of the Elastic Public Cloud

While cost, time, and flexibility advantages are the fundamental reasons to move to the elastic public cloud, there are other important benefits:

- **Near-zero maintenance**: In the public cloud, businesses no longer need to spend significant resources on software and hardware maintenance, such as operating system upgrades and database indexing. Cloud vendors do these for them.

- **Guaranteed availability**: In 2017, a major global airline suffered an outage because an employee accidentally turned off the power at its data center.[18] Such unplanned downtime—due to things like operating system upgrade incompatibility, network issues, or server power outages—virtually vanishes in the public cloud. The leading public cloud providers offer availability guarantees. A 99.99 percent uptime availability, common in the industry, means less than one hour of downtime a year.[19] It is nearly impossible for an in-house IT team to ensure that level of uptime for an enterprise operating globally.

- **Cyber and physical security**: With the public cloud, organizations benefit from cloud providers' extensive investments in both physical and cyber security managed 24/7 to protect information assets. Public cloud providers continuously install patches for the thousands of vulnerabilities discovered every year and perform penetration testing to identify and fix vulnerabilities. Public cloud providers also offer compliance certification, satisfying local and national security and privacy regulations.

- **Latency**: Minimizing latency—the lag time between user action and system response—is critical to enabling real-time operations, great customer experiences, and more. The single biggest determinant is the round-trip time between an end user's application (e.g., a web browser) and the infrastructure. Major public cloud providers offer multiple "availability zones"—i.e., physically isolated locations within the same geographic region, connected with low latency, high throughput, and highly redundant networking. For example, AWS spans 53 availability zones in 18 regions globally. With the public cloud, a game developer in Scandinavia, for example, can deploy a mobile application and provide best-in-class latency in every region worldwide without managing a fleet of far-flung data centers.

- **Reliable disaster recovery**: Today's globally distributed public clouds ensure cross-region replication and the ability to restore to points in time for comprehensive, reliable disaster recovery. For instance, a business whose East Asian data center is impacted by a local political disruption could operate without any interruption from its replica in Australia. Similarly, if files are accidentally destroyed, cloud services allow businesses to restore back to a time when their systems were operating in a normal state. While it is technically possible for any business to set up, manage, and test its own replication and restore services, it would be prohibitively expensive for most organizations.

- **Easier and faster development (DevOps)**: The shift to the cloud enables the new development methodology known as "DevOps" that is gaining widespread popularity and adoption. Software engineers traditionally developed applications on their local workstations but are steadily moving toward developing on the cloud. DevOps combines both software development (Dev) and IT operations (Ops) in much tighter alignment than was previously the case. The cloud gives developers a wider variety of languages and frameworks, up-to-date cloud-based development environments, and easier collaboration and support. With cloud-based containers, engineers can now write code in their preferred development environment that will run reliably in different production environments. All this increases the rate of developing and deploying software for production use.

- **Subscription pricing**: Cloud computing's utility-based pricing has transitioned software pricing to a subscription model, allowing customers to pay only for their usage. Subscription models for SaaS, PaaS, and IaaS have been popularized in recent years, with pricing typically based on the number of users and compute resources consumed. In most cases, subscription pricing is proportional to different levels of software features selected. This allows businesses to pick and choose what they want, for however long they want, and for any number of users. Even small and medium-sized businesses can optimally access best-in-class software.

- **Future-proofing**: SaaS allows software producers to rapidly and frequently upgrade products, so customers always have the latest functionality. In the pre-cloud era, businesses often had to wait six months or more between release cycles to get the latest improvements, and rollout could be slow and error-prone. Now, with cloud-based SaaS, businesses continuously receive seamless updates and upgrades, and know they always operate with the newest version.

- **Focusing on business, not on IT**: In the era of software licenses, businesses had to maintain teams to manage on-premises hosting, software and hardware upgrades, security, performance tuning, and disaster recovery. SaaS offerings free up staff from those tasks, allowing businesses to become nimble and focus on running the business, serving customers, and differentiating from competitors.

Computing without Limits

The elastic cloud has effectively removed limits on the availability and capacity of computing resources—a fundamental prerequisite to building the new classes of AI and IoT applications that are powering digital transformation.

These applications typically deal with massive data sets of terabyte and petabyte scale. Data sets of this size—particularly since they include a wide variety of both structured and unstructured data from numerous sources—present special challenges but are also the essential raw material that makes digital transformation possible. In the next chapter, I turn to the topic of big data in more depth.

Chapter 5

Big Data

As computer processing and storage capacity have increased, it has become possible to process and store increasingly large data sets. Much of the resulting discussion of big data focuses on the significance of that increase. But it's only part of the story.

What's most different about big data, in the context of today's digital transformation, is the fact that we can now store and analyze *all the data* we generate—regardless of its source, format, frequency, or whether it is structured or unstructured. Big data capabilities also enable us to combine entire data sets, creating massive supersets of data that we can feed into sophisticated AI algorithms.

The quantification of information was first conceived of by Claude Shannon, the father of Information Theory, at Bell Labs in 1948. He conceived of the idea of the binary digit (or bit, as it came to be known), as a quantifiable unit of information. A bit is a "0" or a "1". This invention was a prerequisite to the realization of the digital computer, a device that really does nothing more than add sequences of binary numbers—0s and 1s—at high speeds. If we need to subtract, the digital computer adds negative numbers. If we need to multiply, it adds numbers repeatedly. As complex as digital computers may seem, they are essentially nothing more than sophisticated adding machines.

Using base-2 arithmetic, we can represent any number. The ASCII encoding system, developed from telegraph code in the 1960s, enables the representation of any character or word as a sequence of zeros and ones.

As information theory developed and we began to amass increasingly large data sets, a language was developed to describe this phenomenon. The essential unit of information is a *bit*. A string of eight bits in a sequence is a byte. We measure computer storage capacity as multiples of bytes as follows:

One byte is 8 bits.
One thousand (1000) bytes is a kilobyte.
One million (1000^2) bytes is a megabyte.
One billion (1000^3) bytes is a gigabyte.
One trillion (1000^4) bytes is a terabyte.
One quadrillion (1000^5) bytes is a petabyte.
One quintillion (1000^6) bytes is an exabyte.
One sextillion (1000^7) bytes is a zettabyte.
One septillion (1000^8) bytes is a yottabyte.

To put this in perspective, all the information contained in the U.S. Library of Congress is on the order of 15 terabytes.[1] It is not uncommon for large corporations today to house scores of petabytes of data. Google, Facebook, Amazon, and Microsoft collectively house on the order of an exabyte of data.[2] As we think about big data in today's computer world, we are commonly addressing petabyte- and exabyte-scale problems.

There are three essential constraints on computing capacity and the resulting complexity of the problem a computer can address. These relate to (1) the amount of available storage, (2) the size of the binary number the central processing unit (CPU) can add, and (3) the rate at which the CPU can execute addition. Over the past 70 years, the capacity of each has increased dramatically.

As storage technology advanced from punch cards, in common use as recently as the 1970s, to today's solid-state drive (SSD) non-volatile memory storage devices, the cost of storage has plummeted, and the capacity has expanded exponentially. A computer punch card can store 960 bits of information. A modern SSD array can access exabytes of data.

The Intel 8008 processor is a relatively modern invention, introduced in 1972. It was an 8-bit processor, meaning it could add numbers up to 8 bits long. Its CPU clock rate was up to 800 kilohertz, meaning it could add 8-bit binary numbers at rates up to 800,000 times per second.

A more modern processor—for example the NVIDIA Tesla V100 graphics processing unit (GPU)—addresses 64-bit binary strings that it can process at speeds up to 15.7 trillion instructions per second. These speeds are mind numbing.

The point of this discussion is that with these 21st-century advances in processing and storage technology—dramatically accelerated by the power of elastic cloud computing offered by AWS, Azure, IBM, and others—we effectively have infinite storage and computational capacity available at an increasingly low and highly affordable cost. This enables us to solve problems that were previously unsolvable.

How does this relate to big data? Due to the historical computing constraints described above, we tended to rely on statistically significant sample sets of data on which we performed calculations. It was simply not possible to process or even address the entire data set. We would then use statistics to infer conclusions from that sample, which in turn were constrained by sampling error and confidence limits. You may remember some of this from your college statistics class.

The significance of the big data phenomenon is less about the *size* of the data set we are addressing than the *completeness* of the data set and the *absence of sampling error*. With the computing and storage capacity commonly available today, we can access, store, and process the entire data set associated with the problem being addressed. This might, for example, relate to a precision health opportunity in which we want to address the medical histories and genome sequences of the U.S. population.

When the data set is sufficiently complete that we can process all the data, it changes everything about the computing paradigm, enabling us to address a large class of problems that were previously unsolvable. We can build highly accurate predictive engines that generate highly reliable predictive analytics. This in turn enables AI. That is the promise of big data.

As game-changing as it is, there are enormously complex challenges in managing big data and building and deploying large-scale AI and IoT applications fueled by big data. In this chapter, we discuss both the impact of big data in real-world applications and use cases that are driving digital transformation, as well as the significant challenges around harnessing big data. In order to get value from big data, it is clear that organizations will have to adopt new processes and technologies, including new platforms designed to handle big data.

With regard to big data, incumbent organizations have a major advantage over startups and new entrants from other sectors. Incumbents have already amassed a large amount of historical data, and their sizeable customer bases and scale of operations are ongoing sources of new data. Of course, there remain the considerable challenges of accessing, unifying, and extracting value from all these data. But incumbents begin with a significant head start.

To better understand what big data means today, it's useful to briefly review how data technology has evolved over time—and how we got to where we are.

Computer Storage: A Brief History

The First Storage Device

The first recorded storage device is arguably a clay tablet found in the Mesopotamian city of Uruk. It dates to about 3300 B.C. and is now part of the British Museum's collection.[3] The tablet was a record of payment—in beer rations—to workers. Not only is it an early specimen of cuneiform writing but it is also an example of a recorded and stored piece of data for a particular transaction—that could be retrieved and copied to support or quash disagreements and legal disputes.

One can imagine a large warehouse in Mesopotamia holding all possible records of this nature to help bureaucrats enforce agreements. In fact, the Royal Library of Ashurbanipal (in Nineveh, located in today's Iraq) was just this—a collection of 30,000 tablets including the famed *Epic of Gilgamesh*.[4] The library was destroyed in 612 B.C., but many of the clay tablets survived to provide a wealth of data about Mesopotamian literature, religion, and bureaucracy.

Over the ages, the human need to store, retrieve, and manage data has continued to grow. The Great Library at Alexandria, established in the 3rd century B.C.—supposedly inspired by the Royal Library of Ashurbanipal—stored, at its zenith, between 400,000 and a million papyrus scrolls and parchments. The quest to gather these documents—covering mathematics, astronomy, physics, natural sciences, and other subjects—was so important that incoming ships were searched for new books. Information retrieval and copying had a huge cost—one had to pay a top-rated scribe 25 denarii ($3,125 in today's dollars) to copy 100 lines.[5,6]

To our modern eye, we would recognize several more recent projects as precursors of big data. Scientists in Europe in the middle ages captured astronomical data so that by the time Copernicus hit his stride in the early 16th century, his heliocentric ideas could be based on the findings of previous generations.

A century later, Londoners John Graunt and William Petty used public records of bubonic plague deaths to develop a "life table" of probabilities of human survival. This is considered an early statistical model for census methods and a precursor to modern demography. Scientists like Antonie van Leeuwenhoek catalogued microscopic creatures, establishing the study of microbiology.

In the early 1800s, U.S. Navy officer Matthew Maury took advantage of his placement in the Depot of Charts and Implements to data mine decades of captain's logs to create the revolutionary Wind and Current Chart of the North Atlantic Ocean, thereby transforming transatlantic seafaring.

Later in the century, the U.S. Census Bureau, facing the prospect of spending a decade to collect and collate data for the 1890 census, turned to a young inventor from MIT named Herman Hollerith for a solution. Using punch cards, the Hollerith Electric Tabulating Machine turned a 10-year project into a three-month one. Iterations of the machines were used until they were replaced by computers in the 1950s. Hollerith's machine was one of the core inventions that formed the Computing-Tabulating-Recording Company in 1911, later renamed the International Business Machines Company (IBM).

Evolution of Computer Storage from 1940

For thousands of years, the written or printed word had been the primary means of storing data, hypotheses, and ideas about the world. All that changed—first slowly, then rapidly—with the advent of the modern computer.

The earliest computers were room-sized devices. Examples include the Atanasoff-Berry Computer developed at Iowa State University in 1942; the Allies' Bombe and Colossus machines that helped break

German ciphers during World War II; the Harvard Mark I in 1944; and the ENIAC at the University of Pennsylvania in 1946. All these early computers used electro-mechanical relay-based computing approaches that had a limited ability to store data and results.[7]

The earliest computers that made use of stored information ("memory") were the University of Manchester's SSEM (Small-Scale Experimental Machine) and University of Cambridge's EDSAC (Electronic Delay Storage Automatic Calculator), both operational in 1949. EDSAC's memory used delay-line technology—a technique originally used in radar—to keep a unit of information circulating in mercury till it needed to be read. EDSAC's memory was eventually able to hold 18,432 bits of information—organized as 512 36-bit words.[8] Access to stored memory in the EDSAC took more than 200 milliseconds.

Magnetic approaches to storing information started with the Atlas—operational in 1950 and designed and commercialized by U.S. computer pioneering firm Engineering Research Associates (ERA). Atlas's drum memory was designed to hold almost 400 kilobits of information, with data access times around 30 microseconds. Soon after, in 1951, UNISERVO magnetic tapes—each a half-inch wide and 1,200 feet long, made of nickel-plated phosphor bronze—could store 1.84 million bits with data transfer rates of 10-20 microseconds. Other notable milestones in the evolution of data storage technology include MIT's Whirlwind core memory in 1953, IBM's RAMAC disk drive in 1956 (the first magnetic disk drive), and the Signetics 8-bit RAM in 1966 (one of the earliest semiconductor-based memory devices).[9]

Just 30 years after the EDSAC, the Commodore 64 came in 1982 at a price of $595 and could store 64 kilobytes of memory[10]—more than 30 times the primary memory capacity of the EDSAC. Similarly, the IBM 3380 Direct Access Storage Device had a secondary storage capacity of 2.52 gigabytes—54,000 times the capacity of the Atlas just 30 years prior.[11] Over the same time period, the cost per byte of information continued to fall and speed of access continued to increase at similar exponential rates.

Toshiba introduced flash memory in 1984, which gained widespread commercial adoption in multimedia cards, memory sticks, mobile phones, and other use cases. In 2017, Western Digital introduced a 400-gigabyte microSD card the size of a thumbnail and with twice the capacity of its immediate predecessor, available commercially for $250, or less than $1 per gigabyte.[12] Just a year later, capacity increased again as Integral Memory introduced a 512-gigabyte microSDXC card, also with a price under $1 per gigabyte.

Data Center Storage

In parallel, data center storage has advanced significantly. The early days of data centers relied on simple direct-attached storage (DAS) or network-attached storage (NAS) systems—with redundancy—dedicated to specific applications running on dedicated servers. The data center storage model evolved to storage area networks (SANs), which connected storage via high-speed networking to a group of servers and provided more flexibility and scale across applications. This opened the path to virtualization, separating storage from computing and network resources, and creating the framework for highly scalable resources. In the early days, this underpinned the explosive growth of enterprise software such as ERP and CRM, e-commerce, and video and streaming data. With increased performance and reliability, these data center architectures paved the way for real-time, cloud-based services and applications—which are at the heart of big data analytic capabilities today.

CPU Storage

One more foundational element important for big data analysis is the advance in CPU storage—i.e., the in-memory capacity of a computer's CPU that enables very fast access to data for high-speed processing. Today's landscape of CPU storage technologies—including cache, registers, static and dynamic random-access memory (SRAM and DRAM), and SSDs—all play an important role in workload processing. CPU-based processing is fast, but CPU storage is expensive and low capacity. So there is significant activity today in developing lower-cost, higher-performance technologies—like the Intel Optane, phase change RAM (PCRAM), and Redox-based resistive switching RAM (ReRAM)—which will change the landscape and allow organizations to perform even faster calculations on larger data sets.

Data Storage Moves to the Cloud

As we discussed in chapter 4, Amazon Web Services was launched with little fanfare in 2002. It was, on inception, an internal service delivery arm to help different e-commerce teams within Amazon. It came about after an internal reflection session by Amazon's leadership team on their core capabilities. Over the next 15 years, AWS would grow to independently generate over $17 billion in annual revenue. Today, its cloud-based data storage and compute services are available globally.

The value proposition is simple: By sharing resources to compute and store data across many customers, the cost of these services falls below the cost of buying them in-house. AWS has introduced over a thousand individual services, grown to more than a million active customers, and is the leading provider of elastic cloud compute and storage capabilities. Its offerings for data storage include:

- Amazon S3: Simple Storage Service for object storage

- Amazon RDS: a managed relational database

- Amazon Glacier: an online file storage web service for archiving and backup

- Amazon RedShift: a petabyte-scale data warehouse

- Amazon Dynamo DB: a serverless, NoSQL database with low latency

- Amazon Aurora: a MySQL and PostgreSQL-compatible relational database

Today, the price of using S3 storage is a little over $0.02 per gigabyte per month. Prices continue to fall like a knife. Data can be transferred at a blazing rate of 10 Gbps. Competitive offerings from Microsoft, Google, and others are further driving innovation forward and prices down. All this market competition has resulted in an incredibly rich set of services that underpin digital transformation, and at the same time, has brought the cost of storage to almost zero.

The history of data storage—from ancient clay tablets to punch cards to today's nearly free storage in the cloud—shows that organizations have always generated data and acted on whatever data they were able to capture and store. In the past, technical barriers had limited the amount of data that could be captured and stored. But the cloud and advances in storage technology have effectively stripped away those limits—enabling organizations to extract more value than ever from their growing data.

The Evolution of Big Data

Years before big data became a popular business topic (around 2005), technologists discussed it as a technical problem. As noted in chapter 3, the concept of big data emerged some 20 years ago in fields like astronomy and genomics that generated data sets too massive to process practically using traditional computer architectures. Commonly referred to as scale-up architectures, these traditional systems consist of a pair of controllers and multiple racks of storage devices. To scale up, you add storage. When you run out of controller capacity, you add a whole new system. This approach is both costly and ill-suited for storing and processing massive data sets.

In contrast, scale-out architectures use thousands, or tens of thousands, of processors to process data in parallel. To expand capacity, you add more CPUs, memory, and connectivity, thereby ensuring performance does not dip as you scale. The result is a vastly more flexible and less costly approach than scale-up architectures and is ideally suited to handle big data. Software technologies designed to leverage scale-out architectures and process big data emerged and evolved, including Map-Reduce and Hadoop.

Big data as a term first appeared in an October 1997 paper by NASA researchers Michael Cox and David Ellsworth, published in the *Proceedings of the IEEE 8th Conference on Visualization*. The authors wrote: "Visualization provides an interesting challenge for computer systems: data sets are generally quite large, taxing the capacities of main memory, local disk, and even remote disk. We call this the problem of big data."[13] By 2013, the term had achieved such widespread circulation that the *Oxford English Dictionary* confirmed its cultural adoption, including it in that year's edition of the *OED*.

In 2001, Doug Laney—then an analyst at META Group—described three main traits that characterize big data: volume (the *size* of the data set, as measured in bytes, gigabytes, exabytes, or more); velocity (the *speed* of data arrival or change, as measured in bytes per second or messages per second or new data fields created per day); and variety (including its *shape*, form, storage means, and interpretation mechanisms).[14]

Size, Speed, and Shape

Big data continues to evolve and grow along all three of these dimensions—size, speed, and shape. It's important for senior executives—not just the technologists and data scientists in the organization—to understand how each of these dimensions adds value as a business asset.

Size. The amount of data generated worldwide has increased exponentially over the last 25 years, from about 2.5 terabytes (2.5 x 10^{12} bytes) a day in 1997 to 2.5 exabytes (2.5 x 10^{18} bytes) in 2018—and will continue to do so into the foreseeable future. This rapid growth is also true at the enterprise level. According to IDC, the average enterprise stored nearly 350 terabytes of data in 2016, and companies expected that would increase by 52 percent in the following year. Organizations can now access ever-increasing amounts of both internally and externally generated data, providing fuel for data-hungry AI applications to find new patterns and generate better predictions.

Speed. Particularly with the proliferation of IoT devices, data are generated with increasing velocity. And just as a greater volume of data can improve AI algorithms, so too can higher frequency of data drive better AI performance. For instance, time series telemetry data emitted by an engine at one-second intervals contains 60 times more information value than when emitted at one-minute intervals—enabling an AI predictive maintenance application, for example, to make inferences with significantly greater precision.

Shape. Data generated today take myriad forms: images, video, telemetry, human voice, handwritten communication, short messages, network graphs, emails, text messages, tweets, comments on web pages, calls into a call center, feedback shared on a company's website, and so on. Data fall into two general categories—structured and unstructured. Structured data—such as arrays, lists, or records—can be managed efficiently with traditional tools like relational databases and spreadsheets. Unstructured data (i.e., no predefined data model) includes everything else: text, books, notes, speech, emails, audio, images, social content, video, etc. The vast majority of the data in the world—estimates range from 70 percent to 90 percent—is unstructured data.[15] Organizations are now able to bring all these disparate data formats and sources—structured and unstructured—together and extract value through the application of AI.

For example, an oil and gas company created a unified, federated image of its oil field data sets that combines data from numerous sources and in various formats: telemetry from a "data historian" application (software that records time series production data); Excel files containing historical geological analyses; equipment asset records from a pre-existing asset system; geographic information system latitude-longitude files; and more. The unified data view will be augmented with production data from each well, historical and ongoing pictures from well inspections, and other items. The objective is to apply AI algorithms against all these data for multiple use cases, including predictive maintenance and production optimization.

The Promise of Big Data for the Modern Enterprise

Big data—the ability to capture, store, process, and analyze data of any size, speed, and shape—lays the foundation for the broad adoption and application of AI. Organizations can now harness an unlimited array of data sources. Data generated everywhere throughout an organization can have value. Every customer interaction, every on-time and late delivery by a supplier, every phone call to a sales prospect, every job inquiry, every support request—the sources are virtually endless.

Today, organizations capture and store data using all manner of techniques to augment existing enterprise systems. Insurance companies, for example, work with mining and hospitality companies to add sensors to their workforces in order to detect anomalous physical movements that could, in turn, help predict worker injuries and avoid claims.

Similarly, new sources of data from within the enterprise are being constructed or added to. For instance, to power a new fraud detection application at the Italian energy company Enel, investigator feedback on machine learning predictions of fraud is captured with every investigation—the idea is that machine learning predictions augmented with human intelligence will improve over time. The U.S. Air Force uses all maintenance log data going back seven years to extract information correlated with asset performance and critical failure events. Before it started on this project, these data were stored and isolated from other systems. Today, combined with flight logs, those historical data prove invaluable in developing algorithms for predictive maintenance.

Organizations also combine *extraprise* data—i.e., data generated outside of the enterprise—to enhance internal data and enable interesting data correlations. Examples include customer reviews on sites like Yelp, global weather data, shipping logs, ocean current and temperature data, and daily traffic reports, to name just a few. A retailer may find housing construction data useful in modeling potential demand for stores in a new geography. For a utility, data on the number of lightning strikes along a stretch of transmission cable could be valuable. Data scientists are often creative in their use of data. For instance, by using restaurant reviews and times of operation from public sources like OpenTable and Yelp, one utility was able to enhance its machine learning models to detect establishments that consume anomalous levels of energy despite being closed—an indicator of possible energy theft.

Big data capabilities have opened the frontier for organizations to aggressively explore new data sources, both internal and external, and create value by applying AI to these combined data sets. Managing big data, however, presents a number of challenges for organizations that I will cover in the following sections.

Challenges of Big Data in a Modern Enterprise

Enterprises face a multitude of systems, data sources, data formats, and potential use cases. Generating value requires individuals in the enterprise who are able to understand all these data, comprehend the IT infrastructure used to support these data, and then relate the data sets to business use cases and value drivers. The resulting complexity is substantial.

The only tractable way to approach this problem is through a combination of the right tools, computational techniques, and organizational processes. Most organizations will initially require outside expertise to get started with their big data and AI initiatives.

The next several sections discuss five key challenges that organizations face in today's era of big data.

1. Handling a multiplicity of enterprise source systems

The average Fortune 500 enterprise has, at the very least, a few hundred enterprise IT systems. These include everything from human resources, payroll processing, accounting, billing and invoicing, and content management systems to customer relationship management, enterprise resource planning, asset management, supply chain management, and identity management—to name just a few. One leading global manufacturer's IT organization manages and maintains over 2,000 unique enterprise applications.

Consider another example—the electric grid. A typical integrated utility in the U.S. owns and operates its own generation assets, transmission infrastructure, substations, distribution infrastructure, and metering—all to support thousands to millions of customers. The enterprise IT systems to support this operation are typically sourced from leading equipment and IT vendors—supervisory control and data acquisition (SCADA) systems from the likes of Schneider or Siemens; workforce management systems from IBM; asset management systems from SAP; turbine monitoring systems from Westinghouse—the list is long. The only point of integration organizationally for these IT systems is the CEO. Furthermore, these systems were not designed to interoperate. The task of integrating data from two or more of these systems—such as distribution data (e.g., the total consumption on one side of the transformer down the block) and consumer data (e.g., the total consumption of everyone on that block)—requires significant effort.

This effort is further complicated due to different data formats, mismatched references across data sources, and duplication. Often, enterprises are able to put together a logical description of how data in the enterprise and outside the enterprise should relate—these take the form of an object relationship model or an entity relationship diagram. But in practice, integrating these underlying data to create a unified, federated, and updated image of the data accessible via the same object relationship model can be an onerous task. Mapping and coding all the interrelationships between the disparate data entities and the desired behaviors can take weeks of developer effort.

2. Incorporating and contextualizing high-frequency data

While managing data from multiple systems is by itself a complex undertaking, the challenge gets significantly harder with the sensoring of value chains and the resulting inflow of real-time data. Covered in more depth in chapter 7, this phenomenon has accelerated and resulted in a profusion of high-frequency data. These data are seldom useful by themselves. To yield value, they need to be combined with other data.

For example, readings of the gas exhaust temperature for an offshore low-pressure compressor are only of limited value in monitoring the state of that particular asset. However, these readings are far more useful when correlated in time with ambient temperature, wind speed, compressor pump speed, a history of previous maintenance actions, maintenance logs, and other data. A valuable use case would be to monitor anomalous states of gas exhaust temperature across a portfolio of 1,000 compressors in order to send alarms to the right operator at the right offshore rig—which requires a simultaneous understanding of high-frequency sensor readings, external data like weather conditions, associations between raw data and the assets from which those data are drawn, and workforce logs describing who works at each rig at each point in time.

Building an application to support the use case above requires jointly supporting abilities to rapidly retrieve time series data (typically using a distributed key-value store—a specialized type of database); search and sort workforce logs and offshore asset tags (typically using a relational database—often in separate systems); and alert workers (typically through enterprise software applications or commonly available communication tools).

3. Working with data lakes (or data swamps)

In the early 2000s, engineers at Yahoo! built a distributed storage and computational framework designed to scale in a massively parallel fashion. The Hadoop Distributed File System (HDFS) and the Hadoop MapReduce framework went through a wave of enterprise adoption over the next 10 to 15 years—promoted by companies that attempted to commercialize these technologies, such as Hortonworks, Cloudera, and MapR. The Apache Software Foundation has also supported related projects such as Apache Pig, Apache Hive, and Apache Sqoop—all designed independently to support the adoption and interoperability of HDFS. The promise of HDFS was a scalable architecture to store virtually all an enterprise's data—irrespective of form or structure—and a robust way to analyze it using querying and analytic frameworks.

However, the corporate adoption of Hadoop technology remains low.[16] Over 50 percent of corporate IT leaders do not prioritize it. Of those that do, 70 percent had fewer than 20 users in their organization. Technological challenges, implementation challenges, and deployment challenges all played a part in limiting the widespread adoption of Hadoop in the enterprise. In reality, storing large amounts of disparate data by putting it all in one infrastructure location does not reduce data complexity any more than letting data sit in siloed enterprise systems. For AI applications to extract value from disparate data sets typically requires significant manipulation such as normalizing and deduplicating data—capabilities lacking in Hadoop.

4. Ensuring data consistency, referential integrity, and continuous downstream use

A fourth big data challenge for organizations is to represent all existing data as a unified, federated image. Keeping this image updated in real time and updating all "downstream" analytics that use these data seamlessly is still more complex. Data arrival rates vary by system; data formats from source systems can change; and data arrive out of order due to networking delays. More nuanced is the choice of which analytics to update and when, in order to support a business work flow.

Take the case of a telecommunications provider wanting to predict churn for an individual cell phone customer. The unified view of that customer and the associated data update frequencies could look like this:

Data Set	Data Frequency
Call, text, and data volumes and metadata	every second
Network strength for every call placed	every few minutes
Number of bad call experiences historically	every few minutes
Number of low data bandwidth experiences historically	every few minutes
Density/congestion at cell towers used by customer	every few minutes
Ongoing billing	once a day (at least)
Time since last handset upgrade	once a day
Telco app usage and requests	every few days
Published billing	every month
Calls to the call center and their disposition	varies
Visits to the store and their disposition	varies
Visits to the customer service website	varies
Visits to "How do I stop service?" web page or in-app	varies
Calls to a competitor customer service line	varies
Strength/share of in-network calls and texts	every month
Products and services procured	every few months
Customer relationship details	every few months
Third-party customer demographics	every few months

The variance in data arrival frequency is significant. Data errors can further complicate things: If, say, the call center system logging a dissatisfied customer's complaint somehow misrepresents the customer ID, that record is unusable. More critically, if the churn prediction model subsequently used compound aggregates on these data (e.g., the cumulative count of the number of calls to the call center in the last six months within 24 hours of a low bandwidth event and/or a dropped call and with a disposition of "negative sentiment")—keeping these compound aggregates updated can result in an enormous computational burden or out-of-date analytics.

Enterprises have to understand and plan to solve all these challenges as they digitally transform and embed AI into their operations. They will need the right tools to enable seamless data integration at varying frequencies, ensure referential integrity of the data, and automatically update all analytics that depend on these frequently changing data sets.

5. Enabling new tools and skills for new needs

As the availability and access to data within an enterprise grow, the skills challenge grows commensurately. For example, business analysts accustomed to using tools like Tableau—a popular data visualization software application for creating reports with graphs and charts—will need to now build machine learning models to predict business key performance indicators (KPIs) instead of just reporting on them. In turn, their managers, with decades of proficiency in spreadsheet tools, now need new skills and tools to verify their analysts' work in making those predictions.

Enterprise IT and analytics teams need to provide tools that enable employees with different levels of data science proficiency to work with large data sets and perform predictive analytics using a unified data image. These include drag-and-drop tools for novice users and executives; code-light tools for trained business analysts; integrated development environments for highly skilled data scientists and application developers; and data integration and maintenance tools for data engineers and integration architects working behind the scenes to keep the data image updated.

Big Data and the New Technology Stack

Successful digital transformation hinges critically on an organization's ability to extract value from big data. While big data's management demands are complex, the availability of next-generation technology gives organizations the tools they need to solve these challenges. In chapter 10, I will describe in more depth how this new technology stack addresses big data management capabilities. With that foundational capability in place, organizations will be able to unleash the transformative power of artificial intelligence—the subject of the next chapter.

Chapter 6

The AI Renaissance

Cloud computing and big data, which we examined in the preceding two chapters, represent respectively the infrastructure and the raw material that make digital transformation possible. In this chapter and the following one, we now turn to the two major technologies that leverage cloud computing and big data to drive transformative change—artificial intelligence and the internet of things. With AI and IoT, organizations can unlock tremendous value, reinvent how they operate, and create new business models and revenue streams.

Advances in AI have dramatically accelerated in recent years. In fact, AI has progressed to such an extent that it is hard to overstate its potential to drive step-function improvements in virtually every business process.

While the potential upside benefits are enormous, AI is admittedly a deep and complex subject, and most organizations will require the services of technology partners who can get them started and on their way. With the proper technology foundation and expert guidance, organizations that make investments today to harness the power of AI will position themselves for both short- and long-term competitive advantage. Conversely, those that fail to seize this opportunity are putting themselves at a severe disadvantage.

In this chapter, I provide an overview of AI, how it differs from traditional computer science that organizations have relied on for many decades, and how it is being applied across a range of use cases with impressive results. To better understand why there is such growing interest and investment in AI today, it is useful to know a bit about its history. I will touch on some of the highlights from its origins in the 1950s to the advances in recent years that today make AI an absolute imperative for every organization. I will also describe the significant challenges that AI presents and how organizations are overcoming those challenges.

A New Paradigm for Computer Science

Logic-based algorithms represent the core of traditional computer science. For decades, computer scientists were trained to think of algorithms as a logical series of steps or processes that can be translated into machine-understandable instructions and effectively used to solve problems. Traditional algorithmic thinking is quite powerful and can be used to solve a range of computer science problems in many areas—including data management, networking, search, etc.

Logic-based algorithms have delivered transformative value over the last 50 years in all aspects of business—from enterprise resource planning to supply chain, manufacturing, sales, marketing, customer service, and commerce. They have also changed how individuals communicate, work, purchase goods, and access information and entertainment. For example, the application you use to shop online employs numerous algorithms to perform its various tasks. When you search for a particular product by entering a term, the application runs an algorithm to find the products relevant to that term. Algorithms are used to compute taxes, offer you shipping options, process your payment, and send you a receipt.

Traditional logic-based algorithms effectively handle a range of different problems and tasks. But they are not effective at addressing many tasks that are often quite easy for humans to do. Consider a basic human task such as identifying an image of a cat. Writing a traditional computer program to correctly do this would involve developing a methodology to encode and parametrize all variations of cats—all different sizes, breeds, colors, and their orientation and location within the image field. While a program like this would be enormously complex, a two-year-old child can effortlessly recognize the image of a cat. And a two-year-old can recognize many objects beyond cats.

Similarly, many simple tasks for humans—such as talking, reading or writing a text message, recognizing a person in a photo, or understanding speech—are exceedingly difficult for traditional logic-based algorithms. For years these problems have plagued fields like robotics, autonomous vehicles, and medicine.

AI algorithms take a different approach than traditional logic-based algorithms. Many AI algorithms are based on the idea that rather than code a computer program to perform a task, design the program *to learn directly from data*. So instead of being written explicitly to identify pictures of cats, the computer program learns to identify cats using an AI algorithm derived by observing a large number of different cat images. In essence, the algorithm infers what an image of a cat is by analyzing many examples of such images, much as a human learns.

As discussed in previous chapters, we now have the techniques and computing capability to process all the data in very large data sets (big data) and to train AI algorithms to analyze those data. So wherever it is possible to capture sufficiently large data sets across their operations, organizations can transform business processes and customer experiences using AI—making possible the age of AI-driven digital transformation.

Just as the emergence of the commercial internet revolutionized business in the 1990s and 2000s, the ubiquitous use of AI will similarly transform business in the coming decades. AI already touches and shapes our lives today in many ways, and we are still in the infancy of this transition. Google, one of the first companies to embrace AI at scale, uses AI to power all dimensions of its business.[1] AI already powers the core of Google's business: search. The results of any Google search query are provided by an extremely sophisticated AI algorithm that is constantly maintained and refined by a large team of data scientists and engineers.[2] Advertising, the core source of revenue for Google, is all driven by sophisticated, AI-backed algorithms—including ad placement, pricing, and targeting.

Google Assistant uses AI and natural language processing (NLP) to deliver sophisticated, speech-based interaction and control to consumers. Google's parent company, Alphabet, has a self-driving car division called Waymo that already has cars on the streets. Waymo's core technology—its self-driving algorithms—is powered by AI.

Other consumer-facing companies have similar offerings. Netflix uses AI to power movie recommendations. Amazon uses AI to provide product recommendations on its e-commerce platform, manage pricing, and offer promotions.[3] And numerous companies, from Bank of

America to Domino's Pizza, use AI-powered "chat bots" in a variety of use cases including customer service and e-commerce.

While Google, Netflix, and Amazon are early adopters of AI for consumer-facing applications, virtually every type of organization —business-to-consumer, business-to-business, and government—will soon employ AI throughout their operations. The economic benefits will be significant. McKinsey estimates AI will increase global GDP by about $13 trillion in 2030, while a 2017 PwC study puts the figure at $15.7 trillion—a 14 percent increase in global GDP.

AI Is Not a New Idea

To understand why there is such heightened interest in AI today, it's useful to retrace some of its history. Fascinating in its own right, AI's evolution is an instructive lesson in how a few key innovations can catapult a technology into mainstream prominence.

The field of AI is not new. The earliest ideas of "thinking machines" arose in the 1950s, notably with British computer scientist and mathematician Alan Turing's paper speculating about the possibility of machines that think. He posited the "Turing test" to establish a definition of thinking.[4] To pass the Turing test, a computer would have to demonstrate behavior indistinguishable from that of a human.

The term "artificial intelligence" dates back to 1955, when young Dartmouth math professor John McCarthy coined the term as a neutral way to describe the emerging field.[5] McCarthy and others proposed a 1956 summer workshop:

> We propose that a 2-month, 10-man study of artificial intelligence be carried out during the summer of 1956 at Dartmouth College in Hanover, New Hampshire.
>
> The study is to proceed on the basis of the conjecture that every aspect of learning or any other feature of intelligence can in principle be so precisely described that a machine can be made to simulate it.
>
> An attempt will be made to find how to make machines use language, form abstractions and concepts, solve kinds of problems now reserved for humans, and improve themselves. We think that a significant

advance can be made in one or more of these problems if a carefully selected group of scientists work on it together for a summer.[6]

That workshop is largely cited as the creation of AI as a field of research. A rapid explosion of university-led projects followed: MIT launched Project MAC (Mathematics and Computation) with funding from DARPA in 1963,[7] Berkeley's Project Genie started in 1964,[8] Stanford launched its Artificial Intelligence Laboratory in 1963,[9] and University of Southern California founded its Information Sciences Institute in 1972.[10]

Rapid interest in the field grew with the work of MIT's Marvin Minsky—who established the MIT Computer Science and Artificial Intelligence Laboratory.[11] Minsky and John McCarthy at MIT, Frank Rosenblatt at Cornell, Alan Newell and Herbert Simon at Carnegie Mellon, and Roger Schank at Yale were some of the early AI practitioners.

Based on some of the early work, an "AI buzz" set the world aflame in the 1960s and '70s. Dramatic predictions flooded popular culture.[12] Soon machines would be as smart or smarter than humans; they would take over tasks currently performed by humans, and eventually even surpass human intelligence. Needless to say, none of these dire predictions came to pass.

The early efforts by AI practitioners were largely unsuccessful and machines were unable to perform the simplest of tasks for humans. One key obstacle practitioners faced was the availability of enough computing power. Over the course of the 1960s, '70s, and '80s, computing evolved quite rapidly. But machines were still not powerful enough to solve many real-world problems. Over those decades, computers grew in power and shrank in size, evolving from the size of entire buildings, to mainframe computers, minicomputers, and personal computers.

One of the first commercially available IBM computers, the IBM 650 in 1954, cost $500,000 at the time, had memory of 2,000 10-digit words, and weighed over 900 kilograms.[13] In contrast, the iPhone X, launched in 2017, cost $999, has a 64-bit A11 chip and three gigabytes of RAM, and fits in your pocket.[14,15] This dramatic improvement in performance is a powerful testimony to Moore's Law at work. The ubiquitously available, commodity computers of today are a factor of 1,000 more powerful than the machines available to Minsky and his colleagues.

Inadequate computing power was just one limitation the early AI practitioners faced. A second core issue was that the underlying mathematical concepts and techniques were not well developed. Some of the early work in AI in the 1960s focused on advanced algorithmic techniques such as neural nets. But these ideas did not progress very far. For example, Minsky and Seymour Papert coauthored the book *Perceptrons* in 1969.[16] Today the book is considered by some a foundational work in the field of artificial neural networks—now a widely used AI algorithmic technique. However, other practitioners at the time interpreted the book as outlining key limitations of these techniques. In the 1970s, the direction of AI research shifted to focus more on symbolic reasoning and systems—ideas that proved unsuccessful in unlocking economic value.

The Winter of AI

By the mid-1970s, many funding agencies started to lose interest in supporting AI research. The AI research efforts over the past decade had delivered some significant theoretical advancements—including Back-Propagation[17,18] to train neural networks. But there were few tangible applications beyond some rudimentary examples. Areas that had been promised by AI researchers, such as understanding speech, or autonomous vehicles, had not advanced significantly. Reports, such as the Lighthill Report commissioned by the UK Government, were critical of AI.[19]

Following the initial burst of AI research and activity in the 1960s and early 1970s, interest in AI started to dwindle.[20] Computer science practitioners started to focus on other, more rewarding areas of work, and AI entered a quiet period often referred to as "the first AI winter."

AI made a brief resurgence in the 1980s, with much of the work focused on helping machines become smarter by feeding them rules. The idea was that given enough rules, machines would then be able to perform specific useful tasks—and exhibit a sort of emergent intelligence. The concept of "expert systems" evolved and languages like LISP were used to more effectively encode logic.[21] The idea behind an expert system was that the knowledge and understanding of domain experts in different fields could be encoded by a computer program based on a set of heuristic rules.

The concept held the promise that computers could learn from occupational experts (the best doctors, firefighters, lawyers, etc.), encode their knowledge in the expert system, and then make it available to a much broader set of practitioners, so they could benefit from the understanding of the best of their peers.

These systems achieved some initial commercial success and applications in industry. Ultimately, however, none of the expert systems were effective and the promises seemed far ahead of the technical realities. Expert systems were based on a set of explicitly defined rules or logical building blocks—and not a true learning system that could adapt with changing data. Knowledge acquisition costs were high, since these systems had to get their information from domain experts. And they were also expensive to maintain since rules would have to be modified over time. The machines could not easily learn and adapt to changing situations. By the late 1980s, AI had fallen into a second winter.

The AI Renaissance

The field of AI was reinvigorated in the 2000s, driven by three major forces. First was Moore's Law in action—the rapid improvement of computational power. By the 2000s, computer scientists could leverage dramatic improvements in processing power, reductions in the form factor of computing (mainframe computers, minicomputers, personal computers, laptop computers, and the emergence of mobile computing devices), and the steady decline in computing costs.

Second, the growth of the internet resulted in a vastly increased amount of data that was rapidly available for analysis. Internet companies Google, Netflix, and Amazon had access to data from millions to billions of consumers—their search queries, click-throughs, purchases, and entertainment preferences. These companies needed advanced techniques to both process and interpret the vast amount of available data, and to use these techniques to improve their own products and services. AI was directly aligned with their business interests. The internet also enabled the ubiquitous availability of compute resources through the emergence of cloud computing. As we've discussed in chapter 4, inexpensive compute resources were now available in the public cloud—elastic and horizontally scalable. That is, companies could make use of all the computing power they needed, when they needed it.

Third, significant advances in the mathematical underpinnings of AI were made in the 1990s and continued into the 2000s along with the successful implementation of those techniques. A key breakthrough was in the advancement of the subfield of AI called machine learning, or statistical learning. Important contributions came from researchers then at AT&T Bell Labs—Tin Kam Ho, Corinna Cortes, and Vladimir Vapnik—who created new techniques in applying statistical knowledge to develop and train advanced algorithms.

Researchers were able to develop mathematical techniques to convert complex nonlinear problems to linear formulations with numerical solutions—and then apply the increased available computational power of the elastic cloud to solve these problems. Machine learning accelerated as practitioners rapidly addressed new problems and built a family of advanced algorithmic techniques.

Some of the earliest machine learning use cases involved consumer-facing applications driven by companies like Google, Amazon, LinkedIn, Facebook, and Yahoo! Machine learning practitioners at these companies applied their skills to improve search engine results, advertisement placement and click-throughs, and advanced recommender systems for products and offerings.

Open Source AI Software

Many of the machine learning practitioners from these companies, as well as many in the academic community, embraced the "open source" software model—in which contributors would make their source code (for core underlying technical capabilities) freely available to the broader community of scientists and developers—with the idea these contributions would encourage the pace of innovation for all. The most famous of these open source code repositories is the Apache Software Foundation.

At the same time, Python started to emerge as the machine learning programming language of choice—and a significant share of the source code contributions included Python libraries and tools. Many of the most important libraries used today started to emerge as the open source standard.

By the mid-2000s, machine learning had started to make its way into other industries. Financial services and retail were some of the earliest industries to start to leverage machine learning techniques. Financial services firms were motivated by the large scale of data available from transaction processing and e-commerce and started to address use cases such as credit card fraud. Retail companies used machine learning technologies to respond to the rapid growth of e-commerce and the need to keep up with Amazon.

The open source movement was, and continues to be, an important factor in making AI commercially viable and ubiquitous today. The challenge for organizations trying to apply AI is how to harness these disparate open source components into enterprise-ready business applications that can be deployed and operated at scale. Many organizations try to build AI applications by stitching together numerous open source components, an approach that is unlikely to result in applications that can be deployed and maintained at scale. I will outline the complications of that approach in more detail in chapter 10, and describe how an alternative approach addresses the problem.

Deep Learning Takes Off

In the mid-2000s, another AI technology started to gain traction—*neural networks*, or deep learning. This technique employs sophisticated mathematical methods to make inferences from examples. Broad applications of deep neural networks were enabled by the efforts of scientists such as Yann LeCun at New York University, Geoffrey Hinton at the University of Toronto, and Yoshua Bengio at the Université de Montréal—three of the most prominent researchers and innovators in areas like computer vision and speech recognition.

The field of deep learning started to accelerate rapidly around 2009 because of improvements in hardware and the ability to process large amounts of data. In particular, researchers started using powerful GPUs to train deep learning neural nets—which allowed researchers to train neural nets roughly 100 times faster than before. This breakthrough made the application of neural nets much more practical for commercial purposes.

AI has greatly evolved from the use of symbolic logic and expert systems (in the '70s and '80s), to machine learning systems in the 2000s, and to neural networks and deep learning systems in the 2010s.

Neural networks and deep learning techniques are currently transforming the field of AI, with broad applications across many industries: financial services (fraud detection; credit analysis and scoring; loan application review and processing; trading optimization); medicine and health care (medical image diagnostics; automated drug discovery; disease prediction; bone-specific medical protocols; preventive medicine); manufacturing (inventory optimization; predictive maintenance; quality assurance); oil and gas (predictive oilfield and well production; well production optimization; predictive maintenance); energy (smart grid optimization; revenue protection); and public safety (threat detection). These are just some of the hundreds of current and potential use cases.

The Overall Field of AI Today

AI is a broad concept with several key subfields and the overall taxonomy of the space can be confusing. One of the key distinctions is the difference between *artificial general intelligence* (AGI) and AI.

AGI—that I view as primarily of interest to science fiction enthusiasts—is the idea that computer programs, like humans, can exhibit broad intelligence and reason across all domains. AGI does not seem achievable in the foreseeable future, nor is it relevant to real-world AI applications. It is clear that in any given field we will see the development of AI applications that can outperform humans at some specific task. An IBM computer defeated Garry Kasparov at chess in 1996. Google DeepMind can defeat a Go champion. AI techniques can target a laser and read a radiograph with greater accuracy than a human. I believe it is unlikely that we will see AI applications, however, that can perform all tasks better than a human anytime soon. The computer program that can play chess, play Go, drive a car, target a laser, diagnose cancer, and write poetry is, in my opinion, not a likely development in the first half of this century.

AI Evolution from Rules-Based Systems to Deep Learning

AI has evolved from the rules-based, expert systems approaches that characterized its early days, to today's advanced deep learning methods that leverage sophisticated neural networks and powerful hardware.

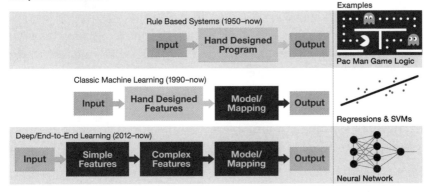

FIGURE 6.1

AI, as I use the term throughout this book, is the area relevant to business and government because it relates to practical applications of artificial intelligence—the applications that you, as a business or government leader, will want to harness for your organization. This is the idea that computer programs can be trained to reason and solve specific dedicated tasks. For example, AI algorithms able to optimize inventory levels, predict customer churn, predict potential equipment failure, or identify fraud. As we've discussed, this field of AI has advanced rapidly in the last couple of decades.

While the different AI subfields fall into three broad categories—machine learning, optimization, and logic—the most exciting and powerful advances are happening in machine learning.

Machine Learning

Machine learning is a subfield of AI based on the idea that computers can learn from data without being explicitly programmed. Machine learning algorithms employ various statistical techniques on the data they are fed in order to make inferences about the data. The algorithms improve as the amount of data they are fed increases and as the inferences they generate are either confirmed or disconfirmed (sometimes by humans, sometimes by machines). For example, a machine learning algorithm for detecting fraud in purchase transactions becomes more accurate as it is fed more transaction data and as its predictions (fraud, not fraud) are evaluated as correct or incorrect.

Machine learning has been central to driving the recent growth of AI. It has proven its ability to unlock economic value by solving real-world problems—enabling useful search results, providing personalized recommendations, filtering spam, predicting failure, and identifying fraud, to name just a few.[22]

Machine learning is a broad field that includes a range of different techniques described in the following section.

Supervised and Unsupervised Learning

There are two main subcategories of machine learning techniques— supervised learning and unsupervised learning.

Supervised learning techniques require the use of training data in the form of labeled inputs and outputs. A supervised learning algorithm employs sophisticated statistical techniques to analyze the labeled training data, in order to infer a function that maps inputs to outputs. When sufficiently trained, the algorithm can then be fed new input data it has not seen before, and generate answers about the data (i.e., outputs) by applying the inference function to the new inputs.

For example, a supervised learning algorithm to predict if an engine is likely to fail can be trained by feeding it a large set of labeled inputs— such as historical operating data (e.g., temperature, speed, hours in use, etc.)—and labeled outputs (failure, nonfailure) for many cases of both engine failure and nonfailure. The algorithm uses these training data to develop the appropriate inference function to predict engine failure for new input data it is given. The objective of the algorithm is to predict engine failure with an acceptable degree of precision. The algorithm can improve over time by automatically adjusting its inference function based on feedback about the accuracy of its predictions. In this case, feedback is automatically generated based on whether the failure occurred or not. In other cases, feedback can be human-generated, as with an image classification algorithm where humans evaluate the prediction results.

There are two main categories of supervised learning techniques. The first is *classification* techniques. These predict outputs that are specific categories—such as whether an engine will fail or not, whether a certain transaction represents fraud or not, or whether a certain image is a car or not. The second category is *regression* techniques. These predict values—such as a forecast of sales over the next week. In the case of forecasting sales over the next week, an oil company might employ an algorithm trained by being fed historical sales data and other relevant data such as weather, market prices, production levels, GDP growth data, etc.

In contrast to supervised learning techniques, *unsupervised* techniques operate without "labels." That is, they are not trying to predict any specific outcomes. Instead, they attempt to find patterns within data sets. Examples of unsupervised techniques include clustering algorithms—which try to group data in meaningful ways, such as identifying retail bank customers who are similar and therefore may represent new segments for marketing purposes—or anomaly detection algorithms, which define normal behavior in a data set and identify anomalous patterns, such as detecting banking transaction behavior that could indicate money laundering.

Neural Networks

Neural networks—and deep neural networks in particular—represent a newer and rapidly growing category of machine learning algorithms. In a neural network, data inputs are fed into the input layer, and the output of the neural network is captured in the output layer. The layers in the middle are hidden "activation" layers that perform various transformations on the data to make inferences about different features of the data. Deep neural nets typically have multiple (more than two or three) hidden layers. The number of required layers generally (but not always) increases with the complexity of the use case. For example, a neural net designed to determine whether an image is a car or not would have fewer layers than one designed to label *all the different objects* in an image—e.g., a computer vision system for a self-driving car, able to recognize and differentiate road signs, traffic signals, lane lines, cyclists, and so on.

In 2012, a neural network called AlexNet won the ImageNet Large Scale Visual Recognition Challenge, a contest to classify a set of several million images that had been preclassified by humans into 1,000 categories (including 90 dog breeds). AlexNet correctly identified images 84.7 percent of the time, with an error rate of only 15.3 percent. This was more than 10 percent better than the next system—a remarkably superior result. Deep learning techniques for image processing have continued to advance since AlexNet, achieving accuracy rates of greater than 95 percent—better than the performance of a typical human.[23]

Organizations in multiple industries are applying deep learning techniques using neural networks to a range of problems with impressive results. In the utilities sector, neural networks are applied to minimize "non-technical loss," or NTL. Globally, billions of dollars are lost each year to NTL as a result of measurement and recording errors, electricity theft from tampering with or bypassing meters, unpaid bills, and other related losses. By reducing a utility's NTL, these AI applications help ensure a more reliable electricity grid and significantly more efficient electricity pricing for customers.

One of the major advantages of using neural networks is the reduction or elimination of feature engineering, a time-consuming requirement when using traditional machine learning algorithms. Neural networks are capable of learning both the output and the relevant features from the data, without the need for extensive feature engineering. However, they usually require a very large amount of training data and are computationally intensive. This is why the use of GPUs has proven crucial for the success of neural networks.

Overcoming the Challenges of Machine Learning

For many AI use cases, organizations can deploy prebuilt, commercially available SaaS applications without having to develop the applications themselves. These include applications for predictive maintenance, inventory optimization, fraud detection, anti–money laundering, customer relationship management, and energy management, among others. In addition to deploying prebuilt SaaS applications, most large organizations will need to develop their own AI applications specifically tailored to their particular needs.

The successful development of applications powered by machine learning AI requires both the right set of skills and expertise, as well as the right tools and technologies. Relatively few organizations in the world have all the necessary internal expertise and capabilities to build, deploy, and operate sophisticated AI applications that will drive meaningful value. The vast majority of organizations will need to engage with partners to provide the required expertise and technology stack to build, test, deploy, and manage the applications.

Machine Learning: Development and Deployment Workflow

There is significant financial upside and business benefit in understanding how to avoid the potential pitfalls of an AI development initiative so that you can quickly capture positive ROI. To get a sense of the challenges in developing and deploying AI applications at scale—and why the right expertise, partners, and development platform are critical—let's look at what's involved in a machine learning development process. In this section, I outline the sequential workflow in developing and deploying a machine learning AI application. This process is well understood by machine learning experts.

1. Data Assembly and Preparation

The first step is to identify the required and relevant data sets, and then assemble the data in a unified image that is useful for machine learning. Because the data come from multiple disparate sources and software systems, there are often issues with data quality such as data duplication, gaps in data, unavailable data, and data out of sequence. The development platform must therefore provide tools to address those issues, including capabilities to automate the process of ingesting, integrating, normalizing, and federating data into a unified image suitable for machine learning.

2. Feature Engineering

The next step is feature engineering. This involves going through the data and crafting individual signals that the data scientist and domain

Workflow for Developing and Deploying a Machine Learning Application

A typical machine learning workflow involves multiple steps, from data loading and labeling, to feature development, algorithm training, and testing. Some deep learning approaches eliminate the need for time-consuming feature engineering.

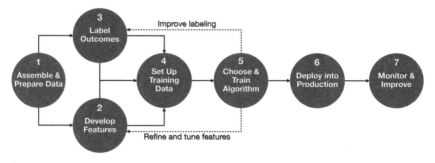

FIGURE 6.2

experts think will be relevant to the problem being solved. In the case of AI-based predictive maintenance, signals could include the count of specific fault alarms over the trailing 7 days, 14 days, and 21 days; the sum of the specific alarms over the same trailing periods; and the maximum value of certain sensor signals over those trailing periods.

3. Labeling the Outcomes

This step involves labeling the outcomes the model tries to predict (e.g., "engine failure"). Often the specific outcomes are not clearly defined in the data since the original source data sets and business processes were not originally defined with AI in mind. For example, in AI-based predictive maintenance applications, source data sets rarely identify actual failure labels. Instead, practitioners have to infer failure points based on combinations of factors such as fault codes and technician work orders.

4. Setting Up the Training Data

Now comes the process of setting up the data set for training the algorithm. There are a number of nuances to this process that may require outside expertise. For classification tasks, data scientists need to ensure that labels are appropriately balanced with positive and negative examples to provide the classifier algorithm enough balanced data. Data scientists also need to ensure the classifier is not biased by artificial patterns in the data. For example, in a recent fraud detection deployment for a utility, a classifier trained on historical cases on a large country-wide data set incorrectly identified a number of suspected fraud cases on a remote island. Further examination revealed that because the island is so remote and hard to access, investigators traveled there *only* if they were certain of fraud. All historical cases investigated on the island were therefore true positive labels. Consequently, the classifier *always* correlated the island location with incidence of fraud, so the algorithm had to be adjusted.

5. Choosing and Training the Algorithm

The next step is to choose the actual algorithm and then train it with the training data set. Numerous algorithm libraries are available to data scientists today, created by companies, universities, research organizations, government agencies, and individual contributors. Many are available as open source software from repositories like GitHub and Apache Software Foundation. AI practitioners typically run specialized searches across these libraries to identify the right algorithm and build the best-trained model. Experienced data scientists know how to narrow their searches to focus on the right classes of algorithms to test for a specific use case.

6. Deploying the Algorithm into Production

The machine learning algorithm then must be deployed to operate in a production environment: It needs to receive new data, generate outputs, and have some action or decision be made based on those outputs. This may mean embedding the algorithm within an enterprise application used by humans to make decisions—for example, a predictive maintenance application that identifies and prioritizes equipment requiring maintenance to provide guidance for maintenance crews. This is where the real value is created—by reducing equipment downtime and servicing costs through more accurate failure prediction that enables proactive maintenance before the equipment actually fails. In order for the machine learning algorithm to operate in production, the under-lying compute infrastructure needs to be set up and managed. This includes elastic scale-out and big data management abilities (e.g., inges-tion, integration, etc.) necessary for large data sets.

7. Closed-Loop Continuous Improvement

Once in production, the performance of the AI algorithm needs to be tracked and managed. Algorithms typically require frequent retraining by data science teams. As market conditions change, business objectives and processes evolve, and new data sources are identified. Organizations need to maintain technical agility so they can rapidly develop, retrain, and deploy new models as circumstances change.

The science of AI has evolved and matured over the last several de-cades. We are now at a point where not only are the underlying tech-nologies available, but also organizations now have access to domain experts, data scientists, and professional services providers that can help them harness the power of AI for competitive advantage.

Business Benefits of AI

AI technologies deliver real business benefits today. In particular, tech-nology companies like Google, LinkedIn, Netflix, and Amazon use AI at large scale. McKinsey Global Institute (MGI) estimates that technology companies spent $20 billion to $30 billion on AI in 2016.[24] Some of the most established applications for AI delivering concrete business ben-efits are in online search, advertising placement, and product or service recommendations.

In addition to technology companies, sophisticated industries ad-vanced in digitization, such as financial services and telecom, are start-ing to use AI technologies in meaningful ways. For example, banks use AI to detect and intercept credit card fraud; to reduce customer churn by predicting when customers are likely to switch; and to streamline new customer acquisition.

The health care industry is just starting to unlock value from AI. Significant opportunities exist for health care companies to use ma-chine learning to improve patient outcomes, predict chronic diseases, prevent addiction to opioids and other drugs, and improve disease coding accuracy.

Industrial and manufacturing companies have also started to unlock value from AI applications as well, including using AI for predictive maintenance and advanced optimization across entire supply chains.

Energy companies have transformed operations using AI. Utility companies use advanced AI applications to identify and reduce fraud, forecast electricity consumption, and maintain their generation, transmission, and distribution assets.

There are several emerging applications of AI in defense. Already, the U.S. military uses AI-based predictive maintenance to improve military readiness and streamline operations. Other use cases include logistics optimization, inventory optimization, and recruiting and personnel management (e.g., matching new recruits to jobs).

I will cover some of these industry use cases in more detail in chapters 8 and 9.

AI in Action: Addressing a $1 Billion Customer Retention Opportunity

To illustrate how AI can address complex concerns shared by virtually every business, let's look at an example of using AI to improve customer retention in the financial services industry. Enterprises focus considerable resources on keeping customers satisfied, successful, and engaged. Particularly in B2B industries, determining the health of a customer account can be challenging. Often, this is a matter of dedicated account managers making calls and manually tracking customer behavior. And in many cases, a company may not learn about a customer's intention to switch to a different provider until it's too late.

In the corporate banking market, banks compete for business based on a number of factors, including product offerings, interest rates, and transaction fees. Banks generate revenue from fees charged on customers' transactions and from interest earned by lending out the funds in customers' accounts. A bank's corporate account managers, therefore, carefully track their customers' transaction activity and cash balances, since these are key revenue drivers. This is largely a manual process, managed using spreadsheets and based on reports generated from the bank's CRM and other systems. But since many internal and external factors—investment activity, mergers and divestitures, competitive dynamics, etc.—can impact a customer's transaction volume and balances in any given period, there is a lot of noise in those indicators.

Corporate account managers therefore struggle to identify, as early as possible, signs that a customer may be permanently reducing or terminating its business with a bank for preventable reasons. If account managers can determine an at-risk customer early enough, they may be able to take action. For instance, a customer might reduce its business because it is financially overextended on some loans. In this case, the account manager might offer to restructure the loans or offer loan counseling services. Or maybe a competitor has offered the customer a better interest rate, in which case the account manager can extend a competitive rate.

Faced with this complexity, a leading financial services company is using an AI suite to develop an AI-powered application to assist corporate account managers in effectively identifying and proactively engaging with potentially at-risk corporate customers. The bank employs hundreds of corporate account managers that serve tens of thousands of corporate customers, representing aggregate cash balances of several hundred billion dollars. Any improvement in customer retention in this high-margin line of business represents significant economic value to the bank.

The AI application ingests and unifies data from numerous internal and external sources, including multiple years of historical data at various levels of frequency: customer transactions and account balances; changes in rates paid on cash balances; credit risk; GDP growth; short-term interest rates; money supply; and account-specific corporate action data from SEC filings and other sources. By applying multiple AI algorithms to these data in real time, the application can identify profiles of at-risk customers, predict those who are likely to reduce their balances for preventable reasons, and send prioritized alerts to account managers, enabling them to take proactive action.

Using the AI application results in far more accurate predictions and timely identification of at-risk customers than the traditional approach used by account managers. The bank estimates the incremental annual economic value of applying this AI application is approximately $1 billion—pure bottom line profit.

The Economic and Social Impacts of AI

AI will have profound consequences for society and business. According to PwC's 2017 study projecting an increase of $15.7 trillion in global GDP by 2030 due to AI, half of that total gain will derive from labor productivity improvements and the other half from increased consumer demand. PwC estimates the potential value creation across specific industries could reach $1.8 trillion in professional services, $1.2 trillion in financial services, $2.2 trillion in wholesale and retail, and $3.8 trillion in manufacturing.

According to the same PwC study, the impact will not be evenly distributed across the globe. While North America currently leads, with Europe and developed Asian economies following, China is expected to eventually surpass others. In fact, China has made it a national priority and goal to be the world leader in AI by 2030. For organizations everywhere, and particularly those competing with Chinese counterparts, the urgency to digitally transform and invest specifically in AI capabilities grows.

AI-driven growth is a welcome antidote to a decades-long slowdown in productivity gains in developed economies. But the potential downside of advances in AI will be sharp and painful for those who do not adapt. For some organizations, their very existence is at risk.

Renowned Harvard Business School professor Michael Porter—whose book on competitive strategy is a classic in the field—speculates a "new world of smart, connected products" underpinned by AI and big data represents a sea change in the fundamental dynamics of competition.[25] Porter suggests this is not simply a matter of competitive advantage; it is *existential*. Recall that 52 percent of Fortune 500 companies have been acquired, merged, or have declared bankruptcy since 2000. The threat of organizational extinction is very real.[26]

For some time, academics, scientists, and market researchers have raised the alarm about AI's impact. The dialogue had been fairly muted, largely constrained to the technology and scientific communities. Occasional press coverage of high-profile AI pessimists—like *Vanity*

Fair's 2017 article on Elon Musk's "crusade to stop the A.I. apocalypse" —appeared, stoking the fire of AI backlash.[27] By the early part of 2018, concerns about the consequences of AI hit the international stage as a main topic at Davos and in subsequent media coverage. Estimates and predictions suddenly took on additional meaning as mass media and pundits stitched together viewpoints on the topic. Dire scenarios such as a robot apocalypse, the elimination of all jobs, and the destruction of civilization hit the media.[28]

Most people with even a casual understanding of the state of AI today interpret this hand-wringing as wildly overblown.[29] History shows the change of magnitude represented by AI is initially met with fear and skepticism, eventually giving way to mass adoption to become business as usual. But that does not diminish the cultural and social downsides. For some types of jobs, the impact will be stark. And the potential for human bias to distort AI analysis is real.

Many jobs will be lost. Retraining existing workforces to adapt will be a challenging public issue. The sooner governments and industry respond with thoughtful policies, the more stable the impact will be. At the same time, most economic AI value cases still require human front-line operators to execute. Certainly, middle managers and white-collar workers will typically work alongside AI in the near term.

As with other technology advances, AI will soon create more jobs than it destroys. Just as the internet eliminated some jobs through automation, it gave rise to a profusion of new jobs—web designers, database administrators, social media managers, digital marketers, etc. In 2020, AI is expected to create 2.3 million jobs while eliminating 1.8 million.[30] Some of these new jobs will be in computer science, data science, and data engineering. Ancillary jobs at consulting firms will continue to grow, both at traditional firms like McKinsey and BCG and at decision science firms like Mu Sigma.

But the reality will likely be a much broader impact on society, and we cannot yet anticipate all the different types of jobs that will result from widespread implementation of AI. Speaking in 2017 about an e-governance initiative, India's prime minister Narendra Modi said: "Artificial intelligence will drive the human race. Experts say that there is a huge possibility of job creation through AI. Technology has the power to transform our economic potential."[31]

Positive viewpoints abound. With the global population growing to 9.7 billion people by 2050, AI-enabled agriculture could help farmers meet the demand for 50 percent more crops on ever-shrinking land resources.[32] AI-powered precision medicine will identify and treat cancer much more effectively. Better cybersecurity will detect and prevent threats. AI-enabled robots will assist the elderly, providing more independence and a better quality of life. AI will dramatically improve the ability to scan billions of online posts and web pages for suspicious content to protect children and others from trafficking and abuse. Climate change, crime, terrorism, disease, famine—AI promises to help alleviate these and other global ills.

I am familiar with a number of AI applications designed to deliver significant social value beyond their commercial impact: An AI application to predict the likelihood of opioid dependency so doctors can make better decisions in prescribing drugs and save millions of people from addiction. An AI application to predict public safety threats so agencies can better protect human lives. An AI application to detect money laundering so financial institutions can better combat the $2 trillion-a-year criminal industry.

In my meetings with organizations around the world, every enlightened business and government leader with whom I've spoken is actively working to understand how to harness AI for social, economic, and environmental good. We have hardly scratched the surface of what's possible in improving human life and the health of the planet with AI.

The Battle for AI Talent

Because AI is now essential for every organization that wants to benefit from the analysis of large data sets, the competition for trained data scientists is robust. Consequently, there is a significant global shortage of AI talent today. Existing talent is extremely concentrated at a few technology companies like Google, Facebook, Amazon, and Microsoft. By some estimates, Facebook and Google alone hire 80 percent of the machine learning PhDs coming into the job market.[33]

While many individuals at companies have job titles related to data science, most are unskilled at machine learning and AI. Businesses still think of data scientists as analysts who perform business intelligence using dashboards, or at best, as statisticians who sample from data sets to draw static inferences. Most organizations are just starting their evolution toward AI and do not have a strong bench of AI practitioners.

Since 2000, the number of AI startups has increased by a factor of 14, while venture investment in AI startups has grown sixfold during the same period. And the share of jobs requiring AI skills has grown by a factor of nearly 4.5 since 2013.[34] The burgeoning global demand for data scientists and managers skilled in analytics has captured the attention of politicians, governments, corporations, and universities worldwide.[35]

Of course, the data scientist pipeline starts with training at university. The rise in high-paying data science jobs has sparked a surge in enrollment in data science programs: Graduates with degrees in data science and analytics grew by 7.5 percent from 2010 to 2015, outpacing other degrees, which grew only 2.4 percent collectively.[36] Today, more than 120 master's programs and 100 business analytics programs are available in the U.S. alone. To train existing workers, boot camps, massive open online courses (MOOCs), and certificates have grown in popularity and availability.

In 2018 LinkedIn reported data scientist roles in the U.S. had grown by 500 percent since 2014 while machine learning engineer roles had increased by 1,200 percent.[37] Another 2017 study found that by 2020 the total number of data science and analytics jobs will increase to 2,720,000 and will have an impact across a broad range of industries.[38] On job sites like Glassdoor and LinkedIn, machine learning engineers, data scientists, and big data developers are among the most popular, with demand coming from numerous industries.

As a result, companies are paying high prices to acquire data scientists. In 2014, for example, Google acquired AI startup DeepMind Technologies, with just 75 employees, for an estimated $500 million—more than $6 million per employee.[39] The acquisition produced at least two significant results: It led to the development of AlphaGo, the first AI program to defeat a top professional player in the ancient Chinese board game Go—which turned out to be a "Sputnik moment" for China, propelling its government to make AI a top strategic priority.[40] More recently, DeepMind's AlphaFold algorithm won the 2018 Critical Assessment of Structure Prediction (CASP) competition—considered the "virtual protein-folding Olympics, where the aim is to predict the 3D structure of a protein based on its genetic sequence data."[41] This is an

Growing Demand for AI Skills

Jobs requiring AI-related skills are growing at a rapid rate, and many are going unfilled. A shortage of talent is leading to a global war for AI software engineers and data scientists.

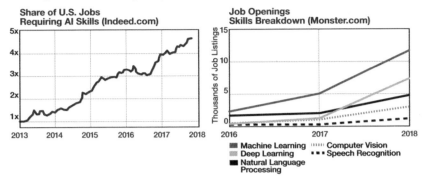

FIGURE 6.3

important area of biomolecular research with significant potential to improve understanding of diseases and the discovery of new drugs.

To address the overall demand for data science skills, governments have begun to act. The UK's Open Data Institute and Alan Turing Institute, the European Commission's 2014 big data strategy, and the U.S. federal government's 2016 Big Data Research and Development Strategic Plan are all examples of coordinated efforts to address the need for trained data scientists. China, which has made AI a central pillar of its thirteenth Five-Year Plan and New Generation of Artificial Intelligence Development Plan, is investing massively in AI research including university programs to train data scientists.[42] But China also estimates it will face data scientist shortfalls: In 2016 the information technology ministry estimated China will need 5 million more AI workers to satisfy its needs.

Globally, more traditional research programs are contributing to core research and are publishing papers at a rapid rate. Leading institutions include MIT, Carnegie Mellon, Stanford, and USC in the U.S.; Nanyang Technological University, National University of Singapore, Hong Kong Polytechnic University, Chinese University of Hong Kong, the Institute of Automation, Tsinghua University, and Chinese Academy of Sciences in Asia; University of Grenada and Technical University of Munich in Europe; as well as others in Canada, Switzerland, Italy, the Netherlands, Australia, and Belgium, to name a few.

Data science programs in the U.S. are expanding across many vectors. In 2014, University of California at Berkeley launched an online data science master's program and now offers an executive education program in data science and analytics. More than 30 high schools in California have started offering data science classes for juniors and seniors.[43] Over the longer term, a significant focus on mathematical and computer science education starting in the K-12 curriculum will be required to address the AI skills gap.

There are also a growing number of "boot camps" and training programs for aspiring data scientists. These programs take in professionals with strong technical backgrounds—e.g., mathematics, physics, or other engineering disciplines—to train and prepare them for AI careers. Some of these boot camp courses are available online. For example, Coursera offers an online curriculum for both machine learning and deep learning.[44] Other courses are in-person, such as the Insight Data Science program in the San Francisco Bay Area.[45]

In addition to data scientists, companies will also increasingly need individuals whom McKinsey calls "translators."[46] Translators can bridge the divide between AI practitioners and the business. They understand enough about management to guide and harness AI talent effectively, and they understand enough about AI to ensure algorithms are properly integrated into business practices.

Without a doubt, we are in a transitional time as organizations retrain their workforces, recruit graduates with AI degrees, and adjust to the many changes driven by AI innovation and adoption. But there is a clear path forward for organizations that realize the inevitability of an AI-powered future and the need to start building AI capabilities now. Today organizations can rely on the expertise of AI advisors and proven technology partners while simultaneously developing their own internal AI competencies.

Succeeding as an AI-Driven Enterprise

We have seen that to succeed with AI, organizations require new technological and business capabilities to manage big data, as well as new skills in data science and machine learning.

A final challenge organizations face in succeeding with AI is to implement changes in business processes that AI requires. Just as the emergence of the internet drove organizations to change business processes in the 1990s and early 2000s, AI drives a similar if not greater scale of change. Organizations may need to adapt their workforce to accept recommendations from AI systems and provide feedback to AI systems. This can be difficult. For example, maintenance practitioners who have been doing their jobs in a specific way for decades often resist new recommendations and practices that AI algorithms may identify. Therefore, capturing value from AI requires strong leadership and a flexible mindset on the part of both managers and front-line employees.[47]

For all these reasons, organizations that embark on digital transformation initiatives increasingly engage experienced technology partners to help overcome the challenges of building, deploying, and operating AI-based applications and driving business process changes required to capture value. Organizations are investing in a new technology stack—that I describe in chapter 10—providing the capabilities to address these requirements in a far more efficient way than traditional approaches.

This new generation of technology is increasingly important as AI applications get larger and more complex, particularly as enterprises and value chains are instrumented with sensors and actuation devices—the phenomenon known as the internet of things (IoT). This increases the amount of data available to organizations by orders of magnitude and also increases the fidelity and accuracy of data sets.

Organizations will be challenged to interpret the large amounts of data IoT generates and to leverage these data to take appropriate action in a timely manner. Interpreting and acting over large data sets will require the application of AI, which will therefore play an important role in unlocking value from IoT. I will describe the IoT phenomenon and its implications for business more fully in the next chapter.

While the threat of missing the digital transformation opportunity is existential, the rewards for embarking on a strategic, organization-wide transformation will be truly game-changing. As studies by PwC, McKinsey, the World Economic Forum, and others show, digital transformation will drive trillions of dollars of new value creation globally over the next decade. Organizations that act now will position themselves to take an outsized share of that prize.

Chapter 7

The Internet of Things

The previous three chapters discussed how the technology trends of elastic cloud computing, big data, and artificial intelligence are driving forces of digital transformation. The fourth trend, the internet of things (IoT), refers to the ubiquitous sensing of value chains so all devices in the chains become remotely machine addressable in real or near-real time.

I first came across the term "internet of things" in 2007 during a business trip in China. Initially, I assumed the internet of things was only about the sensing of value chains. But I have since given this a lot of thought, and I've discovered what's happening is more significant and transformational.

With ever-cheaper and lower-power processors and faster networks, computing is rapidly becoming ubiquitous and interconnected. Inexpensive AI supercomputers the size of credit cards are deployed in cars, drones, surveillance cameras, and many other devices. This goes well beyond just embedding machine-addressable sensors across value chains: IoT is a *fundamental change in the form factor of computing*, bringing unprecedented computational power—and the promise of real-time AI—to every manner of device.

Origin of the Internet of Things

IoT, along with AI, has created one of the most disruptive waves we've ever seen in IT and business. IoT allows us to connect low-cost, high-speed chips and embedded sensors through fast networks. At the root of IoT was the introduction of smart, connected products and the hyper-growth of the internet.

Three decades ago, the notion of smart objects was a new idea. Wearable computing devices were proposed by researchers such as Rank Xerox's Mik Lamming and Mike Flynn, who in 1994 created the Forget-Me-Not, a wearable device that used wireless transmitters "designed to help with everyday memory problems: finding a lost document, remembering somebody's name, recalling how to operate a piece of machinery."[1] In 1995, MIT's Steve Mann created a wearable wireless webcam. That same year, Siemens developed the first wireless machine-to-machine (M2M) communication, used in point-of-sale systems and for remote telematics.

In 1999, MIT Auto-ID Center co-founder and Executive Director Kevin Ashton used the term "internet of things" for the first time. In the title of a presentation designed to get the attention of Procter & Gamble's executive management, he linked the new idea of radio frequency identification (RFID) tags in the supply chain to the intense and growing interest in the internet.[2] The use of RFID tags to track objects in logistics is a well-known early example of IoT, and the technology is commonly used today to track shipments, prevent loss, monitor inventory levels, control entry access, and much more.

In fact, industrial uses of IoT took hold first ahead of consumer uses. In the late 1990s and early 2000s, a wave of industrial applications emerged following the introduction of M2M communication, with companies like Siemens, GM, Hughes Electronics, and others developing proprietary protocols to connect industrial equipment. Often managed by an onsite operator, these early M2M applications evolved in parallel as IP-based wireless networks gained traction with office workers using laptops and mobile phones. By 2010, the idea of moving these largely proprietary networks to IP-based Ethernet protocols was seen as an inevitable direction. Called "Industrial Ethernet," these applications focused on remote servicing of equipment and factory floor monitoring, often from remote locations.

IoT was slower to take hold in the consumer products world. In the early 2000s, companies repeatedly made (largely unsuccessful) forays into connecting products like washing machines, lamps, and other household items. In 2000, for example, LG was the first to introduce an internet-connected "smart refrigerator" (with a $20,000 price tag), but few consumers at the time wanted a fridge that told them when to buy milk. In contrast, wearable computers like the Fitbit and Garmin (both introduced in 2008) started capturing consumer interest, leveraging motion-detecting accelerometers and global positioning system (GPS) capabilities for uses such as fitness and navigation.

Consumer IoT was further sparked in 2011–12, when several successful products like the Nest remote thermostat and the Philips Hue smart lightbulb were introduced. In 2014, IoT hit the mainstream when Google bought Nest for $3.2 billion, the Consumer Electronics Show showcased IoT, and Apple introduced its first smart watch. Consumer IoT is most visible in the fast-growing adoption of wearables (particularly smart watches) and "smart speaker" devices like the Amazon Echo, Google Home, and Apple HomePod—a category growing at nearly 48 percent a year in the U.S.[3]

Today, we see even more changes in the form factor of computing devices. I expect that in the next few years virtually everything will have become a computer—from eyeglasses to pill bottles, heart monitors, refrigerators, fuel pumps, and automobiles. The internet of things, along with AI, creates a powerful system that was barely imaginable at the beginning of the 21st century, enabling us to solve problems previously unsolvable.

The IoT Technology Solution

To take advantage of IoT, businesses and governments need a new technology stack, connecting the edge, an IoT platform, and the enterprise.

The edge consists of a very broad range of communication-enabled devices, including appliances, sensors, and gateways, that can connect to a network. At a minimum, edge devices contain monitoring capabilities, creating visibility into the product's location, performance, and status. For example, a smart meter in an electrical power grid sends status and usage readings to the utility's operations center throughout the day. As the form factor of computing devices continues to evolve, more edge devices are expected to have bidirectional control capabilities. Edge devices that can be monitored and controlled allow for a new set of business problems to be solved. By leveraging a device's monitoring and control capabilities, its performance and operation can be optimized.

IoT Technology: Connecting the Edge to the Enterprise

Taking advantage of the internet of things requires a new technology solution that connects edge devices, an IoT platform, and the enterprise.

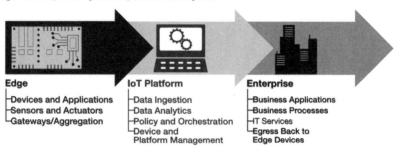

Edge

–Devices and Applications
–Sensors and Actuators
–Gateways/Aggregation

IoT Platform

–Data Ingestion
–Data Analytics
–Policy and Orchestration
–Device and
  Platform Management

Enterprise

–Business Applications
–Business Processes
–IT Services
–Egress Back to
  Edge Devices

FIGURE 7.1

For instance, algorithms can be used to predict equipment failures, allowing a maintenance crew to service or replace the device before it fails.

An IoT platform is the connection between the enterprise and the edge. IoT platforms must be able to aggregate, federate, and normalize large volumes of disparate, real-time operational data. The ability to analyze data on petabyte scale—aggregating all relevant historical and operational data from both modern and legacy information systems into a common cloud-based data image—is a critical requirement.

Today's state-of-the-art IoT platforms function as application development platforms for enterprises. Rapid development of applications that monitor, control, and optimize products and business units greatly increases productivity.

There are many real-world examples of industries that have already integrated IoT as a core element of business transformation. A notable example is the smart grid. The electric power grid, as it existed at the end of the 20th century, was largely as originally designed more than a hundred years earlier by Thomas Edison and George Westinghouse: power generation, power transmission over long distances at high voltage (115 kilovolts or greater), distribution over medium distances at stepped-down voltage (typically 2 to 35 kilovolts), and delivery to electric meters at low voltage (typically 440 volts for commercial or residential consumption).

Composed of billions of electric meters, transformers, capacitors, phasor measurement units, power lines, etc., the power grid is the largest and most complex machine ever developed and, as noted by the National Academy of Engineering, the most important engineering achievement of the 20th century.

The smart grid is essentially the power grid transformed by IoT. An estimated $2 trillion will be spent this decade to sensor this value chain by upgrading or replacing the multitude of devices in the grid infrastructure so that all the devices emit telemetry and are remotely machine addressable.[4] A familiar example is the smart meter. Traditional electromechanical meters are manually read, usually at monthly intervals, by field personnel. Smart meters are remotely monitored and commonly read at 15-minute intervals.

When a power grid is fully sensored, we can aggregate, evaluate, and correlate the interactions and relationships of all the data from all the devices, plus weather, load, and generation capacity in near-real time. We can then apply AI machine learning algorithms to those data to optimize grid performance, reduce the cost of operation, increase resiliency and reliability, harden cybersecurity, enable bidirectional power flow, and reduce greenhouse gas emissions. Combining the power of IoT, cloud computing, big data, and AI results in a digital transformation of the utility industry.

The smart grid is an illustrative example of how value chains in other industries may become interconnected through IoT to create transformative change and value. For example, as self-driving technology develops and takes hold, autonomous vehicles will communicate with one another to optimize traffic flow throughout entire city street networks, resulting in fewer traffic jams, less transit time for commuters, and reduced environmental stress.

The Internet of Things: Potential and Impact

The internet of things is poised to significantly alter how organizations operate. Although this is no longer the controversial statement it was when I first heard the term in 2007, it begs three questions: why, how, and how much?

There are three primary reasons IoT will change the way business is done. First, the volume of data that IoT systems can generate is wholly unprecedented. The internet of things is projected to generate

Digital Transformation of the Smart Grid

$2 trillion is being spent this decade to sensor the power grid value chain.

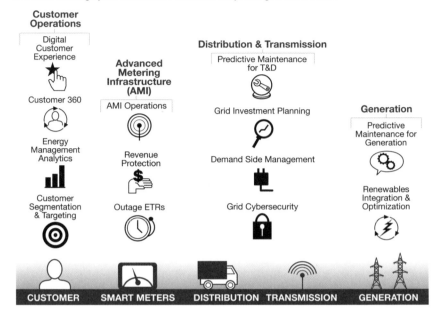

FIGURE 7.2

600 zettabytes of data annually by 2020—that's 600 million petabytes.[5] This number may strike you as almost unbelievable, but recall our discussion of the smart grid: Power plants, transmission substations, transformers, power lines, and smart meters constantly generate data. When properly sensored, these assets often produce multiple reads per second. When you consider that the U.S. electrical grid alone has 5.7 million miles of transmission and distribution infrastructure, 600 zettabytes is not an implausible number.[6]

Second, the data generated are valuable. As organizations sensor and measure areas of their business, those sensor readings help them make better, more profitable decisions. The data generated by IoT, when analyzed by AI, will—and does—enable organizations to better run core business processes. This is true not only in the utility industry but also in oil and gas, manufacturing, aerospace and defense, the public sector, financial services, health care, logistics and transportation, retail, and every other industry I've seen.[7]

The third reason IoT will transform business is the power of Metcalfe's Law—i.e., the value of a network is proportional to the square of the number of its members.[8] In this case, the network is a company's federated data image, and the members are the data points. With the proliferation of sensors in an enterprise's value chain, there is a proliferation of data, both in volume and variety. More data, more value.

Consider an aerospace company looking to implement an AI-driven predictive maintenance solution for its fleet of jet aircraft. Unpredicted equipment failures mean less flight time—clearly a problem for any fleet operator. Most jets already have a wide array of onboard sensors, but many of the readings are not used to predict when maintenance is required. As a result, most organizations today rely on time-based maintenance—i.e., scheduled at predefined time or usage intervals— which leads to over-maintenance and cannot adequately predict when equipment requires service. Wasted resources and costs are the result.

Imagine an alternate approach that takes advantage of *all* data generated by the aircraft systems. Start with one data source: the jet engine forward vibration sensor. On its own, this does not provide enough data to build a comprehensive predictive maintenance application for the entire jet. It may not even provide enough data to predict jet engine failure with an acceptable level of accuracy. But imagine we use data from *20 sensors on each engine*, gathered from every engine across a thousand-jet fleet. Using AI machine learning algorithms on this significantly larger and richer data set, we can predict engine failure with much greater accuracy, resulting in reduced aircraft downtime and more efficient use of maintenance resources—which clearly translate into economic value.

Now consider ingesting and analyzing sensor data from *all* the jet systems and components, not just engine sensors: We can now predict failure for every part of the aircraft—the engines, the fan system, the landing gear—before it happens, because we have sensor data for each part. But this is not the only implication. Because the aircraft is a unified system, the components—and the data—are interrelated. This means data generated by the jet engines may be predictive of failure rates for the fan system and vice versa. This is true for every pair of components. In this way, the value of the data increases exponentially with the volume and diversity of data.

By ingesting more data from more devices and increasing the richness and volume of our data set, the accuracy of our predictive maintenance application is now much higher—and more effective and cost efficient—than traditional methods. Additionally, predictive maintenance paves the way for more efficient management of inventory parts and supply chain operations—a compound benefit. Returning to the old, scheduled aircraft maintenance operations is inconceivable. In much the same way and for the same reasons—data volume, value, and Metcalfe's Law—IoT will transform business processes across industries.

As another example, IoT has significant impact on agriculture. A potato farmer in the Netherlands now runs one of the world's most advanced potato farms because of IoT.[9] Multiple types of sensors on his farm—monitoring things like soil nutrients, moisture levels, sunlight, temperature, and other factors—provide large amounts of valuable data, enabling the farmer to use his land more efficiently than other farms. By connecting every piece of the farming process through IoT, he knows exactly which parts of his land need more nutrients, where pests are eating leaves, or which plants are not getting enough sunlight. Equipped with these insights, the farmer can take the right actions to optimize his farm's production.

The business world is in the early days of capturing the value that IoT—in conjunction with cloud computing, big data, and AI—can unlock. Our Cambrian Explosion of IoT is still ahead of us. But one thing is clear: IoT will change business in a major way. The question remains *how*. I argue it will profoundly change three fundamental aspects of business: how we make decisions, how we execute business processes, and how we differentiate products in the marketplace.

First, decision-making will change, with data-driven decision-making in particular taking on an entirely new meaning.[10] Algorithms will become an integral part of most, if not all, decisions. This is particularly true for the day-to-day decisions that keep a business running. Think of decisions made on the factory floor, inside a fulfillment warehouse, or even in a bank's lending division. With product usage information, equipment health data, and environmental measurements, problems can be assessed in real time and recommendations can immediately be surfaced to operators. This means less reliance on simple but suboptimal "rule-of-thumb" practices. It also means less reliance on operational expertise. Human expertise is only required when the AI-produced output seems off-base. If it is, the system can learn from human intervention to better address similar cases in the future. This means fewer staff, less human involvement, and superior business results. Sensored value networks enable fact-based, AI-driven predictive decision-making.

Second, IoT will change how business processes are executed, resulting in faster, more accurate, and less expensive decision-making. Instead of consulting one's own intuition and experience and doing "what feels right," operators will consult an algorithmic recommendation that clearly explains why it suggests a certain course of action. The onus will be on employees to override the system, but this will happen only in a fractional number of cases. Employees will be freed up to focus less on operational minutiae and more on adding strategic and competitive value.

Third, IoT will change the way products are differentiated in the marketplace. We will see a new level of individualization of product behaviors. Smartphones already adapt to how their owner speaks or types. Smart thermostats learn the temperature preferences of residents and automatically accommodate them. In health care, intelligent glucose monitors equipped with algorithms can automatically adjust insulin delivery via an implanted pump.

This is just the beginning—IoT changes the relationships we form with physical objects. IoT gives manufacturers unprecedented visibility into how customers use their products. Not only does this enable companies to know their customers better and thus make better products, but it also enables new warranty and equipment rental models—such as guaranteeing products under certain usage constraints and deactivating rented items when the customer stops paying a subscription fee.[11] These models may not seem appealing to end users at first glance, but they can radically change the economics of owning or renting certain products, and customers absolutely do respond to better pricing models. IoT has unlocked new possibilities in decision-making, operations, and product differentiation, and it will continue to do so—often in ways we have not yet imagined.

How much will all this IoT-driven change impact the economy? With the total number of connected devices projected to grow from about 20 billion today to 75 billion by 2025,[12] analysts expect IoT will contribute

Exponential Growth of Connected Devices
The total number of connected devices will reach 75 billion by 2025.

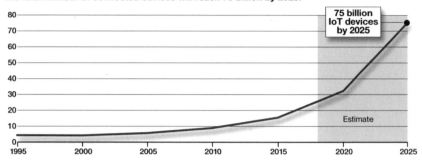

FIGURE 7.3

up to $11.1 trillion in annual global economic value by 2025.[13] That is a staggering amount, equivalent to approximately 11 percent of the global economy, based on the World Bank's projection of $99.5 trillion in global GDP in 2025.

Significant workforce displacement will be a byproduct of IoT adoption and the corresponding automation it enables. I expect the level and timing of job displacement to vary dramatically across industries, but the aggregate statistics are undeniable.

Almost half (47 percent according to the *Economist*) of American jobs are at risk due to automation, and a substantial portion of this automation is due to IoT. In Britain and Japan, the numbers are similar: 35 percent and 49 percent of jobs are at risk, respectively.[14]

Individual firms also weigh the impact of automation. UBS CEO Sergio Ermotti predicts that automation caused by new technology adoption could cause the company to downsize by 30 percent. At UBS alone, that is almost 30,000 employees.[15] Former Deutsche Bank CEO John Cryan predicted the firm will cut its 97,000-person organization in half due to automation.[16] Goldman Sachs estimates that self-driving cars could destroy 25,000 driving jobs every month in the U.S. alone.[17]

However, job displacement doesn't mean people will no longer work. New jobs will emerge even as traditional jobs disappear. As I noted in chapter 6, advanced technologies will create more jobs than they will eliminate, and this change will happen quickly.

Business Value by Industry from IoT in 2025

IoT is projected to create up to $11 trillion in business value in 2025.

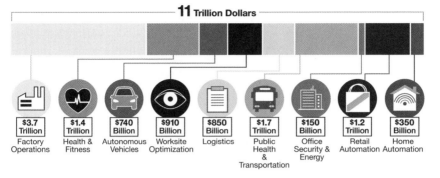

$3.7 Trillion	$1.4 Trillion	$740 Billion	$910 Billion	$850 Billion	$1.7 Trillion	$150 Billion	$1.2 Trillion	$350 Billion
Factory Operations	Health & Fitness	Autonomous Vehicles	Worksite Optimization	Logistics	Public Health & Transportation	Office Security & Energy	Retail Automation	Home Automation

FIGURE 7.4

New opportunities will abound for those with immediately relevant skill sets and new types of roles will emerge that we cannot even imagine today. In 2018, 7 of the top 10 fastest-growing job titles on LinkedIn were data science and engineering roles.[18] This growth in data science will continue for the foreseeable future: In 2020, there are expected to be about 700,000 job openings for data scientists and similar roles in the U.S.[19] Similarly, operational roles for those who manage IoT devices of all sorts, as well as new types of IT, networking, and telecommunications jobs, are likely to grow. These high-value jobs will often be cross-disciplinary, grounded in business and technical knowledge.

There is every reason to be optimistic. But as we've noted, employers, governments, and schools will need to train and retrain millions of people for these new jobs. Millions of existing workers will have to find new jobs. I believe we in the commercial sector have a responsibility to promote training and education for these new roles. IoT, when paired with AI, is causing a structural shift in the employment landscape. IoT and the technologies it enables will affect our world at a scale that is difficult to overstate.

How IoT Creates Value

A broad and growing range of use cases is driving the tremendous impact of the internet of things. All these involve different parts of the technology stack, ranging from the actual hardware of connected devices to services, analytics, and applications. From a customer's or end user's perspective, IoT's real value comes from services, IoT analytics, and applications, while the rest of the technology stack serves as an enabler with lower value and growth potential.[20] Ultimately, organizations using IoT technologies (factory owners, operators, manufacturers, etc.) will capture most of the potential value over time.

For business leaders to adopt IoT solutions, they need to know how these offerings will add value to their organization by solving critical business challenges: reducing asset maintenance costs, optimizing inventory, increasing revenue through better demand forecasting, increasing customer satisfaction and product quality, and more.

By focusing on these concrete business problems, IoT offerings can be rolled out rapidly across industries and gain widespread adoption. In the following section, I will discuss some of the most promising use cases and how they can add value to businesses.

IoT Use Cases

Smart Grid

As previously noted, the utilities sector was one of the first industries to make use of IoT on a large scale. By deploying millions of smart meters across their operations, utilities have created what we today call a smart grid.

Enel, the large utility based in Rome, manages more than 40 million smart meters across Europe. These meters generate an unprecedented amount of data: more than 5 billion readings per day. IoT phasor measurement units (PMUs) on transmission lines emit power quality signals at 60 Hz cycles (i.e., 60 times per second), with each PMU generating 2 billion signals per year.

The combination of inferring the power consumption, production, and storage capacity of each customer in real time (using cloud computing and AI)—in conjunction with the network effect of interconnected customers, local power production, and storage—is the essence of the smart grid. The more connected sensors and the more data available for analysis, the more accurate the deep learning algorithms will be, resulting in an increasingly efficient smart grid. Recall Metcalfe's Law:

Increasing the number of connected sensors drives exponential value in the network. All this sensor data provides near-real-time information on the condition of the grid—its status, equipment issues, performance levels, etc. This allows the algorithms to adapt their predictions and recommendations in near real time. Enel estimates the application of AI algorithms on all this smart grid data across its entire network will yield more than €600 million in annual economic value.

Predictive Maintenance

Companies can apply AI to data captured with IoT technologies—sensors, meters, embedded computers, etc.—in order to predict failure of equipment before it happens. This reduces unplanned downtime and enables flexible work schedules that extend equipment life and drive down service labor and parts replacement costs. A wide range of industries—from discrete manufacturing, energy, and aerospace to logistics, transportation, and health care—will be able to capture these benefits.

Consider, for example, Royal Dutch Shell, one of the world's largest energy companies with 86,000 employees operating in more than 70 countries, and annual revenue of more than $300 billion. Shell is developing AI applications to address numerous use cases across its global operations, which span a vast number of assets throughout more than 20 refineries, 25,000 oil and gas wells, and over 40,000 service stations. Several AI applications are live in production, with numerous others to follow.

In one use case, Shell developed and deployed an application to predict failure of hydraulic power units (HPUs)—which are critical in preventing well blowouts—for 5,000 gas wells at its Australian QGC operation. The AI-powered application ingests high-frequency data from multiple sensors at these remote, hard-to-access well sites in order to predict both when an HPU will fail and the root cause of the issue. This enables maintenance teams to proactively address issues before failure occurs. The demonstrated benefits of the application include higher asset runtime, optimized resource utilization, reduced operational costs, and millions of dollars in realized annual revenues.

In another example, Shell developed and deployed an application that predicts performance deterioration for more than 500,000 valves operating at refineries around the world that produce gasoline, diesel, aviation fuel, lubricants, and other products. Valves of multiple types are critical components in controlling the flow of fluids throughout refineries. A valve's performance deteriorates over time based on multiple factors, including the type of valve, its historical usage, exposure to heat, pressure, rate of fluid flow, etc. Multiple sensors continuously record various measures of a valve's operation and status.

For this use case, Shell automated the training, deployment, and management of more than 500,000 AI models—one for each individual valve. The application ingests more than 10 million sensor signals at very high frequency; applies valve-specific AI models to predict deterioration; and prioritizes the most critical valves for operator attention. The application enables Shell's operations to shift from being reactive and rule-based to predictive and prescriptive. Based on these changes, which reduce maintenance costs and increase operating efficiency, deployment of the application for this use case alone is estimated to deliver *several hundred million dollars in annual economic value.*

Inventory Optimization

From manufacturing to consumer packaged goods and many other industries, companies across the world struggle to get inventory planning right. In fact, many large organizations with complex supply chains and inventory operations miss their "on time in full" (OTIF) delivery targets 50 percent of the time when employing inventory optimization solutions from traditional enterprise resource planning (ERP) providers. IoT-based solutions—combined with AI-based big data analysis—can help companies dramatically improve their OTIF achievement rates, significantly increasing processing speed while reducing response times, stock-outs, and inventory pileups.

For example, a \$40 billion U.S. discrete manufacturer of large complex machines uses an AI-powered inventory optimization solution to balance optimal inventory levels and minimize inventory costs. The company's machines select from 10,000 different options and as many as 21,000 components in each bill of materials. Unlike traditional

ERP-based inventory solutions, the AI application applies advanced sto-chastic, AI-based optimization on top of the company's large IoT-based data set. As a result, this manufacturer is able to reduce inventory costs by up to 52 percent on its $6 billion holding inventory—freeing up $3 billion of capital that it can deploy and invest elsewhere.

Patient Care

The potential for IoT in health care is vast. IoT gives doctors the oppor-tunity to track patient health remotely in order to improve health outcomes and reduce costs. By harnessing all these data, IoT supports doctors in predicting risk factors for their patients.

For example, pacemakers are a kind of IoT sensor—they can be read remotely and can issue alarms to doctors and patients, warning if a heartbeat is irregular. The wearable industry has given people the abil-ity to easily track all sorts of health-related metrics: steps taken, stairs climbed, heart rate, sleep quality, nutrition intake, and so on.

Other applications take advantage of large sets of IoT-generated data to uncover insights and make predictions. Health care organiza-tions use AI predictive analysis to find potential barriers to medication treatment and to identify potential contraindications. This gives doctors the tools to more effectively support patients, improve outcomes, re-duce relapse, and enhance quality of life. Imagine pill bottles that track adherence to prescribed medications, alerting doctors and users when patients fail or forget to take their medication. Also in development are smart pills that can transmit information on vital signs after being ingested.

Significant additional value can be created when consumer IoT sys-tems are linked to business-to-business (B2B) systems. For example, data from personal fitness tracking devices like a Fitbit or Apple Watch combined with clinical information can create a holistic view of the pa-tient, allowing doctors to deliver better care.

The burgeoning array of IoT use cases, ranging from production optimization and demand response to fleet management and logistics, paint a good picture of the power and value of IoT. Most of the economic potential of IoT lies in B2B applications rather than consumer applica-tions. However, simple applications like IoT-enabled baggage handling, so travelers know exactly where their luggage is, can go a long way toward increasing customer satisfaction across numerous consumer sectors. We are certain to see more of these IoT applications in the future.

Industries Mostly Impacted by IoT

IoT's largest impact will be on companies operating in asset-intensive industries. Approximately 50 percent of IoT spending will be accounted for by three industries: discrete manufacturing, transportation and logistics, and utilities.[21,22] Many of these companies increasingly face competition from powerful technology companies. For example, FedEx needs to invest heavily in IoT to stave off competition from Amazon, which has built its own delivery capabilities—including Amazon Air (a fleet of cargo jets), Amazon Delivery Services Partners (Amazon-branded delivery vans operated by licensed partners), and Amazon Flex (independent drivers who deliver packages using their own vehicles). With annual shipping costs greater than $20 billion, Amazon has substantial incentive to invest in its own delivery capabilities, putting pressure on FedEx, UPS, and others to innovate.[23]

Integrating digital IoT capabilities will have a profoundly transformative effect on companies in these industries, particularly in terms of reduced costs and increased operational efficiencies. Two major use cases alone—predictive maintenance and inventory optimization—will drive significant economic value. In the utilities sector, ongoing investment in smart grid capabilities will also create substantial value, as we have seen at ENGIE and Enel.

Closely following these industries, we will see a large impact on business-to-consumer (B2C), health care, process, and energy and natural resources companies. In health care, IoT will deliver great value—in terms of both economic benefit and human well-being—through new solutions for monitoring and managing illness in real time such as automated insulin pumps for diabetes patients. Similarly, in natural resource industries like forestry and mining, IoT solutions for monitoring resource conditions and improving safety will produce economic benefits and help save human lives and the environment. The IoT-enabled world promises to be wealthier, safer, and healthier.

IoT Spending by Sector

Discrete manufacturing, transportation and logistics, and utilities will dominate IoT spending in 2020.

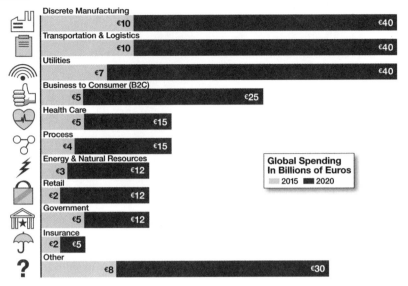

FIGURE 7.5

The IoT Market Landscape

IoT Solution Providers

Many players in the IoT market are positioned to deliver valuable solutions:

- Industrial companies and manufacturers like Siemens, John Deere, and Caterpillar can extend their digital capabilities to create new IoT offerings and enhance their existing products—from jet engines, motors, and vehicles to farm and mining equipment—delivering more value to end customers.

- Telecommunication companies like AT&T, Verizon, and Vodafone can leverage their vast networks of communication assets and rich customer data to provide IoT connectivity and value-added services such as IoT-enabled home security.

- Enterprise software giants like SAP, Microsoft, and Oracle are attempting to incorporate capabilities into their platforms to support IoT devices for end customers.

- Internet and tech giants such as Google, Amazon, and Apple—already established in the consumer IoT space with products like Google Home, Amazon Echo, and Apple HomePod—will continue to enhance and expand their IoT offerings. Whether they attempt to offer B2B solutions—or will be successful if they do—remains to be seen.

- Across a broad range of other industries—energy, mining, oil and gas, health care, automotive, aerospace—IoT presents opportunities for companies to innovate, not only in how they harness IoT to operate more efficiently but also in how they incorporate IoT into the products and services they offer.

- Finally, some of the most exciting IoT offerings and solutions are certain to come from current and future startups.

Enablers and Barriers

As organizations look to harness IoT technology for their internal use or to develop IoT products and services, they need to consider several factors that will either further enable or potentially slow down IoT adoption and market evolution.

Security, privacy, and confidentiality will become increasingly important. Individuals entrust companies with their data and will require a compelling value proposition to allow for the data to be collected. They will also want to understand exactly what data are collected and how companies ensure data security. Failing to deliver on these promises will create significant barriers to adoption. Moreover, when IoT is used to control physical assets, security breaches can have potentially dire consequences.

For IoT technology to deliver on the promise of real-time decision-making, infrastructure developments in the area of 5G wireless communication must first come to fruition. Telecommunications companies across the world are in the process of investing billions of dollars in this infrastructure, with the first 5G networks beginning to roll out in 2019. When in place, this infrastructure will be a huge boost to the adoption of IoT, because it will provide the capability to move data wirelessly at speeds fast enough for real-time decision-making.

Mainstream mass adoption of IoT products will also require the continuing price decline of sensors, connectivity hardware, and batteries. Computing and storage prices must also continue their decline, as the increasing volume of IoT-generated data will require IoT product providers to consume more of these resources.

Regulation and public policy can also either spur development of the IoT market or significantly impede it. For example, regulation can set market rules and data practices that protect consumers and therefore increase adoption. Having the appropriate incentives in place will also be a market enabler. Certain technologies and use cases, such as self-driving cars, cannot proceed without government action. Those products risk delay if governments fail to act.

Finally, organizations may have to make changes to the company culture to fully leverage IoT's power. In many cases, new IoT technologies will reduce the need for certain jobs and create new ones, requiring employees to develop new skills through training.

Implications for Businesses

Transforming the Value Chain

Every aspect of the value chain, from product development to after-sales service, is affected when companies embrace IoT in their product thinking.

In the past, product development was often very discontinuous, with companies focusing on periodic product releases. Going forward, design of IoT-enabled products will become increasingly iterative, particularly for products with embedded software that requires frequent updates via the cloud. Product teams will need new skills. Manufacturing companies will need not only mechanical engineers but also software engineers and data scientists.

As companies gather data through IoT devices, they gain new insights into customers and can better customize products to consumer needs. IoT will form a new basis for an ongoing dialogue with consumers, and new business models will emerge as products can be offered as a service. Sales and marketing teams will need broader knowledge to effectively position offerings as part of these connected systems.

For many companies, IoT will also have a major impact on after-sales services, since IoT makes remote service feasible. In addition, sensor data can be used to predict when parts are about to break, which makes predictive maintenance possible, enabling companies to significantly expand their value proposition to customers.

With IoT, security concerns become amplified, as IoT devices become targets of potential cyberattacks. Companies now are tasked with protecting thousands or millions of products in the field. Security must be embedded as a first principle in product design and across the value chain.

Redefining Industry Boundaries

Large-scale IoT adoption will affect companies' strategies and how they differentiate themselves, create value, and compete. IoT will change the structure of entire industries, blurring the boundaries within industries and shifting bargaining power.

IoT products will change the basic principles of product design. Products will be designed to be part of systems and able to be continuously serviced and upgraded. Real transformation will happen when IoT brings what Harvard Business School professor Michael Porter calls "smart, connected products" together into a "product system"—where IoT products are integrated with other products to optimize the entire system. As an example, Porter points to John Deere, which is creating a "farming equipment system" by connecting and integrating its products (e.g., tractors, tillers, combines) with the goal of optimizing overall equipment performance for the farm customer.[24] In the "smart home" space, Apple for example is creating the foundation of a product system with its Apple HomeKit framework, enabling third-party manufacturers to develop products—such as lights, sprinklers, locks, fans, etc.—that can be controlled with the Apple Home app. Competition in this sense will also move from competing on the best single product to competing on the best system.

This represents a fundamental change in a company's business model—from making and selling a product to making entire product systems or platforms. The possibilities now available require companies to answer major strategic questions such as what business they are in. Companies have to decide if they want to be the system integrator that provides the entire platform or one discrete product on a larger platform.

Effect on Business Models

Embracing IoT is forcing companies to assess new strategic options. These important choices include which capabilities to pursue and what functionality to embed; whether to create an open or a proprietary system; what type of data to capture and how to manage it; what business model to pursue; the scope of the offering; and more.

The organizational changes I previously described will be evolutionary, with old and new structures often needing to operate in parallel. Many companies will have to pursue hybrid or transitional structures to allow scarce talent to be leveraged and experience pooled. Some firms will need to partner with focused software companies and experienced consultants to inject new talent and perspectives into their organizations. At the corporate level in multi-business companies, overlay structures are being put in place to evangelize IoT and AI opportunities:

- **Stand-Alone Business Unit**. This is a separate new unit, with profit and loss responsibility, in charge of executing the company's strategy to design, launch, market, sell, and service IoT products and services. The business unit aggregates the talent and mobilizes the technology and assets needed to bring new offerings to market. It is free from constraints of legacy business processes and organizational structures.

- **Center of Excellence (CoE)**. Supplemental to stand-alone business units, the CoE is a separate corporate unit, housing key expertise on smart, connected products. It does not have profit and loss responsibility but is a shared services cost center that other business units can tap. The CoE brings together cross-functional expertise in digital technologies (AI, IoT) and transformation strategy, helping guide IoT product strategy and providing expert resources for other business units.

- **Cross-Business-Unit Steering Committee**. This approach involves convening a committee of thought leaders across various business units who champion opportunities to share expertise and facilitate collaboration. This organization will typically play a key role in setting overall digital transformation strategy.[25]

IoT products will reshape not only competition, but the very nature of the manufacturing firm, its work, and how it is organized. They are creating the first true discontinuity in the organization of manufacturing firms in modern business history.

It is important for organizations to see IoT products first and foremost as a chance to improve economies and society. IoT products are poised to contribute great advances in the human condition—a cleaner planet through more efficient energy and resource usage and healthier lives through better health monitoring. They position us to change the trajectory of society's overall consumption. Exponential opportunities for innovation presented by IoT products, together with the huge expansion of data they create, will be a net generator of economic growth.

IoT represents a major opportunity for organizations across industries—expected to create more than $11 trillion in global economic value by 2025—and will profoundly change how products are designed, supported, and used, as everything becomes a computing device. Many of the companies I talk with today are making IoT a first-level business imperative. Many more will follow. IoT, combined with the ability to analyze large data sets residing in the cloud and to apply sophisticated AI algorithms for specific use cases, will dramatically transform how businesses operate and create value.

The Ultimate AI and IoT Computing Platform

IoT devices are sensors—sensors that can remotely monitor the state of devices, systems, and organisms in real or near real time. They are proliferating across all value chains: travel, transportation, energy, aerospace, health care, financial services, defense systems, and government. They are becoming ubiquitous: smart watches, smart meters, home camera monitors. All modern aircraft, vehicles, and construction equipment are being equipped with sensors allowing the operator or manufacturer to monitor the equipment. Today humans wear Fitbits. Tomorrow humans will be fitted with heart monitors with sensors. Brain waves will be monitored. Pills with sensors will be ingested to report on the state of the gut, blood chemistry, heart arrhythmia, cortisol levels—all will be remotely monitored.

As discussed above, the rate of IoT sensor proliferation in the 21st century is breathtaking. Soon over 50 billion sensors will have been installed across industrial, government, and consumer value chains.

Taking a closer look at these IoT devices, when we peel off the cover, we find that—although it might only cost a few dollars or a few cents—each has computational and communication capacity. It is a computer connected to a network.

Recall Moore's Law, coined by Intel co-founder Gordon Moore. In 1965 Moore described a trend he saw that the number of transistors on an integrated circuit was doubling every two years at half the cost. This cost economy proved the driving force behind the increase in computer and memory performance we have seen in the past 50 years.

Moore's Law

Moore's Law, postulated by Intel co-founder Gordon Moore, states that the number of transistors on an integrated circuit doubles every two years at half the cost.

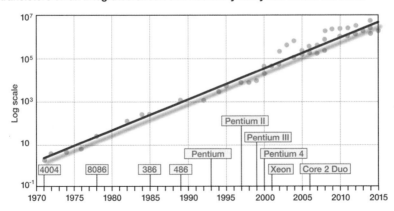

FIGURE 7.6

As a scientist at Xerox PARC in the 1970s, Bob Metcalfe invented Ethernet—a breakthrough that made it possible to connect previously discrete computers into interactive networks. It was clear that the power of the computer network is greater than the sum of its components. In an attempt to describe that power, Metcalfe's Law was first presented in 1980. Metcalfe's Law states that the power of the network is a function of the square of the number of devices connected to the network.

You can think of digital transformation as a result of the collision and confluence of Moore's Law and Metcalfe's Law. With IoT we have 50 billion computers connected into a network. Fifty billion squared is on the order of 10^{21}.

10^{21} is roughly equivalent to the number of stars in our universe. That's *1 billion trillion!* IoT may be the single most important defining feature of the 21st-century economy. Yes, it's a network of sensors. Yes,

Metcalfe's Law

The internet of things, soon to have 50 billion connected devices, creates a computing platform the power of which was inconceivable only a few years ago.

CONNECTIONS IN A NETWORK = n(n-1)/2

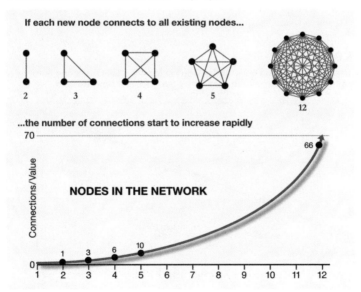

FIGURE 7.7

they collect massive amounts of data that can be used in new and powerful ways. But most importantly, this IoT constellation is a *computing platform*. Much of the computing takes place in the sensors themselves—that is, on the edge—that collectively constitute a computing platform the power of which was inconceivable only a few years ago.

IoT and AI are two sides of the same coin. It is this computing platform that fully enables AI and digital transformation.

Chapter 8

AI in Government

"Artificial intelligence is the future, not only for Russia, but for all human-kind. Whoever becomes the leader in this sphere will become the ruler of the world."[1]

Vladimir Putin
September 2017

Throughout this book I have argued that digital transformation will touch every industry. It will profoundly impact every facet of business and society. It will create enormous value globally.

It will also determine the future geopolitical power balance and the security of the world's nations and their citizens. War is being digitally transformed.

AI is the new battleground in the competition for global economic and military power, with the U.S. and European democracies in the West vying with China in the East for AI leadership. Russia, while not a significant economic power, clearly understands and prioritizes the military importance of AI.

In this chapter I provide an overview of the battle for AI leadership, focusing primarily on the two central players: the U.S. and China. I also outline some of the ways in which AI can and is being applied today to drive significant readiness improvements, operational efficiencies, and cost savings in the U.S. military.

I believe it is incumbent on senior executives and government leaders to understand the dynamics of the global competition for AI leadership and its implications for national and global security. The private sector, as innovators and technology providers, will play a key role in the outcome of this competition. There is nothing bigger at stake.

We Are at War

The next cyber-war has begun. China, Russia, North Korea, Iran, Al-Qaeda, and others are engaged in full frontal cyber-war today, attacking Western institutions including the U.S. government, banks, high tech companies, critical infrastructure, and social media.

This is all well-documented by the U.S. Director of National Intelligence in a January 2019 report, *Worldwide Threat Assessment of the U.S. Intelligence Community.* The report concluded the critical cyber threats to U.S. national security are originating primarily from China and Russia; they are ongoing and increasing in intensity and impact.

> Our adversaries and strategic competitors will increasingly use cyber capabilities—including cyber espionage, attack, and influence—to seek political, economic, and military advantage over the United States and its allies and partners....
>
> At present, China and Russia pose the greatest espionage and cyber-attack threats, but we anticipate that all our adversaries and strategic competitors will increasingly build and integrate cyber espionage, attack, and influence capabilities into their efforts to influence US policies and advance their own national security interests.[2]

The highly successful Russian efforts to weaponize Facebook and other social media in an attempt to co-opt the 2016 U.S. presidential election are well documented and still under investigation.

China is particularly active. China's cyber-espionage division, known as Unit 61398, over 100,000 strong, has successfully completed numerous devastating cyber-war missions directed against the U.S. and others. In 2009, Operation Aurora exploited vulnerabilities in Internet Explorer to penetrate Google, Adobe, and two dozen additional companies to access the source code for many computer software products. The goal was to better enable China to monitor and contain dissidents.[3]

Unit 61398 has stolen reams of trade secrets from Alcoa, U.S. Steel, and Westinghouse. Included in this plunder were Westinghouse's IP and trade secrets for designing and operating nuclear power plants.

In 2015, it was revealed that a foreign enemy, generally thought to be China, succeeded in stealing 21.5 million documents—including the personnel records of 4 million people—from the U.S. Office of Personnel Management. These data include the background checks and extensive personal and highly confidential information on 4 million people who had been considered for employment by the U.S. government, including those who had been granted or considered for a security clearance.[4]

Facebook, Sony Pictures, Target, Visa, Mastercard, Yahoo!, Adobe, JP Morgan Chase, Equifax, the U.S. Department of State, the Democratic National Committee—the frequency of these nefarious attacks by foreign nations and other bad actors is sufficiently ubiquitous that we are no longer surprised to open the morning paper to find that another few hundred million top secret documents or highly personal financial or medical records have been stolen by a foreign enemy. If this is not war, what is it?

The Strategic Role of AI

National governments around the globe clearly view AI as a strategic technology, with more than 25 countries having published national AI strategies in recent years.[5] These strategy papers cover AI policy across scientific research, talent development, education, public and private sector adoption and collaboration, ethics, data privacy standards and regulations, and data and digital infrastructure.

No country has been more ambitious in its national strategy for global AI supremacy than China. Backed by massive investments in R&D, China foresees a future where AI infuses every aspect of its industrial, commercial, governmental, and military operations, including advanced AI-powered weapons in every domain: land, air, sea, space, and cyberspace.

Just as AI is playing a central role in the digital transformation of business and industry, AI is driving the transformation of 21st-century warfare.

The AI Race Is the First Phase in the War between China and the U.S.

In July 2017, China released its "Next Generation Artificial Intelligence Development Plan," with the explicit goal of becoming the world leader in artificial intelligence by 2030. It will increase government spending on core AI programs to $22 billion in the next few years, with plans to spend nearly $60 billion per year by 2025. China's defense budget has doubled during the past decade, reaching an estimated $190 billion in 2017.[6]

Of particular note is the role of AI-enabled cyber warfare in China's military strategy. In a 2018 report to Congress, the U.S. Defense Department highlighted that cyber warfare figures prominently in China's goal to turn the People's Liberation Army (PLA) into a "world-class" military force:

> Chinese military writings describe informatized warfare as the use of information technology to create an operational system-of-systems allowing the PLA to acquire, transmit, process, and use information to conduct joint military operations across the domains of land, sea, air, space, cyberspace and the electromagnetic spectrum during a conflict. Ongoing military reforms are aimed at accelerating the incorporation

China Is on Track to Outspend the U.S. in R&D

With ambitions to be the world's undisputed technology leader, including AI, China is making massive investments in R&D.

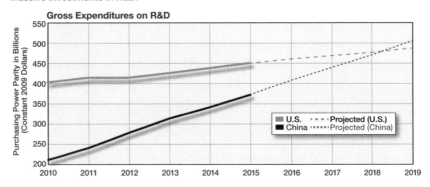

FIGURE 8.1

of information systems enabling forces and commanders to carry out missions and tasks more effectively to win informatized local wars. The PLA continues to expand the scope and regularity of military exercises simulating these operations and likely views conventional and cyber operations as means of achieving information dominance.[7]

China is working to apply AI across its arsenal of weaponry, including advanced aircraft, missiles, autonomous vehicles, and cyber weapons:[8]

- According to Yang Wei, former chief designer of the Chengdu Aircraft Corp J-20 stealth fighter, China's next-generation fighter will utilize AI to achieve air superiority

- AI will enable future unmanned combat aircraft (UCAV) that are more responsive than human-controlled aircraft, as well as new space-combat platforms equipped with energy-based weapons

- AI will also enable deep-sea, unmanned underwater combat vehicles (UUCVs) to assert control over the ocean floor and defend the large sensor grids that make up China's "Underwater Great Wall"

- Future cruise missiles will deploy AI that enables commanders to control missiles in real time, add tasks in-flight, or operate them in "fire-and-forget" mode

- To dominate in electronic warfare, AI-enabled cyber weapons will be used against enemy networks, utilizing advanced methods to "make the opponent unable to perceive, or perceive garbage information and false information"

Weaponization of Critical Infrastructure

The use of AI-enabled cyber weapons as a precursor to—or perhaps in place of—a military conflict in itself poses potentially catastrophic risks. Consider the U.S. power grid. The electricity grid is the engine that powers all mechanisms of commerce and civilization in the United States. Should this engine fail, all dependent activities immediately cease to function, including water and sanitation, the food supply chain, financial institutions, health care, communications, media, transportation, and law enforcement.

The U.S. power grid is brittle, fragile, and highly susceptible to destructive cyberattack by bad actors, terrorists, rogue states, and foreign enemies. And they know it. The U.S. power grid is subject to incessant attacks employing phishing and spear-phishing, identity theft, denial of service attacks, and a spectrum of viral injection techniques delivering and embedding clandestine malware, bots, and worms that, if and when enabled, have the capability of disabling critical portions of the power system if not the entire grid itself. If and when that happens, the world as we know it comes to an end. Think *Mad Max* meets Peoria.

How vulnerable is the grid? The North American Electric Reliability Corporation has predicted that the malicious software used in the sophisticated Russian attack that brought down the Ukrainian grid in 2015 could be modified to use against utilities in the U.S.[9] One email-delivered virus could wipe out the reboot sequence on the computer SCADA (Supervisory Control and Data Acquisition) system of any large grid operator—effectively hitting the "off" switch. A 2017 survey of North American utility executives found that more than three-quarters believe there is a likelihood that the U.S. grid will be subject to a cyberattack in the next five years.[10]

The risk is not just cyber but also physical. Rebecca Smith of the *Wall Street Journal* has reported that if nine specific substations in the U.S. were to be disabled, the entire U.S. power grid could be offline for weeks to months.[11] In 2014, Jim Woolsey, former head of the CIA, warned of the increasingly likely threat of a nuclear electromagnetic pulse (EMP) attack.[12] One high-altitude EMP explosion would disable the grid for years. A decade ago the EMP Commission determined that as a result of a long-term shutdown of the grid—in a social milieu of total chaos— only 1 out of 10 Americans would survive after one year.[13,14]

The vulnerability of the grid, the new reality of cyber-physical attacks on critical infrastructure, and the almost unimaginable devastation that would result have been well-known and documented by U.S. national leadership and media for decades. Nevertheless, the U.S. has no cohesive national policy to secure critical grid infrastructure— especially for local distribution systems. There is no national policy to deal with the aftermath of an effective cyberattack on the power grid.

The national Armageddon nightmare has changed from the prospect of a 20th-century nuclear winter to the potential of a 21st-century digital winter.

In 2010, William Perry, Stephen Hadley, and John Deutsch reported in a confidential, but now public, bipartisan letter to the chairman of the House Energy and Commerce Committee that *"the grid is extremely vulnerable to disruption by a cyber or other attack. Our adversaries...have the capability to carry out such an attack. The consequences...would be catastrophic."*[15]

Recent reports in the *Wall Street Journal* and other outlets describe numerous successful state-sponsored penetrations of U.S. utilities by Russia.[16] The effect of these penetrations is to weaponize the U.S. grid. Why would adversaries need nuclear or biological weapons, when they have the ability to bring the United States to its knees with a few taps of a keyboard from Tehran, Pyongyang, or Moscow?

Leaders from agencies charged with protecting national security, including the CIA, DIA, NSA, FBI, FEMA, DHS, and DoD, have attested to the significance of the vulnerability and the scale of possible devastation. Both the government and the media have confirmed that this is no longer just a threat; it is happening every day.

The digitalization of the grid and exponential growth in interconnected distributed energy resources dramatically expands the vulnerable attack surface, multiplying what today are a few critical network nodes to millions.

This is a solvable engineering and governance problem. From a science and engineering perspective, this is an order of magnitude less complex than the Manhattan Project or the Space Program. Critical infrastructure can be secured. Distributed digital resources can be made a strength.

The legal framework governing the regulation of U.S. utilities was first outlined when Franklin Delano Roosevelt was president and fewer than 1 in 10 American households had a refrigerator. Federal and state governments need to bridge antiquated jurisdictional and regulatory boundaries to collaborate, cooperate, and coordinate in this age of new technology and new threats. The cyber-physical security of the grid is a matter of national security and requires a commensurate degree of attention, resources, and coordination.

It is a simple matter of priority and budget. There is no need to wait until—as some think inevitable—a catastrophic 9/11-type attack on the U.S. power grid wreaks untold devastation on the country.

It is time for the White House, Congress, governors, and state legislatures to set the priority. It is time for the public and private sectors to step up to the plate; to acknowledge that the problem is critical; to implement a plan to address the vulnerability; and fix it.

AI-Driven Hyperwar

Retired U.S. Marine Corps General John Allen provides a vividly imagined description of what AI-driven warfare—or "hyperwar"—might look like in the near future:

> The battle damage was devastating and constituted the leading edge of what the United States soon would discover was a widespread, strategic attack. The guided-missile destroyer had not "seen" the incoming swarm because it had not recognized that its systems were under cyberattack before things turned kinetic. The undetected cyber activity not only compromised the destroyer's sensors, but also "locked-out" its defensive systems, leaving the ship almost helpless. The kinetic strikes came in waves as a complex swarm. The attack appeared to be conducted by a cloud of autonomous systems that seemed to move together with a purpose, reacting to each other and to the ship.
>
> The speed of the attack quickly overwhelmed nearly all the ship's combat systems, and while the information technology specialists were able to release some defensive systems from the clutches of the cyber intrusion, the sailors in the combat information center (CIC) simply were unable to generate the speed to react. Decision-action times were in seconds or less. Indeed, it appeared from the now very limited situational awareness in the CIC that some of the enemy autonomous weapons were providing support to other systems to set up attacks of other systems. The entire event was over in minutes.[17]

This new kind of hyperwarfare, with its unprecedented speed and massively concurrent action, is made possible by AI-powered decision-making.

These autonomous weapon systems are available today. In early 2018, Russia completed testing of its hypersonic glider, Avangard, that can travel at Mach 20—more than 15,000 miles per hour—and is designed to sneak under U.S. ballistic missile defenses.[18] The U.S. Air Force doesn't anticipate fielding an equivalent hypersonic weapon system until 2021.[19]

The U.S. Technology Lead Is at Stake

In response to the threat posed by AI-enabled adversaries, the U.S. Congress is holding hearings on the Defense Department's progress on artificial intelligence and in 2018 established a new National Security Commission on Artificial Intelligence, mandated by the National Defense Authorization Act. Its members are appointed by senior congressional leaders and agency heads to develop recommendations for advancing the development of AI techniques to bolster U.S. national security.

The Defense Advanced Research Projects Agency (DARPA) announced plans to spend more than $2 billion on research into so-called "third wave" artificial intelligence capabilities over the next few years. This is a small fraction—just 10 percent—of the $22 billion China intends to spend on AI in the near term. The DARPA initiative is called "AI Next" and aims to develop AI technology that adapts to changing situations as human intelligence does, as opposed to the current mode of processing high-quality training data in myriad situations to calibrate an algorithm.

U.S. National Defense Strategy

"We face a more competitive and dangerous international security environment than we have faced in decades," Heather Wilson, U.S. Air Force Secretary, said. "Great power competition has re-emerged as the central challenge for U.S. security and prosperity."[20] The 2018 National Defense Strategy articulates the U.S. strategy to compete, deter, and win in an increasingly complex security environment.

Rapid technology change—AI, autonomy, robotics, directed energy, hypersonics, biotech—largely defines this complex environment. Long-term strategic competitions with China and Russia are the principal priorities for the Department of Defense requiring both increased and sustained investment due to the magnitude of the threats to U.S. security.

For decades the U.S. enjoyed dominant superiority in every operating domain. Today, every domain is contested—air, land, sea, space, and cyberspace. Competitors and adversaries target U.S. battle networks and operations, while also using other areas of competition short of open warfare to achieve their ends (e.g., information warfare, ambiguous or denied proxy operations, and subversion).

China is leveraging military modernization, influence operations (e.g., propaganda, misinformation, social media manipulation), and predatory economics to coerce neighboring countries to reorder the Indo-Pacific region to its advantage. As China continues its economic and military ascendance, asserting power through an all-of-nation long-term strategy, it will continue to pursue a military modernization program that seeks Indo-Pacific regional hegemony in the near term and displacement of the U.S. to achieve global preeminence in the future.[21]

According to U.S. defense analysts, China's cyber activities directed against the U.S. and Department of Defense are sophisticated and extensive:

> To support China's military modernization, it uses a variety of methods to acquire foreign military and dual-use technologies, including targeted foreign direct investment, cyber theft, and exploitation of private Chinese nationals' access to these technologies. Several recent cases and indictments illustrate China's use of intelligence services, computer intrusions, and other illicit approaches to obtain national security and export-restricted technologies, controlled equipment, and other materials.
>
> Computer systems around the world, including those owned by the U.S. Government, continue to be targeted by China-based intrusions. These intrusions focus on accessing networks and extracting information. China uses its cyber capabilities to support intelligence collection against U.S. diplomatic, economic, academic, and defense industrial base sectors. China can use the information to benefit China's defense high-technology industries, support China's military modernization, provide the CCP insights into U.S. leadership perspectives, and enable diplomatic negotiations, such as those supporting China's Belt and Road Initiative. Additionally, targeted information could enable PLA cyber

forces to build an operational picture of U.S. defense networks, military disposition, logistics, and related military capabilities that could be exploited prior to or during a crisis. The accesses and skills required for these intrusions are similar to those necessary to conduct cyber operations in an attempt to deter, delay, disrupt, and degrade DoD operations prior to or during a conflict.[22]

The 2018 National Defense Strategy outlines a comprehensive strategy comprised of multiple priorities, including readiness, modernization (nuclear, space and cyber, intelligence, surveillance and reconnaissance, missile defense, autonomous systems, and contested logistics), agility, and cultivating workforce tech talent.

AI's Role in Defense Preparedness: Aircraft Readiness

The U.S. Air Force has about 5,600 aircraft with an average age of 28 years, some introduced into service 60 years ago. According to Air Force data, about 71.3 percent of the Air Force's aircraft were flyable, or mission-capable, at any given time in fiscal 2017,[23] which represents a drop from the 72.1 percent mission-capable rate in fiscal 2016, and a continuation of the decline in recent years.

In September 2018, the Secretary of Defense ordered the Air Force and Navy to raise mission-capable rates for four key tactical aircraft above 80 percent within a year, a number well above the mission-capability rates those aircraft now achieve:

- F-35 (readiness of 55 percent)

- F-22 (readiness of 49 percent)

- F-16 (readiness of 70 percent)

- F-18 (readiness of 53 percent for F/A-18E/F Super Hornet fleet, 44 percent for reserve fleet of F-18C Hornets)

Many of these aircraft are nearing the end of their service life. The Congressional Budget Office projects that replacing the aircraft in the current fleet would cost an average of $15 billion a year in the 2020s.

That figure would rise to $23 billion in the 2030s and then fall back to $15 billion in the 2040s. In comparison, appropriations for procuring new aircraft averaged about $12 billion per year between 1980 and 2017.

The flying branch needs to replace a lot of planes in a short span of time, U.S. Air Force Secretary Heather Wilson said in a March 2018 statement: "The Air Force must manage a bow wave in modernization over the next ten years."[24]

A significant improvement in aircraft readiness, along with the resulting cost savings (such as reduced maintenance and inventory holding costs), could have a major impact in bridging the modernization budget gap.

Improving aircraft readiness requires anticipating unplanned maintenance, ensuring availability of spare parts in the right locations, and scheduling maintainers to perform maintenance. The U.S. Air Force has demonstrated that by applying sophisticated AI algorithms to aircraft flight, environmental, and maintenance data, we can correctly identify at least 40 percent of unscheduled aircraft maintenance.

Based on the success of the demonstration project, the USAF plans to make the predictive maintenance application available to any USAF aircraft platform. When widely deployed, the USAF expects it will improve overall readiness by 40 percent.

This AI-based approach does not require the time and expense of retrofitting older jets with system sensors. These algorithms can be deployed in conjunction with the Air Force's current maintenance systems to recommend additional aircraft subsystem maintenance while an aircraft is undergoing scheduled maintenance. The outputs of these algorithms can also inform spare parts demand planning and maintenance scheduling.

AI algorithms can not only increase the throw-weight (i.e., weapon delivery capacity) of the Air Force by 40 percent but also free up operations and maintenance budget for fleet modernization and expansion. The cumulative impact of this AI-driven predictive maintenance application for the USAF—which includes sizeable reductions in time, labor, spare parts and inventory holding costs, and reporting costs—adds up to a 10 percent efficiency improvement on $50 billion in annual operations and maintenance costs. That is *$5 billion a year* that can help bridge the modernization budget gap.

Projected Costs for Procuring New Aircraft, 2019–2050

The U.S. Congressional Budget Office projects that costs to procure new military aircraft will substantially increase over the next decade. Using AI to improve aircraft availability and reduce operations costs can free up billions of dollars for modernization efforts.

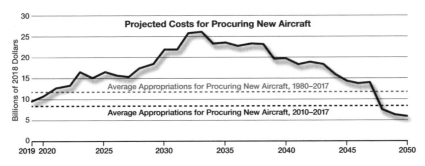

FIGURE 8.2

The Department of Defense's Operations and Maintenance budget request for fiscal 2019 is $283.5 billion.[25] Application of these AI algorithms across assets employed in the Army, Navy, and Marines can drive similar readiness improvements and budget savings.

Defense Modernization at the Speed of Relevance

U.S. Defense Department investments in AI provide the opportunity to upgrade military operational capabilities while improving affordability and streamlining key business functions to deliver military competitive advantage. Doing so at an accelerated pace and in partnership with innovative companies is a Defense Department priority.

The Department has made important strides in addressing the mismatch between the pace of start-ups and traditional government procurement through the creation in 2015 of the Defense Innovation Unit (DIU), a Silicon Valley–based office that has more flexibility to fund small defense contracts quickly and facilitate interaction between the Pentagon and Silicon Valley.

"My fundamental view is we are in a technology race. We didn't ask to be in this, but we're in it," said Michael Brown, Director of DIU. "I'm concerned that if we don't recognize that we're in a race and take appropriate action, then we let China move forward and we don't put our best foot forward in terms of leading in these key technology areas."[26]

The Pentagon has also created a new Joint Artificial Intelligence Center to coordinate and advance defense-related AI activities. These efforts make it easier for the government to work with start-ups and other companies not used to working with the federal government.

In 2018 the Army established the Army Futures Command to streamline and accelerate acquisition and rapidly deliver warfighting capabilities, with an objective of reducing the requirements development process from nearly five years to one year or less.

With cross-functional teams, the command is tackling six modernization priorities: Long Range Precision Fires (missiles); Next Generation Combat Vehicle (tanks, troop carriers); Future Vertical Lift (helicopters); Network Command, Control, Communication, and Intelligence; Air and Missile Defense; and Soldier Lethality (troop combat capabilities).[27]

The fiscal year 2019 National Defense Authorization Act that was signed by the President in August 2018 earmarked $10.2 billion to help fund those efforts. The command itself has an annual budget of about $100 million.

"Army Futures Command has been an opportunity for us to bring two key stakeholders together—acquisitions and requirements," said Under Secretary of the Army Ryan D. McCarthy during a panel at the 2018 Association of the U.S. Army (AUSA) annual meeting.[28]

The Defense Department is investing broadly in military application of autonomy, artificial intelligence, and machine learning. Efforts to scale Department-wide use of AI to expand military advantage include:[29]

Space and cyberspace as warfighting domains. The Department will prioritize investments in resilience, reconstitution, and operations to ensure U.S. space capabilities. The U.S. will also invest in cyber defense, resilience, and the continued integration of cyber capabilities into the full spectrum of military operations.

Resilient and agile logistics. Investments in this area prioritize distributed logistics and maintenance to ensure logistics sustainment while under persistent multidomain (ground, air, sea, and space) attack, as well as transitioning from large, centralized, unhardened infrastructure to smaller, dispersed, resilient, adaptive bases.

In the private sector, AI algorithms are in use to achieve similar goals such as high levels of on-time customer delivery and power network resiliency. The algorithms operate by continuously characterizing and compensating for uncertainty in demand, logistics, and supply networks; these techniques can be applied to ensure guaranteed delivery of military forces and supplies. Similarly, AI algorithms are used to track the state of power networks and ensure their resiliency; in the case of unanticipated equipment failure, power is instantaneously re-routed to ensure continuous power delivery. These techniques are equally applicable to operating in contested military environments.

Command, control, communications, computers, intelligence, surveillance, and reconnaissance (C4ISR). Investments prioritize developing resilient, survivable, federated networks and information systems from the tactical level up to strategic planning. Investments also prioritize capabilities to gain and exploit information, deny adversaries those same advantages, and enable the U.S. to identify and hold accountable both state and non-state perpetrators of attempted cyberattacks.

An example is the F-35 Joint Strike Fighter operational threat library—the "mission data files." The mission data files—the "brains" of the airplane—are extensive on-board data systems that compile information on geography, air space, and potential threats such as enemy fighter jets in areas where the aircraft might be deployed in combat.[30]

The mission data files work with the F-35's Radar Warning Receiver that detects approaching threats and hostile fire. Information from the aircraft's long-range sensors is compared in real time against the library of enemy threats. If this happens quickly enough and at a sufficient standoff range, the F-35 can identify and destroy enemy targets before it is vulnerable to enemy fire. For example, the mission data system could rapidly identify a Chinese J-10 fighter if detected by the F-35's sensors.

Keeping the mission data files current requires assimilating information gathered from numerous government intelligence agencies in varying formats (image, video, comments, documents, and structured data). Analysts must review, analyze, organize, and update these data manually and determine which intelligence is most relevant for a given mission data file. AI algorithms can be used to automate the aggregation, analysis, and correlation of these disparate data, which will accelerate the process and ensure the F-35 is operating on relevant and up-to-date information.

Workforce AI Talent

Increasing the pipeline of AI talent in both the private and public sectors is critical to ensuring AI leadership and national security. AI researchers and data scientists currently command increasingly high salaries, a sign of the shortfall in top-tier talent. The U.S. must educate, recruit, and retain the best researchers in the world. Increasing education funding and opportunities for science, technology, engineering, and mathematics (STEM) is a top priority. The federal government plan for STEM education released in December 2018 takes some important steps to expand the pipeline of students acquiring advanced STEM degrees.[31]

Another significant obstacle to progress is the security clearance process. There are 500,000 new federal employees, contractors, and military personnel whose ability to work is impeded or limited by a security clearance process that is unable to keep up with demand.[32] Some individuals are able to obtain interim security clearances and begin working, but others are left waiting a year or more before being able to begin work at all.[33] There is a similar backlog of reinvestigations that are required periodically of cleared personnel.

Defense Security Services is implementing innovative techniques to assess personnel risk, including a "continuous evaluation" (CE) system. Using AI algorithms, the CE system regularly scans a range of data sources—such as court proceedings and bank and credit bureau records—looking for indications that an existing clearance holder or applicant may pose a security risk. If it uncovers any risk indicators for an individual, the CE system alerts a security agent for follow-up review and action.[34] These systems are more efficient and more effective at identification of risk and can easily be scaled to federal employees and suppliers.

No Bigger Stakes

AI will fundamentally determine the fate of the planet. This is a category of technology unlike any that preceded it, uniquely able to harness vast amounts of data unfathomable to the human mind to drive precise, real-time decision-making for virtually any task—including the operation of hypersonic missiles; energy-powered space-based weapons; autonomous air, land, and water combat vehicles; and advanced cyber-weapons aimed at information systems, communications networks, power grids, and other essential infrastructure. In short, AI will be the critical enabling technology of 21st-century warfare.

Today the U.S. and China are engaged in a war for AI leadership. The outcome of that contest remains uncertain. China clearly is committed to an ambitious and explicitly stated national strategy to become the global AI leader. Unless the U.S. significantly steps up investment in AI across the board—in government, industry, and education—it is at risk of falling behind. You can think of this as the 21st-century equivalent of the Manhattan Project.

The fate of the world hangs in the balance.

Chapter 9

The Digital Enterprise

As we've covered in the preceding chapters, the confluence of elastic cloud computing, big data, AI, and IoT drives digital transformation. Companies that harness these technologies and transform into vibrant, dynamic digital enterprises will thrive. Those that do not will become irrelevant and cease to exist. If the reality sounds harsh, that's because it is.

The price of missing a transformational strategic shift is steep. The corporate graveyard is littered with once-great companies that failed to change. Blockbuster, Yahoo!, and Borders stand out as companies crushed by sector-wide changes to which they could not adapt. At its peak, Blockbuster, an American video and videogame rental company, employed 60,000 people, earned $5.9 billion in revenue, and boasted a $5 billion market capitalization.[1] Six years later, Blockbuster filed for bankruptcy, a shell of its former self.[2] In 2000, Netflix CEO Reed Hastings proposed a partnership with Blockbuster—Netflix wanted to run Blockbuster's online presence as part of a $50 million acquisition—and Blockbuster declined.[3] As I'm writing this, Netflix has a market capitalization of over $160 billion and Blockbuster no longer exists. Netflix saw the shift happening, discarded mail order, and transformed into a streaming video company. Blockbuster did not.

In 2000, Yahoo! was the poster child of the internet. It was valued at $125 billion at the height of the dot-com bubble.[4] In the following years, Yahoo! had opportunities to buy both Google and Facebook, and in both cases, they failed to execute the deals due to pricing issues: $3 billion was simply too much to pay for a company like Google.[5] In 2008, Microsoft attempted a hostile takeover of Yahoo! at a price tag of about $45 billion, which Yahoo! successfully rebuffed, and in 2016, Verizon acquired Yahoo! for $4.8 billion.[6] The downhill slope for Yahoo! was dramatic.

The consumer internet became mobile, social, and driven by interactions around photos and videos. Yahoo! did not, so it was acquired and disintegrated. At the time of this writing, Google and Facebook have market capitalizations of $840 billion and $500 billion, respectively.

Borders, an American book retailer, had 1,249 stores at its peak in 2003.[7] Just two years earlier, Borders contracted its e-commerce business to Amazon.com, a famously grave mistake that disincentivized internal executives from establishing a proprietary online presence.[8] Amazon's e-books and data-driven logistics were an existential threat, but Borders failed to act. Unsurprisingly, by sending its online business to Amazon and failing to enter the e-book business, the Borders brand eroded and it became irrelevant. In 2010, Borders attempted to launch its own e-reader and e-book store, but it was too late.[9] One year later, Borders closed its doors for the last time.[10]

These stories—Blockbuster, Yahoo!, and Borders—are not exceptional. They are not anomalies. They are not unusual. These stories are the product of mass corporate extinctions driven by fundamental shifts in the way business is done. They represent the guaranteed outcome for companies that do not transform. This time around, digital transformation is the do-or-die impetus. Companies that do not succeed in this vital task will go the way of Blockbuster, Yahoo!, and Borders.

While the cost of failing to adapt is perilous, the future has never looked brighter for large companies embracing digital transformation. This is primarily for two reasons. The first is Metcalfe's Law, as we have discussed in chapter 7: Networks grow in value as the participants increase. Large corporations stand to benefit from a similar paradigm regarding data. If properly used, the value of enterprise data also increases exponentially with scale. Large companies tend to have dramatically more data than the upstart competitors seeking to supplant them and can collect data considerably faster. If incumbent organizations can digitally transform, they will establish "data moats," which are an asymmetric advantage that could dissuade competitors from easily entering their industries. The impact of such data moats should not be underestimated. The advantage Amazon or Google already has, thanks to years of consumer and user data, is enormous. Similarly, early market entrants with disruptive offerings—think Uber, Zappos, Slack, or Instagram—quickly gain competitive advantage by capturing and using large amounts of data, creating a formidable time-to-market scale advantage.

The second reason large companies are well positioned to exploit digital transformation is they typically have access to substantial capital. Digital transformation offers highly attractive investment opportunities. One such opportunity is hiring large numbers of top-flight data scientists and engineers. Another is investing in digital transformation technologies.

As it turns out, these two factors—data moats and access to capital—work synergistically. Large companies with proprietary data, the right technologies in place, and the capital to recruit top talent will find themselves in almost unprecedented—and extremely favorable—positions.

For data scientists and engineers, more data means more interesting problems to solve—and the best data scientists and engineers want to work on the most interesting problems. If a large company is able to execute a successful digital transformation, its data moat—i.e., its advantage in having more and better data than competitors—translates into the ability to attract superior data scientists, build superior artificial intelligence algorithms and outputs, generate superior insights, and ultimately achieve superior economic performance. Google, Amazon, and Netflix are clear examples of how such a data advantage plays out.

We are in the very early days of digital transformation. As we've seen, the technologies driving this change have matured only within the last 5 to 10 years. In this chapter, I share case studies of successful digital transformation initiatives at six large organizations—ENGIE, Enel, Caterpillar, John Deere, 3M, and the U.S. Air Force—based on work we do at C3.ai with these customers.

The following case studies—which involve solving some of the world's most complex data science problems—encompass a number of different use cases, including predictive maintenance, inventory optimization, fraud detection, process and yield optimization, and customer insights. Common to all these case studies are the strategic nature of the approach—in particular, the focus on specific, high-priority objectives to drive significant, measurable value—and the CEO-level mandate for change.

ENGIE: Company-Wide Digital Transformation

ENGIE, the integrated French energy company I've previously mentioned, is in many ways the archetype of a large enterprise embracing digital transformation. With more than 150,000 employees and operations spanning 70 countries, ENGIE reported €60.6 billion in revenue in 2018. ENGIE generates vast amounts of data from its 22 million IoT devices and hundreds of enterprise and operational systems. In 2016, ENGIE CEO Isabelle Kocher recognized two inextricable forces shaking the core of ENGIE's industry: digital and energy transformations. In ENGIE's own words, the revolution in the energy industry is being driven by "decarbonization, decentralization, and digitalization."[11] Kocher recognized that, in order to survive and thrive in this new energy world, ENGIE would have to undergo a fundamental digital transformation.

As we've discussed, successful digital transformation has to start at the top. At ENGIE, it starts with Kocher. She has painted the vision for ENGIE's digital transformation and announced that €1.5 billion will be devoted to the company's digital transformation from 2016 to 2019. She created ENGIE Digital, a hub for digital transformation efforts across the company. ENGIE Digital includes its Digital Factory—a Center of Excellence (CoE) where the company's software developers, alongside its partners, incubate and roll out innovative IT tools across the organization. Finally, Kocher has appointed Yves Le Gélard as chief digital officer to oversee these efforts.[12]

ENGIE's first step in this transformation was to identify high-value use cases, and to craft a roadmap that prioritizes its trajectory toward full digital transformation. ENGIE's Digital Factory has created and prioritized a comprehensive project roadmap. Use cases span the company's lines of businesses. Here are some examples:

- For its gas assets, ENGIE uses predictive analytics and AI algorithms to perform predictive maintenance on its assets and optimize electricity generation—identifying drivers of efficiency loss, reducing asset failures, and improving uptime.

- In customer management, ENGIE is rolling out an entire suite of on-line services for customers, including self-service applications that allow them to manage their own energy use. For individual residents and building managers, ENGIE has developed an application that analyzes data from smart sensors to pinpoint opportunities to save energy.

- In renewables, ENGIE has developed a digital platform of applications to optimize generation of electricity from renewable sources. These applications use predictive analytics and AI to forecast maintenance requirements, identify underperforming assets, and provide field operators with a real-time view of assets and maintenance needs. The platform already covers more than 2 gigawatts of installed capacity and by 2020 will cover more than 25 gigawatts, making it one of the largest AI deployments in the world for renewable energy management. Today, more than 1,000 machine learning models are continuously trained to adapt to changing operating conditions, providing 140,000 predictions per day at 10-minute intervals for more than 350 wind turbines across the world. By 2020, its digital platform will address more than 20 additional machine learning use cases, unlocking significant economic value.

- In smart cities, ENGIE plans to develop and deploy a number of applications—including efficient district heating and cooling, traffic control, green mobility, waste management, and security—to create sustainable, energy-efficient connected cities, as the percentage of the world population living in cities increases from 50 percent today to 70 percent in 2050.

The list of use cases for ENGIE goes on and on. Across its organization, ENGIE will develop and deploy 28 applications over a three-year period and train over 100 employees. To coordinate and drive this change, ENGIE has established a sophisticated CoE, applying best practices to collaborate with business unit leaders, define requirements, create roadmaps, and develop and deploy applications in a systematic way that achieves measurable results.

One year in, the first four applications are already live. ENGIE is starting to see results, and the potential economic benefits are substantial: for example, the value of just two use cases—predicting and preventing equipment failures and optimizing planned downtime and dispatch operations—is expected to exceed €100 million annually.

Enel: Digital Transformation One Step at a Time

Enel, the Italian utility, is the second largest power producer in the world, with over 95 gigawatts of installed capacity, more than 70 million customers globally, €75.7 billion in 2018 revenue, and 69,000 employees. A smart-grid pioneer, Enel was the first utility in the world to replace traditional electromechanical meters with digital smart meters, a major operation carried out across Enel's entire Italian customer base. By 2006, Enel had installed 32 million smart meters across Italy; Enel has since deployed a total of more than 40 million smart meters in Europe, representing more than 80 percent of the total smart meters on the continent.

Enel's digital transformation has been monumental: The company has the largest deployment of AI and IoT applications in the world. Enel's journey toward digital transformation also started at the top, led by CEO Francesco Starace who appointed Fabio Veronese, Head of Infrastructure & Technological Services, to lead Enel's digital transformation initiative. Enel projects to spend €5.3 billion to digitize its assets, operations, and processes, and to enhance connectivity.[13]

Let's dive into two specific use cases along Enel's digital transformation journey. First is the predictive maintenance of Enel's 1.2-million-kilometer distribution network in Italy that comprises numerous assets—substations, distribution lines, transformers, and smart meters—with sensors throughout. To further improve grid reliability and reduce the occurrence of outages and service interruptions due to asset failure, Enel deployed a prebuilt AI-powered predictive maintenance application. The SaaS application applies advanced machine learning to analyze real-time network sensor data, smart meter data, asset maintenance records, and weather data to predict failures along distribution network "feeders" (i.e., distribution lines that carry electricity from substations to transformers and end customers) before they happen. Enel can monitor assets in real time, assign day-by-day risk scores to assets, and immediately catch any anomalies or changed operating conditions that forecast emerging maintenance issues. This AI-powered predictive capability enables Enel to improve reliability, reduce its operations costs, provide greater flexibility in scheduling of maintenance tasks, significantly extend the life cycle of its assets, and improve customer satisfaction.

Key innovations in this project include (a) the ability to construct Enel's as-operated network state at any point in time using an advanced graph network approach, and (b) the use of an advanced machine learning–based framework that continuously learns to improve the performance of predicting asset failures. Leveraging elastic cloud computing, the predictive maintenance application is able to aggregate petabyte-scale, real-time data from Enel's grid sensors and smart meters, correlate those data with operational systems data, and, importantly, extend operational insight by subjecting those data to a comprehensive set of power analytics and machine learning algorithms.

The second use case to highlight is revenue protection. Enel transformed its approach to identifying and prioritizing electricity theft ("non-technical loss") to drive a significant increase in the recovery of unbilled energy, while improving productivity. Enel's vision for this transformation was an enterprise AI and IoT SaaS application that could be deployed across all of Enel's operating entities globally within a six-month period. Delivering on this vision required building a machine learning algorithm to match the performance delivered by Enel experts, who used a manual process honed over 30 years of experience. While this was a significant challenge in and of itself, Enel set an ambitious target to double the performance achieved in recent operating years.

A key innovation that enabled this transformation was replacing traditional non-technical loss identification processes. This focused primarily on improving the success of field inspections with advanced AI algorithms to prioritize potential cases of non-technical loss at service points, based on a blend of the magnitude of energy recovery and likelihood of fraud. The AI-powered revenue protection application enabled Enel to reach its target and *double the average energy recovered per inspection*—a significant achievement, given that Enel's original process was based on three decades of expert experience.

Digital transformation has delivered enormous value and impact for Enel. Its efforts even earned the company a spot on *Fortune*'s 2018 "Change the World" list (one of only 57 companies globally)—for the third time in four years. The *Fortune* list recognizes companies that, through their core business strategy, improve living conditions on both a social and environmental level. Enel has imbued innovation and digital transformation throughout its organization, and it has paid off—with a projected annual economic benefit that exceeds €600 million per year.

Caterpillar: Enterprise Data Hub

Switching gears to the industrial manufacturing sector, we can look to the world's leading manufacturer of construction and mining equipment—Caterpillar. It is an example of a company that produces extremely complex engineered products and understands the potential value in fundamentally transforming this intensive production process. In 2016, Caterpillar's then-CEO Doug Oberhelman announced, "Today, we've got 400,000 connected assets and growing. By this summer, every one of our machines will come off the line being able to be connected and provide some kind of feedback in operational productivity to the owner, to the dealer and to us." He pointed to a further vision "where we can show the customer on his iPhone everything going on with his machine, his fleet, its health, its run rate, its productivity and so on."[14]

Caterpillar's digital transformation strategy hinges on the company's digitally connected equipment—today comprising some 470,000 assets (and expected to grow to over 2 million) in operation across customers worldwide. Caterpillar's first step was to create an extensible Enterprise Data Hub to act as the source of enterprise data from more than 2,000 of Caterpillar's applications, systems, and databases globally. These data include business application data, dealer and customer data, supplier data, and machine data. The data will be aggregated, unified, normalized, and federated into a single data image that supports a variety of machine learning, predictive analytics, and IoT applications across Caterpillar's business units.

Leveraging the Enterprise Data Hub, Caterpillar is building a host of applications to enable its digital transformation. In a first instance, Caterpillar turned to its inventory. How do you manage a supply network that brings together over 28,000 suppliers to ship to 170 dealers, all with fluctuating demand? Having visibility across its supply network, understanding the transit time of parts shipped from overseas, and reducing excess inventory and spare parts inventory are critical business questions that Caterpillar is solving through the use of AI, big data, and predictive analytics.

With an AI-powered application, Caterpillar now has the ability to search and view inventory across its supply chain, receive AI-powered recommendations on optimal stocking levels, and understand the trade-offs between stockout risks and holding excess inventory. Caterpillar has developed and deployed advanced AI-enabled solutions that provide its dealer network with visibility into finished goods inventory and sophisticated "similarity search" capability. This enables dealers to effectively meet customer demand by surfacing recommendations of in-stock products that very closely match customer requirements. The application also provides Caterpillar's production planners and product managers with recommendations on configuration options and inventory stocking levels.

Next, Caterpillar is focused on leveraging telemetry from its entire fleet of connected assets along with data related to ambient operating conditions for each asset. Some of this telemetry is being continuously ingested in real time at a rate of over 1,000 messages per second. Such AI-enabled analytics allow Caterpillar to pinpoint anomalies in equipment health, predict asset failure, design competitive warranty offerings, and leverage the full set of operating data to design the next generation of products and features.

Caterpillar makes all these changes to its operations through the establishment of a CoE—a cross-functional team that brings together outside experts and Caterpillar developers for intensive training on how to design, develop, deploy, and maintain applications using AI and predictive analytics. The CoE's role is to define a prioritized use case roadmap, and then implement a scalable, repeatable program to develop, deploy, and operate a portfolio of high-value applications to transform the enterprise.

John Deere: Transforming Supply Chain and Inventory

John Deere is another industrial manufacturer embarking on a digital transformation strategy to transform its supply chain. Founded in 1837, John Deere is the largest farm equipment manufacturer in the world, with more than $38 billion in annual revenue and over 60,000 employees.

A critical component of John Deere's digital transformation is managing its inventory. John Deere operates hundreds of factories globally and makes highly complex industrial equipment. The company allows customers to configure hundreds of individual options, leading to products that have thousands of permutations. The customized nature of the product creates significant complexity in managing inventory levels during the manufacturing process. Previously, John Deere had to manage key uncertainties like fluctuations in demand, supplier delivery times, and product line disruptions. Due to these uncertainties, and since the final configuration of a product is often not known until close to the submission of a product's order, John Deere would often hold excess inventory to fulfill orders on time. This excess inventory is expensive and complicated to manage.

Like other manufacturers in the industry, John Deere deployed material requirements planning (MRP) software solutions to support production planning and inventory management. John Deere had also experimented with different commercial inventory optimization software offerings. However, the existing software solutions were unable to dynamically optimize inventory levels of individual parts at scale while managing uncertainty and learning continually from data. Key sources of uncertainty include variability in demand, supplier risk, quality issues with items delivered by suppliers, and production line disruptions.

To address these issues, John Deere built an AI-powered application to optimize inventory levels, starting with one of its product lines that has over 40,000 unique parts. The company used an algorithm to calculate daily historical inventory levels based on a range of parameters. With the AI-powered application, John Deere was able to simulate and optimize order parameters, quantify the planned use of materials based on production orders, and minimize safety stock levels. The operational impact of these insights is significant—John Deere could potentially reduce parts inventory by 25 to 35 percent, delivering between $100 million and $200 million in annual economic value to the company.

3M: AI-Driven Operational Efficiency

Headquartered in Minnesota, 3M is a multinational conglomerate that produces tens of thousands of product variants derived from 46 core technology platforms. The company is primarily in the business of physical products, although one of its divisions, 3M Health Information Systems, provides software.

3M's origins go back to 1902, when a group of enterprising young men founded the Minnesota Mining and Manufacturing Company, a mining venture that promptly failed. The founders, in conjunction with a group of investors and employees, refused to fold. Instead they tried commercializing many different products, eventually finding success in manufacturing sandpaper. Along the way they developed a robust culture of innovation that is deeply embedded in the company today. Its numerous industrial and consumer products include many familiar brands such as Scotch Tape, Post-it Notes, and Scotchgard. Today, the 3M Company (renamed in 2002) employs more than 91,000 people and generated more than $32 billion in revenue in 2018.

CEO Mike Roman, a 30-year 3M veteran, and his leadership team are executing against the "3M Playbook"—a set of strategies that are fundamentally about simplification, optimization, innovation, and building on 3M's strengths. As part of the playbook, 3M's "business transformation" program is focused on increasing operational productivity while reducing costs. "In fast-changing times, companies have to constantly adapt, change and anticipate," Roman stated shortly after taking over as CEO in 2018. "This is one reason why our transformation efforts are so critical, as we become more agile, more contemporary, more efficient, and even better equipped to serve the evolving needs of customers."[15]

3M sees numerous opportunities to apply AI to drive significant improvements in operational efficiency and productivity across a wide range of business processes with direct bottom-line benefits. The company is developing and deploying multiple AI-enabled applications focused on specific high-value use cases. Let me highlight two use cases that may be of interest to any large manufacturing company.

In one use case, 3M has developed an AI application to dramatically improve its "order-to-promise" process, enabling the company to provide significantly more accurate commitments for when products will be delivered to corporate customers. Given 3M's extensive supply chain, logistics network, and the tens of thousands of product variants it makes, this is a complex problem to solve.

With the AI-powered application, 3M integrates and unifies data from disparate enterprise systems—order, customer, demand, manufacturing, inventory, customer service—to predict expected delivery dates for individual orders and provide accurate promises to customers when they place orders. This type of AI-enabled process makes business-to-business procurement feel more like shopping on Amazon, dramatically enhancing 3M's customer service by ensuring orders arrive when they are promised. It also has the significant secondary benefit of revealing bottlenecks in the supply and logistics network, enabling further network optimization. Authorized users in 3M can access relevant KPIs across every location globally, which are updated in real time, via an intuitive user interface. They can also use these insights to make important operating decisions, such as ordering additional stock, redirecting orders, and sending out service alerts to potentially affected customers.

A second use case focuses on the "order invoice escalation" process, with the objective of dramatically reducing the number of invoice-related customer complaints. Given the complexity of many purchase orders—numerous invoice lines, cross-border deliveries, multiple applicable discounts and taxes—a significant number of customer complaints are related to invoicing issues. 3M developed an AI-powered application to predict invoices that may cause customer complaints, enabling 3M specialists to review and amend those invoices before they are sent. 3M's invoicing system previously relied solely on a rules-based approach to flag potential issues and lacked AI-enabled predictive capabilities. The new application employs sophisticated AI methods along with the existing rules and achieves far greater accuracy in identifying problematic invoices. For a company of 3M's scale and global reach, the resulting benefits—in terms of both reduced costs of investigating invoice-related issues and increased customer satisfaction—are significant.

By 2020, 3M expects the impact of its business transformation initiative will result in $500 million to $700 million in annual operational savings and another $500 million reduction in working capital. That's over $1 billion—*three percent of the company's 2018 revenue.*

United States Air Force: Predictive Maintenance

While many industrial organizations have embraced AI predictive analytics to optimize inventory, protect revenue, improve customer relations, and more, the advantages of digital transformation are not limited to private enterprise.

The U.S. military spends a third of its annual budget on maintenance. Any reduction in that number has profound implications for military readiness—not to mention impacts on available resources, morale, and more. Starting in mid-2017, several internal groups in the U.S. Air Force began to consider whether applying AI to aircraft maintenance would alleviate unplanned failures, increase aircraft availability, and improve the regularity of maintenance schedules.

The Air Force maintains a fleet of almost 5,600 aircraft that are on average 28 years old. The USAF relies on 59 air bases in the U.S. and over 100 airfields overseas. Planes are flown by 17,000 pilots and maintained by thousands of different personnel in many different groups. The factors that contribute to an aircraft needing maintenance, or to the failure of any one of its six main systems (engine, flight instruments, environmental control, hydraulic-pneumatic instrumentation, fuel, and electrical) or subsystems, can range wildly. Base temperatures and humidity, maintenance crew behaviors, flight conditions and duration, and of course, equipment condition and age can all impact maintenance needs.

To solve this challenge, the Silicon Valley outpost of the Defense Innovation Unit (DIU) that is chartered with accelerating commercial technologies for military use worked with several USAF divisions to develop a project for AI-based predictive maintenance. The teams started with the E-3 Sentry (Airborne Warning and Control System, or AWACS) and compiled seven years of all relevant structured and unstructured data: sorties, workforce experience, subsystem interdependencies, external weather, maintenance text logs, oil samples, and even pilot notes.

In three weeks, the teams aggregated these operational data from 11 sources with 2,000 data points for a single E-3 Sentry subsystem to build a prototype. After a 12-week effort, the teams delivered an initial application that used 20 AI machine learning algorithms to calculate the probability of failure of high-priority aircraft subsystems, so maintenance could be done on those systems just prior to failure.

The predictive maintenance application also provided capabilities to optimize maintenance schedules to align with usage and risk, prioritize maintenance across equipment, directly initiate activities through existing work order management systems, identify root causes of potential

Artificial Intelligence Predictive Maintenance Drives 40 Percent Improvement in Aircraft Readiness

Based on initial results of deploying AI-driven predictive maintenance for its fleet of E-3 Sentry aircraft (left), the USAF expanded the project to include its fleet of F-16 Fighting Falcon (center) and C-5 Galaxy (right) aircraft.

FIGURE 9.1

failures, and recommend technical actions to an operator. The USAF team can now analyze equipment health at any level of aggregation, including systems and subcomponents, risk profiles, operational status, geographic location, and deployment.

Overall, the initial project improved aircraft availability by 40 percent. Because the initial project was successful, the USAF expanded the project to the C-5 Galaxy and the F-16 Fighting Falcon and plans to make the application for predictive maintenance available to any USAF group or aircraft platform. Once the application is widely deployed, the USAF expects it will improve *overall* USAF readiness by 40 percent.

As these case studies demonstrate, digital transformation can have a potentially revolutionary impact on large enterprises and public sector entities. The changes go deep into process and culture.

But success in these efforts is contingent on two fundamental pillars: a technology infrastructure able to support these new classes of AI and IoT applications, and direct leadership from the CEO. In the next chapter, I describe the new "technology stack" that digital transformation requires. And in the final chapter, I outline how CEOs can take concrete action and move forward on their digital transformation journey.

Chapter 10

A New Technology Stack

In the four decades that I have participated in the information technology revolution, the industry has grown from the order of $50 billion to about $4 trillion annually. That growth is accelerating today.

I have seen the transition from mainframe computing to minicomputers, to personal computing, to internet computing, and to handheld computing. The software industry has transitioned from custom application software based on MVS, VSAM, and ISAM, to applications developed on a relational database foundation, to enterprise application software, to SaaS, to handheld computing, and now to the AI-enabled enterprise. I have seen the internet and the iPhone change everything. Each of these transitions represented a replacement market for its predecessor. Each delivered dramatic benefits in productivity. Each offered organizations the opportunity to gain sustainable competitive advantage.

Companies that failed to take advantage of each new generation of technology ceased to be competitive. Imagine trying to close the books at a major global corporation without an ERP system or to run your business solely on mainframe computers. It is unimaginable.

A New Technology Stack

The current step function in information technology that I have been discussing has a number of unique requirements that create the need for an entirely new software technology stack. The requirements of this stack to develop and operate an effective enterprise AI or IoT application are daunting.

To develop an effective enterprise AI or IoT application, it is necessary to aggregate data from across thousands of enterprise information systems, suppliers, distributors, markets, products in customer use, and sensor networks, to provide a near-real-time view of the extended enterprise.

Data velocities in this new digital world are quite dramatic, requiring the ability to ingest and aggregate data from hundreds of millions of endpoints at very high frequency, sometimes exceeding 1,000 Hz cycles (1,000 times per second).

The data need to be processed at the rate they arrive, in a highly secure and resilient system that addresses persistence, event processing, machine learning, and visualization. This requires massively horizontally scalable elastic distributed processing capability offered only by modern cloud platforms and supercomputer systems.

The resultant data persistence requirements are staggering in both scale and form. These data sets rapidly aggregate into hundreds of petabytes, even exabytes, and each data type needs to be stored in an appropriate database capable of handling these massive volumes at high frequency. Relational databases, key-value stores, graph databases, distributed file systems, blobs—none is sufficient, and all are necessary, requiring the data to be organized and linked across these divergent technologies.

Do It Yourself

In the 1980s, when I was at Oracle Corporation, we introduced relational database management system (RDBMS) software to the market. There was a high level of market interest. RDBMS technology offered dramatic cost economies and productivity gains in application development and maintenance. It proved an enabling technology for the next generation of enterprise applications that followed, including material requirements planning (MRP), enterprise resource planning (ERP), customer relationship management (CRM), manufacturing automation, and others.

The early competitors in the RDBMS market included Oracle, IBM (DB2), Relational Technology (Ingres), and Sperry (Mapper). But the primary competitor to Oracle, the one that became the world's leading provider, was not any of these companies. It was in many cases the CIO. He or she was going to build the organization's own RDBMS with IT personnel, offshore personnel, or the help of a systems integrator. No one succeeded. After a few years and tens to hundreds of millions of dollars invested, the CIO would be replaced and we would come back and install a commercial RDBMS.

When we introduced enterprise application software to the market, including ERP and CRM in the 1990s, the primary software competitors included Oracle, SAP, and Siebel Systems. But in reality, the primary obstacle to adoption was the CIO. Many CIOs believed they had the knowledge, the experience, and the skills to develop these complex enterprise applications internally. Hundreds of person-years and hundreds of millions of dollars were expended on these wasteful projects. A few years later, there would be a new CIO and we would return to install a working system.

I remember even some of the most technologically astute companies—including Hewlett-Packard, IBM, Microsoft, and Compaq—repeatedly failed at internally developed CRM projects. And after multiple efforts, all ultimately became large and highly successful Siebel Systems CRM customers. If *they* couldn't do it, what were the chances a telecommunications company, bank, or pharmaceutical company could succeed? Many tried. None succeeded.

Reference AI Software Platform

The problems that have to be addressed to solve the AI or IoT computing problem are nontrivial. Massively parallel elastic computing and storage capacity are prerequisite. These services are being provided today at increasingly low cost by Microsoft Azure, AWS, IBM, and others. This is a huge breakthrough in computing. The elastic cloud changes everything.

In addition to the cloud, there is a multiplicity of data services necessary to develop, provision, and operate applications of this nature.

The software utilities shown in Figure 10.1 are those necessary for this application domain. You can think of each as a development problem on the order of magnitude of a relatively simple enterprise software application like CRM. This assembly of software techniques necessary to address the complexity of the AI and IoT enterprise problem approximates the union of the commercially viable software development methodologies invented in the past 50 years. This is not a trivial problem.

Let's take a look at some of these requirements.

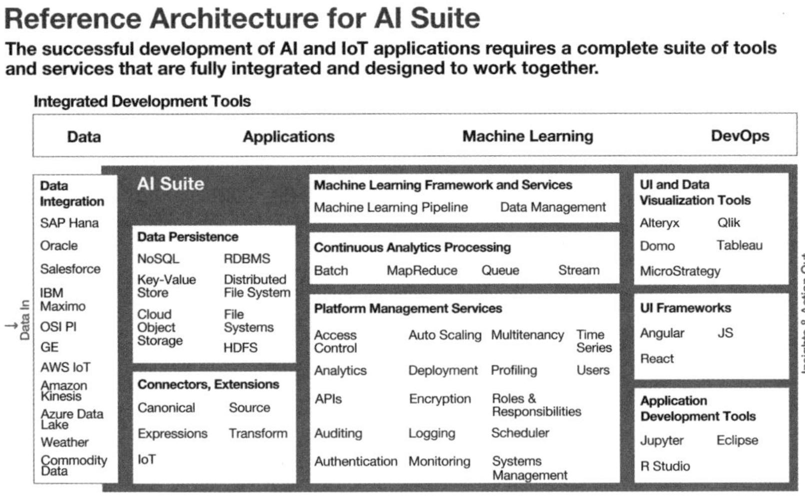

Reference Architecture for AI Suite

The successful development of AI and IoT applications requires a complete suite of tools and services that are fully integrated and designed to work together.

Integrated Development Tools

Data	Applications	Machine Learning	DevOps

Data Integration	AI Suite	Machine Learning Framework and Services	UI and Data Visualization Tools
SAP Hana		Machine Learning Pipeline Data Management	Alteryx Qlik
Oracle	**Data Persistence**		Domo Tableau
Salesforce	NoSQL RDBMS	**Continuous Analytics Processing**	MicroStrategy
IBM	Key-Value Distributed	Batch MapReduce Queue Stream	
Maximo	Store File System		**UI Frameworks**
OSI PI	Cloud File	**Platform Management Services**	Angular JS
GE	Object Systems	Access Auto Scaling Multitenancy Time	React
AWS IoT	Storage HDFS	Control Series	
Amazon Kinesis		Analytics Deployment Profiling Users	**Application Development Tools**
Azure Data Lake	**Connectors, Extensions**	APIs Encryption Roles & Responsibilities	Jupyter Eclipse
Weather	Canonical Source	Auditing Logging Scheduler	R Studio
Commodity Data	Expressions Transform	Authentication Monitoring Systems Management	
	IoT		

Data In →   ← Insights & Action Out →

FIGURE 10.1

Data Integration: This problem has haunted the computing industry for decades. Prerequisite to machine learning and AI at industrial scale is the availability of a unified, federated image of all the data contained in the multitude of (1) enterprise information systems—ERP, CRM, SCADA, HR, MRP—typically thousands of systems in each large enterprise; (2) sensor IoT networks—SIM chips, smart meters, programmable logic arrays, machine telemetry, bioinformatics; and (3) relevant extraprise data—weather, terrain, satellite imagery, social media, biometrics, trade data, pricing, market data, etc.

Data Persistence: The data aggregated and processed in these systems includes every type of structured and unstructured data imaginable. Personally identifiable information, census data, images, text, video, telemetry, voice, network topologies. There is no "one size fits all" database that is optimized for all these data types. This results in the need for a multiplicity of database technologies including but not limited to relational, NoSQL, key-value stores, distributed file systems, graph databases, and blobs.

Platform Services: A myriad of sophisticated platform services are necessary for any enterprise AI or IoT application. Examples include access control, data encryption in motion, encryption at rest, ETL, queuing, pipeline management, autoscaling, multitenancy, authentication, authorization, cybersecurity, time-series services, normalization, data privacy, GDPR privacy compliance, NERC-CIP compliance, and SOC2 compliance.

Analytics Processing: The volumes and velocity of data acquisition in such systems are blinding and the types of data and analytics requirements are highly divergent, requiring a range of analytics processing services. These include continuous analytics processing, MapReduce, batch processing, stream processing, and recursive processing.

Machine Learning Services: The whole point of these systems is to enable data scientists to develop and deploy machine learning models. There is a range of tools necessary to enable that, including Jupyter Notebooks, Python, DIGITS, R, and Scala. Increasingly important is an extensible curation of machine learning libraries such as TensorFlow, Caffe, Torch, Amazon Machine Learning, and AzureML. Your platform needs to support them all.

Data Visualization Tools: Any viable AI architecture needs to enable a rich and varied set of data visualization tools including Excel, Tableau, Qlik, Spotfire, Oracle BI, Business Objects, Domo, Alteryx, and others.

Developer Tools and UI Frameworks: Your IT development and data science community—in most cases, your IT development and data science *communities*—each have adopted and become comfortable with a set of application development frameworks and user interface (UI) development tools. If your AI platform does not support all of these tools—including, for example, the Eclipse IDE, VI, Visual Studio, React, Angular, R Studio, and Jupyter—it will be rejected as unusable by your development teams.

Open, Extensible, Future-Proof: It is difficult to describe the blinding pace of software and algorithm innovation in the systems described above. All the techniques used today will be obsolete in 5 to 10 years. Your architecture needs to provide the capability to replace any components with their next-generation improvements, and it needs to enable the incorporation of any new open source or proprietary software innovations without adversely affecting the functionality or performance of any of your existing applications. This is a level-zero requirement.

Awash in "AI Platforms"

As discussed, the technology vectors that enable digital transformation include elastic cloud computing, big data, AI, and IoT. Industry analysts estimate this software market will exceed $250 billion by 2025. McKinsey estimates that companies will generate more than $20 trillion annually in added value from the use of these new technologies. This is the fastest-growing enterprise software market in history and represents an entire replacement market for enterprise application software.

Digital transformation requires an entirely new technology stack incorporating all the capabilities described above. This is not about using structured programming and 3,000 programmers in Bangalore or your favorite systems integrator to develop and install yet another enterprise application.

The market is awash in open source "AI Platforms" that appear to the layperson to be solutions sufficient to design, develop, provision, and operate enterprise AI and IoT applications. In this era of AI hype, there are literally hundreds of these in the market—and the number increases every day—that present themselves as comprehensive "AI Platforms."

Examples include Cassandra, Cloudera, DataStax, Databricks, AWS IoT, and Hadoop. AWS, Azure, IBM, and Google each offer an elastic cloud computing platform. In addition, each offers an increasingly innovative library of microservices that can be used for data aggregation, ETL, queuing, data streaming, MapReduce, continuous analytics processing, machine learning services, data visualization, etc.

If you visit their web sites or sit through their sales presentations, they all appear to do the same thing and they all appear to provide a complete solution to your AI needs.

While many of these products are useful, the simple fact is that none offers the scope of utility necessary and sufficient to develop and operate an enterprise AI application.

Take Cassandra. It is a key-value data store, a special-purpose database that is particularly useful for storing and retrieving longitudinal data,

A Sea of "AI Platforms"

The market is awash with hundreds of open source components that purport to be an "AI platform." Each component can provide value, but none provides a complete platform by itself.

FIGURE 10.2

like telemetry. And for that purpose, it is a great product. But that functionality represents perhaps 1 percent of the solution you require. Or take HDFS, a distributed file system, useful for storing unstructured data. Or TensorFlow, a set of math libraries published by Google, useful in enabling certain types of machine learning models. Databricks enables data virtualization, allowing data scientists or application developers to manipulate very large data sets across a cluster of computers. AWS IoT is a utility for gathering data from machine-readable IoT sensors. Again, these are all useful, but by no means sufficient. Each addresses a small part of the problem required to develop and deploy an IoT or AI application.

These utilities are written in different languages, with different computational models and frequently incompatible data structures, developed by programmers of varying levels of experience, training, and professionalism. They were never designed to work together. Few, if any, were written to commercial programming standards. Most have not proven commercially viable and the source code has been contributed to the "open source" community. You can think of the open source community as a kind of superstore in the cloud with a growing collection of hundreds of computer source code programs available for anyone to download, modify at will, and use at no cost.

"Do It Yourself" AI?

Just like relational databases, just like ERP, and just like CRM, the knee-jerk reaction of many IT organizations is to try to internally develop a general-purpose AI and IoT platform using "free" open source software with a combination of microservices from cloud providers like AWS and Google.

The process starts by taking some subset of the myriad of proprietary and open source solutions and organizing them into the reference platform architecture that I described above.

The next step is to assemble hundreds to thousands of programmers, frequently distributed around the planet, using a programming

The AI Software Stack

The "build it yourself" approach requires stitching together dozens of disparate open source components from different developers with different APIs, different code bases, and different levels of maturity and support.

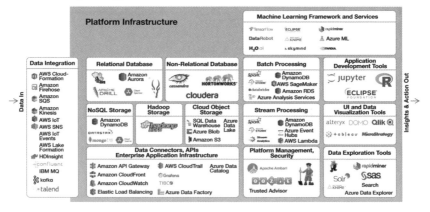

FIGURE 10.3

technique called structured programming and application programming interfaces (APIs) to attempt to stitch these various programs, data sources, sensors, machine learning models, development tools, and user interface paradigms together into a unified, functional, seamless whole that will enable the organization to excel at designing, developing, provisioning, and deploying numerous enterprise scale AI and IoT applications. How hard can this be? The truth is, if it's not impossible, it is close. The complexity of such a system is two orders of magnitude greater than building a CRM or ERP system.

Many have attempted this, but to my knowledge no one has succeeded. The classic case study is GE Digital that expended eight years, 3,000 programmers, and $7 billion trying to succeed at this task. The end result of that effort included the collapse of that division and the termination of the CEO, and it contributed to the dissolution of one of the world's iconic companies.

Were someone to succeed at such an effort, the resultant software stack would look something like Figure 10.4. I refer to this as the AI Software Cluster.

AI Software Cluster

The "build it yourself" approach requires numerous integrations of underlying components that were not designed to work together, resulting in a degree of complexity that overwhelms even the best development teams.

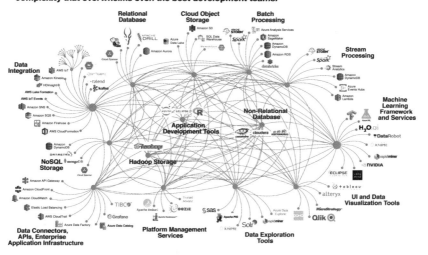

FIGURE 10.4

There are a number of problems with this approach:

1) Complexity. Using structured programming, the number of software API connections that one needs to establish, harden, test, and verify for a complex system can approach the order of 10^{13}. (Putting this into perspective, there are an order of 10^{21} stars in our universe.) The developers of the system need to individually and collectively grasp that level of complexity to get it to work. The number of programmers capable of dealing with that level of complexity is quite small.

Aside from the platform developers, the application developers and data scientists also need to understand the complexity of the architecture and all the underlying data and process dependencies in order to develop any application.

The level of complexity inherent in these efforts is sufficiently great to assure project failure.

2) Brittleness. Spaghetti-code applications of this nature are highly dependent upon each and every component working properly. If one developer introduces a bug into any one of the open source components, all applications developed with that platform may cease to function.

3) Future Proof. As new machine libraries, faster databases, and new machine learning techniques become available, you will want to make those new utilities available within your platform. In order to do so you will likely have to reprogram every application that was built on the platform. This may take months to years.

4) Data Integration. An integrated, federated common object data model is absolutely necessary for this application domain. Using this type of structured programming API-driven architecture will require hundreds of person-years to develop an integrated data model for any large corporation. This is the primary reason why tens to hundreds of millions of dollars get spent, and five years later, no applications are deployed. The Fortune 500 is littered with these disaster stories. The systems integrator makes out like a bandit, and the customer is left with his or her pockets inside out.

The Gordian Knot of Structured Programming

Structured programming is a technique developed in the mid-1960s to simplify code development, testing, and maintenance. Prior to structured programming, software was written in large monolithic tomes replete with APIs and "go-to" statements. The resultant product might consist of millions of lines of code with thousands of such APIs and go-to statements that were difficult to develop, understand, debug, and maintain.

The essential idea of structured programming was to break the code into a relatively simple "main routine" and then use something called an application programming interface (API) to call subroutines that were designed to be modular and reusable. Example subroutines might provide services like complete a ballistics calculation, or a fast Fourier transform, a linear regression, an average, a sum, or a mean. Structured programming remains the state of the art for many applications today, and has dramatically simplified the process of developing and maintaining computer code.

While this technique is appropriate for many classes of applications, it breaks down with the complexity and scale of the requirements for a modern AI or IoT application, resulting in a Gordian knot described in Figure 10.4 above.

Cloud Vendor Tools

An alternative to the open source cluster is to attempt to assemble the various services and microservices offered by the cloud service providers into a working seamless and cohesive enterprise AI platform. As you can see in Figure 10.5, leading vendors like AWS are developing increasingly useful services and microservices that in many cases replicate the functionality of the open source providers and in many cases provide new and unique functionality. The advantage of this approach over open source is that these products are developed, tested, and quality assured by highly professional enterprise engineering organizations. In addition, these services were generally designed and developed with the specific purpose that they would work together and interact in a common system. The same points hold true for Google, Azure, and IBM.

Cloud Vendor Tools—AWS

Public cloud platforms like AWS, Azure, and Google Cloud offer an increasing number of tools and microservices, but stitching them together to build enterprise-class AI and IoT applications is exceedingly complex and costly.

FIGURE 10.5

The problem with this approach is that because these systems lack a model-driven architecture like that described in the following section, your programmers still need to employ structured programming to stitch together the various services. A reference architecture for a relatively simple predictive maintenance application is shown in Figure 10.6. The time to develop and deploy this application is 200 person-days at a cost in 2019 dollars of $600,000. The result of the effort is 83,000 lines of code that need to be maintained over the life of the application. The resulting application will run only on AWS. If you wanted to run this application on Google or Azure, it would have to be completely rebuilt for each of those platforms at a similar cost, time, and coding effort.

By contrast, using a modern model-driven architecture described in the next section, the same application, employing the same AWS

Architecture to Build a Basic Predictive Maintenance Application on AWS

Building even a simple AI predictive maintenance application using microservices of a public cloud (AWS in this example) and a structured programming approach takes 40 times the work effort of using a model-driven architecture.

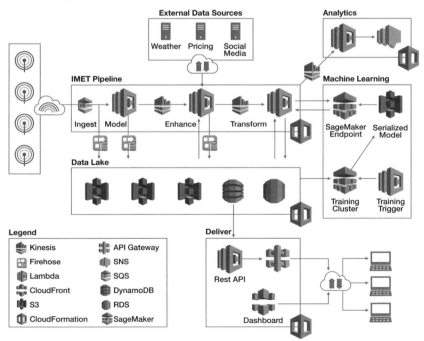

FIGURE 10.6

services, can be developed and tested in 5 person-days at a cost of approximately $2,000. Only 1,450 lines of code are generated, dramatically decreasing the lifetime cost of maintenance. Moreover, the application will run on any cloud platform without modification, so you would not incur the additional effort and cost of refactoring the application should you want to switch to a different cloud vendor.

Model-Driven Architecture

Developed at the beginning of the 21st century, you can think of a model-driven architecture as the knife used to cut the Gordian knot of structured programming for highly complex problems.

Central to a model-driven architecture is the concept of a "model" that serves as an abstraction layer to simplify the programming problem. Using models, the programmer or application developer does not have to be concerned with all the data types, data interconnections, and processes that act on the data associated with any given entity, e.g., customer, tractor, doctor, or fuel type. He or she simply needs to address the model for any given entity—e.g., customer—and all the underlying data, data interrelationships, pointers, APIs, associations, connections, and processes associated with or used to manipulate those data are abstracted in the model itself. This reduces the number of elements, processes, and connections of which the programmer or application developer needs to be aware from an order of 10^{13} to 10^3, making the intractable now quite tractable.

Using a model-driven architecture, *anything* can be represented as a model—even, for example, applications including databases, natural language processing engines, and image recognition systems. Models also support a concept called inheritance. We might have a model called relational database, that in turn serves as a placeholder that might incorporate any relational database system like Oracle, Postgres, Aurora, Spanner, or SQL Server. A key-value store model might contain Cassandra, HBase, Cosmos DB, or DynamoDB.

The use of a model-driven architecture provides an abstraction layer and semantics to represent the application. This frees the programmer from having to worry about data mapping, API syntax, and the mechanics of the myriad of computational processes like ETL, queuing, pipeline management, encryption, etc.

By reducing the number of entities, objects, and processes the developer needs to understand from an order of 10^{13} to 10^{3} and by freeing the developer from wrestling with all this minutiae, a model-driven architecture decreases the cost and complexity of designing, developing, testing, provisioning, maintaining, and operating an application by as much as 100 times or more.

The optimal design for an object model to address AI and IoT applications uses abstract models as placeholders to which a programmer can link an appropriate application. The relational database model might link to Postgres. A report writer model might link to MicroStrategy. A data visualization model might link to Tableau. And so on. A powerful feature of a model-driven architecture is that as new open source or proprietary solutions become available, the object model library can simply be extended to incorporate that new feature.

Another important feature of a model-driven architecture is that the application is entirely future-proofed. If, for example, you began developing all your applications using Oracle as your relational database and then later decide to switch to an alternate proprietary or open source RDBMS, all you have to do is change the link in your RDBMS meta-model to point to the new RDBMS. Importantly, all the applications you deployed previously using Oracle as the RDBMS will continue to run without modification after the replacement. This enables you to immediately and easily take advantage of new and improved product offerings as they become available.

Platform Independence

In my professional experience I have never seen anything like the adoption rate of cloud computing. It is unprecedented. As recently as 2011, the message delivered by CEOs and corporate leadership worldwide was clear: "Tom, what don't you understand about the fact that our data will never reside in the public cloud?" The message today is equally clear and exclamatory: "Tom, understand that we have a cloud-first strategy. All new applications are being deployed in the cloud. Existing applications

Model-Driven AI Architecture

A model-driven architecture provides an abstraction layer that vastly simplifies and accelerates the development and deployment of AI and IoT applications.

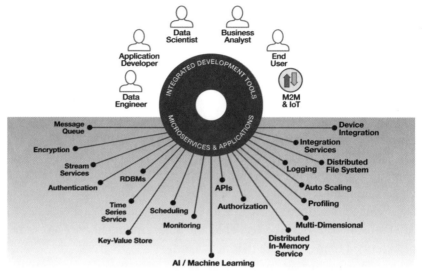

FIGURE 10.7

will be migrating to the cloud. *But understand, we have a multi-cloud strategy."*

Wow. How did that happen? I am not certain that I can explain the 180-degree turn at global scale in the span of a few years, but there is no question it happened. And as discussed previously, it is clearly reflected in the revenue growth of the leading cloud vendors. It is also clear that corporate leaders are afraid of cloud vendor lock-in. They want to be able to continually negotiate. They want to deploy different applications in clouds from different vendors, and they want to be free to move applications from one cloud vendor to another.

So this becomes an additional requirement of a modern model-driven software platform. When you develop your AI application, it needs to run without modification on any cloud and on bare metal behind the firewall in a hybrid cloud environment.

The final requirement for the new AI technology stack is what I call polyglot cloud support—the ability to "mix and match" various services

Multi-Cloud Deployment

Organizations require an AI architecture that enables them to deploy applications on multiple public cloud platforms as well as on bare metal behind the firewall in a private cloud or data center.

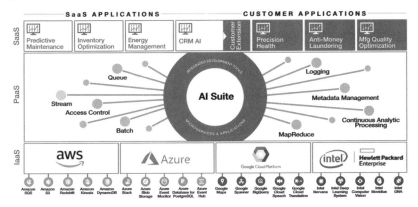

FIGURE 10.8

from multiple cloud providers and to easily swap and replace those services. The cloud vendors are providing the market a great service. Today they provide instant access to virtually unlimited horizontally scalable computing capacity and effectively infinite storage capacity at exceptionally low cost. By the time these aggressive competitors are through with one another, I believe the cost of cloud computing and storage will approach zero.

The second important service cloud vendors provide is rapid innovation of microservices. Microservices like TensorFlow from Google accelerate machine learning. Amazon Forecast facilitates deep learning for time-series data. Azure Stream Analytics integrates with Azure IoT Hub and Azure IoT Suite to enable powerful real-time analytics in IoT sensor data. It seems not a week goes by without another announcement of yet another useful microservice from Azure, AWS, Google, and IBM.

Polyglot cloud support is, in my opinion, an essential capability of the New AI Technology Stack. This capability not only allows application portability from one cloud vendor to another but also affords the capability to run your AI and IoT applications on multiple clouds simultaneously. This is important, because as these vendors continue to out-innovate one another, you can pick and choose microservices from

Polyglot Cloud Deployment

Polyglot capability enables application portability from one cloud vendor to another and the ability to run AI and IoT applications on multiple clouds simultaneously.

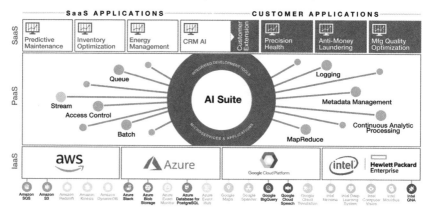

FIGURE 10.9

multiple vendors to optimize the capability of your AI applications. And when a new and more powerful microservice becomes available, you can simply unplug the old microservice and plug in the new one. Your applications keep on ticking but now with greater performance, precision, and economic benefit.

Chapter 11

The CEO Action Plan

Greater Stakes, Greater Threats, Greater Rewards

Consider these facts: The average lifespan of an S&P 500 corporation in the 1950s was 60 years; by 2012 it was less than 20 years.[1] Half of the companies that composed the Fortune 500 in 2000 are no longer on the list today.[2] From 2013 to 2017, median CEO tenure at large corporations dropped by one full year, from six to five years.[3] Acquisitions, mergers, privatizations, and bankruptcies have decimated the status quo.

I expect these trends will accelerate. The technologies driving digital transformation are now robust, mature, and widely available. Digital leaders will emerge across industries, harnessing AI and IoT to achieve step-function improvements in their business processes and outcompete slower rivals.

At the same time, capital markets become more efficient every day—adding to the pressure on underperforming companies that will be treated ruthlessly. Hawk-eyed hedge fund and private equity professionals constantly search for opportunities to acquire, merge, demerge, and liquidate corporations that show traces of vulnerability. The private equity industry manages $2.5 trillion, with nearly $900 billion in "dry powder" waiting to be deployed.[4] This capital will not only be used in takeover bids—it will also be used to fund rapidly growing digital-native competitors. If history is any indicator, these funds will back growth enterprises that leverage modern technologies and will mercilessly exploit, dismantle, and destroy companies that do not. Companies that fail to digitally transform will be prime targets.

Competitive threats on the digital landscape can come from any and every direction, in unexpected ways. In January 2018, Amazon, Berkshire Hathaway, and JP Morgan Chase announced a joint venture into the health care industry. In a single day of trading, $30 billion of market capitalization was erased from the 10 largest U.S. health care companies, with some dropping by as much as 8 percent.[5] This example may seem extreme. I assure you, it is just the beginning.

Although the threat of extinction is great and the need for action urgent, companies that succeed will be richly rewarded. Every significant study of the potential economic impact of digital transformation—by leading researchers like McKinsey, PwC, BCG, and the World Economic Forum—shows that organizations have the opportunity to create *trillions of dollars of value* through AI and IoT.

This is as close to a winner-take-all situation as I've seen. Companies that transform will be operating on an entirely different level from their lagging competitors. This will be tanks versus horses.

Digital transformation is the next do-or-die imperative. How CEOs respond will determine whether their companies thrive or perish.

The Transformative CEO

As we've noted previously, digital transformations are both pervasive—touching every part of the organization—and go to the *core* of the enterprise, the capabilities and assets that define and differentiate the business. For those reasons, digital transformation—to be successful—must be driven from the top down by the CEO, with full support from, and alignment across, all senior leaders and business functions.

In fact, digital transformation has completely inverted the technology adoption cycle that prevailed in prior decades. Previously new technologies frequently came out of research labs, new companies were formed to commercialize the technologies, and over time they were introduced to industry through the IT organization. And eventually, after gradual adoption, they gained the attention of the CIO. Only after years (if ever) did they reach the CEO's desk—and this was usually only in the form of a brief or a budget approval requiring the CEO's signature.

Today, CEOs initiate and mandate digital transformations. This is a big change—it is an entirely new paradigm for innovative technology adoption, driven by both the existential nature of the risk (transform or die), as well as the magnitude of the challenge. Whereas the CEO was generally not involved in IT decisions and strategy, today he or she is the driving force.

Over the last decade, the C3.ai team and I have deeply engaged in a number of CEO-led digital transformations with customers across multiple industries and geographies. Through that experience, we have developed a proven methodology—the 10-point CEO Action Plan—to accelerate digital transformation success.

Getting started with a digital transformation initiative can be a daunting undertaking due to the challenges of both implementing new technologies and managing the associated business process changes. Many organizations are paralyzed into inaction. Others hurtle headlong into transformation projects without a proven methodology, reducing their likelihood of success. Employed by multiple organizations that have approached their digital transformation initiatives in a strategic and methodological way to great effect, the CEO Action Plan encapsulates best practices, providing a clear guide for organizations to move forward with confidence.

Rather than a sequential, step-by-step process, think of the CEO Action Plan as a set of 10 principles—or key success factors—to guide the transformation initiative. Some actions will be taken in parallel, some in sequence, and every organization will adapt to fit their particular situation. Ultimately, however, all 10 points are essential, as they touch on the key areas of leadership, strategy, implementation, technology, change management, and culture.

CEO Action Plan for Digital Transformation
The Opportunity Is Exceeded Only by the Existential Threat

1. Marshal the senior CXO team as the digital transformation engine.
2. Appoint a Chief Digital Officer with authority and budget.
3. Work incrementally to get wins and capture business value.
4. Forge a strategic vision in parallel, and get going.
5. Draft a digital transformation roadmap and communicate it to stakeholders.
6. Pick your partners carefully.
7. Focus on economic benefit.
8. Create a transformative culture of innovation.
9. Reeducate your leadership team.
10. Continually reeducate your workforce—invest in self-learning.

1. Marshal the CXO team as the digital transformation engine.

A leadership team committed to the digital transformation agenda is an absolute requirement and a first priority. Your C-suite must become the engine of digital transformation. Don't take this to mean the CEO or CMO are suddenly writing code or wrangling new technologies. As Stephanie Woerner, a research scientist at the MIT Sloan School of Management's Center for Information Systems Research, writes: "This need for digital savviness doesn't mean that CEOs are going to be coding, but it does mean that enterprises are demanding that CEOs and other top-level executives know what opportunities digital opens up for their enterprise and how to create a digital value proposition that distinguishes their enterprise from others."[6]

This is a change from previous eras when CEOs required only a rudimentary understanding of how technology worked. Today, CEOs have to keep up with a deluge of information about ever-changing technologies, able to decide what is relevant to the business and prioritize which new technologies to focus on, and which to filter out.[7] Because competition, particularly from digital natives, can come from out of the blue, this task takes on more weight.

The senior CXO team needs to marshal the funding, resources, and relationships necessary to enable digital transformation.[8] Reinventing a company requires this commitment from the C-suite to ensure the entire workforce is aligned behind the vision.

This is not a trivial task. It can be hard to get the C-suite on board. The CEO of a large European heavy-equipment manufacturer experienced this lesson firsthand. His mission to own and drive digital transformation as a core evolution across the business was clear—transform the company for agility, insight, and growth. But each business unit had individual priorities and an unclear understanding initially of what digital transformation meant. This created confusion and the misperception that the answer was to "buy IT." Only after establishing a common understanding of the digital transformation mandate and clarity about its goals was the CEO successful in getting his CXOs on board.

Digital transformation requires adopting a long-term perspective. It requires moving beyond just measuring financial performance for the next quarter to also thinking toward a broader, bigger picture of the future and how the enterprise will fit within it.

It also requires a certain personality type. Leaders need to be able to handle risk, they need to be willing to speak out, and they need an experimentation mindset.[9] Leaders must also be comfortable with technology and conversant with technology terms and concepts. This means spending time to understand the capabilities of relevant technologies and what the development teams are doing. CEOs need to surround themselves with a C-suite and a board that share these traits in order to propel transformation.

2. Appoint a Chief Digital Officer with authority and budget.

While the entire C-suite must be the driving force behind the digital transformation agenda, there needs to be a dedicated senior executive singularly focused on digital transformation results—a chief digital officer (CDO) who is empowered with authority and budget to make things happen. I have seen this model work very effectively.

The CDO's primary role is chief evangelist and enabler of digital transformation—the one focused on the transformation strategy and who communicates across the organization on the action plans and results. The CDO needs to have, or be able to establish, strong relationships throughout the organization to help business line leaders transform their processes.

The CDO's role is focused not just on IT implementation or technology change, but on enabling the full spectrum of digital transformation. The CDO's role is to think about what's next and how the organization needs to evolve in order to seize new opportunities, create new value for customers and the business, and manage potential risks and disruptions. Just as the chief security officer role took on importance as a result of threats posed by cyberattacks and breaches, the chief digital officer has taken on new urgent meaning in the age of digital transformation.

The CDO role is an important one but insufficient to broker all the functional innovation that needs to happen across the organization in order to transform. Best practice also requires a central organization to act as the hub of digital transformation—i.e., a Center of Excellence. A CoE is a cross-functional team of software engineers, data scientists, product specialists, and product managers who work collaboratively in an enterprise to develop and deploy AI and IoT applications. The CEO and CDO play key roles in forming, supporting, and engaging with the CoE.

The CoE is particularly important for training the broader enterprise to be self-sufficient in digital transformation efforts. The CoE team should locate together, as they need to work closely and with the rest of the enterprise to affect change.

The CDO may recommend complementing internal capabilities with outside partner help. This can be a useful strategy to jump-start a digital transformation initiative.

The CDO needs to have the full support of the CEO and the clear authority to assume responsibility for the digital transformation roadmap, vendor engagement, and project supervision. He or she needs to act as the CEO's full-time partner responsible and accountable for the result.

3. Work incrementally to get wins and capture business value.

Just as vital as assembling and aligning internal forces is the need to capture business value as soon as possible. Three simple pieces of advice:

- Do not get enmeshed in endless and complicated approaches to unify data.

- Build use cases that generate measurable economic benefit first and solve the IT challenges later.

- Consider a phased approached to projects, where can you deliver demonstrable ROI one step at a time, in less than a year.

Many organizations get hopelessly mired in complex "data lake" projects that drag on for years at great expense and yield little or no value. The landscape is littered with such examples. Trying to solve the issue of building an all-encompassing data lake for analytics and insight is an unfortunately common occurrence. One oil and gas company took years to create a unified data lake that materialized only on paper. A U.S. heavy-equipment manufacturer wasted two years with 20 outside consultants to build a unified data model, only to see no results at all.

GE spent over $7 billion trying to develop its moon-shot digital transformation software platform, GE Digital—an effort that ultimately contributed substantially to the failure of the company and the replacement of its iconic CEO.

A large UK bank invested over €300 million with a major systems integrator, attempting to develop a custom-built digital transformation platform to solve its anti–money laundering problems. Three years later, nothing has been delivered, the bank continues to be fined, and it now operates under strict regulatory supervision.

The corporate landscape is littered with lengthy, expensive IT experiments that attempted to build digital capabilities internally. Is this really your corporate core competency? Perhaps you should leave that to experts with demonstrated track records of delivering measurable results and ROI in less than a year.

The way to capture business value is to work out the use case first, identify the economic benefit, and worry about the IT later. While this may sound like heresy to a CIO, a use-case-first model allows for focus on the value drivers.

By adopting a phased delivery model—this is essentially the agile development model popular in software development today—teams can achieve results faster. With a phased model, projects get addressed and delivered in short, iterative cycles aimed at continuous incremental improvement, each contributing additional economic benefit, enabling teams to focus on the end result and the "customer" (whether internal or external). For team members, this has the psychological benefit of helping them feel involved in productive efforts that contribute to company growth, instilling motivation around concrete digital transformation efforts.

4. Forge a strategic vision in parallel, and get going.

Digital transformation strategy should be focused on creating and capturing economic value. A proven approach is to map out your industry's full value chain, and then identify steps of this value chain that have been, or that you expect to become, digitized. This will help you

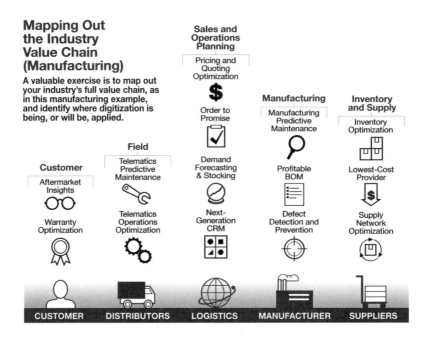

Mapping Out the Industry Value Chain (Manufacturing)

A valuable exercise is to map out your industry's full value chain, as in this manufacturing example, and identify where digitization is being, or will be, applied.

FIGURE 11.1

understand where your gaps are. Figure 11.1 shows an example of this mapping in the manufacturing industry.

Your value chain map—and your strategy—might initially center on inventory optimization, production optimization, AI predictive maintenance, and customer churn. How you sequence your strategy depends on how and where you can find business value. You should sequence these projects in the order that offers the highest probability of delivering immediate and ongoing economic and social benefit. Don't boil the ocean. Tackle these projects in a phased approach proving out your strategy, fine-tuning your processes, and adding value to the enterprise incrementally with each project deliverable.

Two key elements of developing your strategy are benchmarking and assessing the forces of disruption in your industry.

Benchmarking

Like all aspects of business, digital transformation happens in a competitive context. You will want to benchmark your enterprise's digital capabilities against those of your peers and best-of-breed exemplars. Where is your industry as a whole on the digital maturity spectrum? Who are the digital frontrunners in your industry? How do you compare with them? These are the critical questions you'll need to answer to get an effective lay of the land.

A benchmarking process might be as follows: (1) audit current approaches to digital transformation in your industry; (2) rank your capabilities against peers; (3) identify best practices from more advanced peers; and (4) develop a roadmap for improving capabilities. Online benchmarks for measuring an enterprise's level of digital transformation abound.

Once you've taken stock of your organization's digital capabilities, you can begin to try to understand how your industry might be changing and how you need to be prepared for that future. Clearly identify the existential threats to your company in the coming decade. Think about alternatives to turn those threats into areas of strategic competitive advantage.

Assessing the Forces of Disruption

Developing your strategy requires an assessment of your industry and the forces of disruption likely to shake it up. This is challenging. It means identifying threats not only from known competitors but also from unexpected areas, as countless examples in recent years have amply demonstrated. These could be competitors pursuing a higher-quality approach, low-cost upstarts, more nimble digital natives, companies that provide more visibility/insight, or existing entities expanding into new areas. Threats from foreign competitors are possible. Reputational threats, from security issues or PR problems, are more pressing than in previous eras.

Consider, for example, the impact Amazon, JP Morgan, and Berkshire Hathaway had when they announced in January 2018 intentions to enter the health care market. Stocks of existing insurers and drug retailers plummeted.[10] Or the impact of Netflix on Blockbuster. Or Uber and Lyft on taxis, and so on.

Bain & Co. uses a model to focus on industries that could be digitally disrupted. Those industries that could benefit from real-time information, improved allocation of goods or resources, intelligent automation of highly routine processes, or improved customer experiences are all ripe for disruption. (See Figure 11.2.)

A few key measures help to indicate if your industry is particularly vulnerable. The first is *operational efficiency*. Are incumbents operating with high operating costs and facing pressure to improve efficiency? This could foretell the potential for new entrants that can operate with lower margins and greater efficiency.

Next, think about *barriers to entry*. Are regulation or capital requirements the sole reason large incumbent players are able to thrive in your industry? This could be an indicator of the potential for a new entrant to completely shake things up by bypassing these barriers. Look at how Airbnb has upended the lodging industry by sidestepping existing regulations.

Finally, think about to what degree your industry has *high dependency on fixed assets*. In the age of digital transformation, a high dependency on fixed assets can be a potential weakness rather than a strong barrier to entry. For example, banks need to reassess their investments in physical branch offices as consumers increasingly embrace digital banking channels. In today's world, investing in AI-enabled processes is likely to deliver a significantly higher ROI than opening a new branch office.

On the flip side, the existence of proprietary technology, high operational efficiency, and control of distribution channels are all indicators that your market is less likely to be disrupted in the near future.

Understanding where your company and your industry sit in terms of their susceptibility to disruption will help guide critical strategic choices. The right time to start taking control of your unique state of disruption is now.[11]

5. Draft a digital transformation roadmap and communicate it to stakeholders.

At this point, you've convinced your C-suite to get on board, you've surveyed your industry landscape, taken stock of your own digital capabilities, benchmarked yourself against your peers, and taken lessons from digital leaders. It's time to draft your enterprise's own roadmap

Signposts of Potential Digital Disruption

How vulnerable is your industry? This model from Bain points out signposts of potential digital disruption along three vectors: cost, customer experience, and business model.

Radically Lower Cost $

- Low-Yield Processes
- Underutilized or Poorly Allocated Resources
- Highly Routine Processes

Vastly Better Customer Experience

- Poor Customer Understanding and Slow Learning
- Generic Customer Experiences and Value Propositions
- Generic and Excess Pricing

New Business Models

- Intermediaries
- Value Chain Redefiners
- Data and Analytics Platforms

FIGURE 11.2

and set a game plan for communicating it to stakeholders across the organization.

As BCG writes, "This involves building a portfolio of opportunities—identifying and prioritizing functions or units that can benefit most from transformation. It also involves locating and starting to address roadblocks to transformation. During the design phase, companies also invest in framing and communicating the vision for the transformation to build support for needed changes, and they invest in systems to industrialize data analytics—making analytics a resource for every operation."[12]

First, clearly define a future vision for your digital business. What does your ideal future state look like in terms of your organizational structure, people and leadership, product and services, culture, and adoption of technology? Use this ideal future state to compare against your current state and zoom in on any gaps. Put your transformation on a timeline with clear milestones—make the timeline aggressive, but not so aggressive that it becomes unfeasible and just gets ignored.

The best digital transformation roadmaps involve concrete plans and timelines to bring advanced AI applications into production. The development and rollout pace will depend on your specific objectives and circumstances, but in our experience a relatively small group can bring two large-scale AI applications into production every six months. A typical roadmap for a large global company is outlined in Figure 11.3.

Your roadmap will serve several purposes throughout your journey. First, it will be a concrete, actionable game plan against which to

Digital Transformation Roadmap

A digital transformation roadmap—as shown in this example for a financial services organization—provides an actionable plan to guide and measure progress.

		Operation & Incremental Application Development	Retail Banking Predictive Credit Risk Analytics
		Active Application Development	Private Banking Anti-Money Laundering
		Commercial Banking Transaction Value Optimization	Commercial Banking Transaction Value Optimization
		Commercial Banking Securities Lending Optimization	Commercial Banking Securities Lending Optimization
	Merchant Banking Fraud Detection	Merchant Banking Fraud Detection	Merchant Banking Fraud Detection
	Retail Banking Cross Sell/Upsell Recommendations	Retail Banking Cross Sell/Upsell Recommendations	Retail Banking Cross Sell/Upsell Recommendations
Merchant Banking Fraud Detection	Commercial Banking Transaction Value Optimization	Retail Banking Predictive Credit Risk Analytics	Trading Trading Policy Compliance
Retail Banking Cross Sell/Upsell Recommendations	Commercial Banking Securities Lending Optimization	Private Banking Anti-Money Laundering	Trading Intraday Liquidity Management
2019 1st Half	2019 2nd Half	2020 1st Half	2020 2nd Half

FIGURE 11.3

measure your company's progress. Your plan might change, of course, but this roadmap will still be a useful bellwether for your progress. It will help keep your transformation on track. And it will help you unlock and measure business value early and often. Finally, it will be an actionable plan for your entire organization to align behind. Remember, associated with each project you should assign an expected recurring annual economic benefit. Focus every project on the attainment of that target. If you cannot quantify the expected benefit, scrap the project.

Organizational alignment is critical. As a business leader, you need to communicate effectively and sell your vision to stakeholders across the organization. Changing the organization, its culture, and its mindset requires buy-in from across product lines and stakeholders, not just at the C-suite level. As McKinsey senior partner Jacques Bughin writes:

> It's now widely understood that a digital transformation needs active CEO support throughout the journey. This top-down support, however, has to go beyond the chief executive. Companies should start by putting a chief digital officer in charge of the full digital agenda. Truly changing culture, moreover, requires that support for a digital reinvention

flow through the management hierarchy right down to every front-line employee, so the full organizational pyramid is tuned towards digital. All leaders need to shift their style from top-down decision-maker to coach.[13]

I will talk more about change and creating an innovation culture at the end of this chapter.

6. Pick your partners carefully.

To fulfill your vision of digital transformation, it's vital to pick the right partners. This applies to the full ecosystem of partnerships the CDO and CEO need to establish—software partners, cloud partners, and a spectrum of other partnerships and alliances. In a digitally transforming world, partners play a bigger role than in the past. There are four key areas in AI-based transformations where partners can add significant value: strategy, technology, services, and change management.

Strategy

Management consulting partners can help flesh out your AI strategy: Map out your value chain, uncover strategic opportunities and threats, and identify key AI applications and services you will need to develop in order to unlock economic value. They can also assist in setting up your organizational structure for the transformation, including the design of your AI/Digital Center of Excellence, and help establish the appropriate processes and incentive plans for your business.

Technology

Software partners can provide the right technology stack to power your digital transformation. My recommendation is to avoid the "accidental" open source Hadoop architectures, low-level services offered by the large cloud providers, and consulting firm–supported data lake approaches.

These may all seem manageable at first. But as you scale your transformation, the complexity of your system will grow exponentially. Each individual AI application or service will require cobbling together a large number of low-level components, and your engineers will spend a majority of their time working on low-level technical code rather than solving business problems. Your technical agility will also be severely impacted.

My recommendation is to seek out technology providers that can offer a cohesive set of higher-level services for building advanced AI applications with large data volumes. As you evaluate software partners, look for companies with proven track records of enabling AI applications at scale.

Services

Professional services partners can help build your advanced AI applications and/or augment your staff. They can provide teams of developers, data integration specialists, and data scientists if you do not have those talent profiles in house (or are not interested in acquiring some or all of these skilled resources). My recommendation is to look for services partners that have a proven model of agile development that delivers high-value applications in months, not years—partners that can efficiently transfer working solutions and knowledge to your team through well-structured training programs.

Change Management

Once you have developed AI applications and services, a key next step involves all the business transformation and business process change required to capture economic value. You will have to work on integrating AI into your business processes in conjunction with your software solution development.

This will involve understanding how humans and machines can work together—e.g., the machine generating recommendations and augmenting human decision-making. Humans must also be able to give the AI systems feedback so they can learn and evolve.

Human practitioners will often mistrust recommendations from algorithms, and you will have to ensure recommendations are examined objectively and followed to the extent possible.

The incentive structures and organizational structures of human teams may have to be changed to capture value. The organizational issues can be extremely complex in certain situations—e.g., with large labor forces that have historically been trained to operate and contractually rewarded in the same way for a long time.

Personnel will have to be retrained and employment contracts rewritten. New leaders will need to be hired. Compensation and incentive structures will have to be reengineered. Organization structures will require new architectures. Recruiting, training, and management practices will need to be overhauled. The nature of work will change and unless your workforce is trained, incented, organized, and *motivated* to take advantage of these new technologies, the economic and social benefits will not accrue. This is the hard part. Dealing with this is why you make the big bucks.

7. Focus on economic benefit.

Harold Geneen, the iconic CEO of ITT, is famous for his counsel that management's job is to manage. From Peter Drucker we learned that if it is important, we measure it. Andy Grove taught us that only the paranoid survive.

As much as you would like to delegate digital transformation to an outside agency, you can't do it. This is your job. As you approach it, I encourage you to stay focused on economic and social benefit. Benefit for your customers, for your shareholders, and for society at large. If you and your team cannot identify projects for digital transformation that return significant economic value within one year, keep looking. If the solution cannot be delivered within a year, don't do it. The market is moving too rapidly. Demand near-term results.

In the course of this journey you will be presented with many digital project proposals that just don't seem to make sense. Many projects will be sufficiently complex that they appear incomprehensible. A rule to live by is that if the project does not seem to make sense, it's because it doesn't make sense. If it appears incomprehensible, it is likely impossible. If you do not personally understand it, don't do it.

I have been actively engaged with the CEOs and management teams of many Fortune 100 companies assessing and selecting such projects for the past decade. We discourage our customers from moving forward on probably 7 out of 10 projects presented. We do that because the project is likely to fail, or in some cases certain to fail. The most important decisions you make in this journey will be the projects you decline to fund.

This is a team sport. Engage with your management team, your business leaders, and your trusted partners. If you make the effort to wrestle with enough ideas—if you throw enough spaghetti at the wall in your conference room enveloped with whiteboards—one project will emerge from the process that is tractable, offers clear and substantial economic benefit, can be completed in six months to a year, and once completed successfully presents the opportunity to be deployed and scaled across the enterprise. Jump on that one and don't stop until the value is realized. Your digital transformation journey has now begun.

When you have identified one or more such projects, bring in experts to provide the software technology. Personally sponsor the project. Review progress weekly. Set clear and objectively quantifiable milestones, and mandate that they be met. When a milestone slips, require a mitigation plan to get it back on schedule. Walk around daily to talk to the people doing the work so you can feel the progress, or lack thereof—don't just read a weekly executive report. And most importantly, assume that unless you do all of the above, the project will fail.

8. Create a transformative culture of innovation.

A CEO may have a clear vision of what needs to happen to transform the organization. But senior management, middle management, and rank and file employees must also fully understand that vision and operate in an environment conducive to success. A 2018 Forrester Consulting thought leadership paper on digital transformation noted that nearly half of lower-level decision makers struggle to meet digital transformation objectives.[14] It's easy to say that all good plans die outside senior leadership. But without understanding how the organizational culture needs to shift, that axiom could be all too true.

In order to effectively drive digital transformation, CEOs need to understand what the world of digital transformation and disruption looks like, and what digital products can do. As part of this effort to gather information and inform their own visualizations of their company's future, CEOs should conduct corporate executive visits at the sources of disruption. As a February 2017 McKinsey article pointed out, "Companies must be open to radical reinvention to find new, significant, and sustainable sources of revenue."[15] Where better to find inspiration for such radical reinvention than the source of disruption itself?

At C3.ai, I personally host many CXOs, as well as delegations from governments around the world, who are trying to understand the agile, nimble culture of Silicon Valley. Most often, these visitors spend a work week meeting with leaders and smaller organizations in the Bay Area across a wide swath of industries and use cases.

Think of Uber, Airbnb, Amazon, Apple, Tesla, Netflix. These companies outcompete traditional players, disrupt entire industries, and create new business models. They've created entirely new ways of approaching their business, entirely new business models and new services. Through corporate executive visits, the C-suite can see what a disruptive organization looks like, how it goes about setting the course for disruption, and how to emulate this for their own enterprises.

Most importantly, corporate leaders can learn from these companies what it means to have an innovation culture. This does not simply mean superficial traits such as offices arrayed with beanbag hangouts, sushi for lunch, and daily massages. Rather, it means cultivating a culture of core values—one that rewards collaboration, hard work, and continuous learning.

Executive visitors to our C3.ai headquarters in Silicon Valley, for example, frequently comment on the energy and focus they see exhibited by our team members, who work in an open office environment and often self-aggregate in small groups to solve problems together. Visitors ask about our four core values—innovation, curiosity, integrity, and collective intelligence—that are posted in our open dining area. And they see our "Wall of Fame," where we display certificates of every employee who has completed outside course work to advance their careers, for which they are financially rewarded with cash bonuses—an effective way to reinforce a learning culture.

The way you attract, the way you retain, and most importantly, the way you motivate and organize people today has changed dramatically from what we experienced in recent decades. With the baby boomers, we could focus primarily on compensation plans to motivate individuals.

Today, we oversee multi-generational workforces comprised of a complex tapestry of baby boomers, Gen Xers, and millennials—a very rich and complex group. Individuals in today's workforce have divergent value systems and diverse motivations and skill sets. You need to figure out how to take that powerful mix of diverse attitudes, goals, and motivations and turn it into something cohesive, focused, and productive, with a shared mission and common purpose.

Study after study tells us the companies able to innovate effectively are those that share certain characteristics: a high tolerance for risk, agile project management, empowered and trained employees, collaborative cultures, lack of silos, and an effective decision-making structure. As a 2016 MIT Sloan study on digital transformation found: "So for companies that want to start down the road to digital maturity, the 'one weird trick' that will help is developing an effective digital culture. The cultural characteristics we identified—appetite for risk, leadership structure, work style, agility, and decision-making style—are by no means all your company needs to successfully compete in a digital world, but you cannot compete without them."[16]

Without a culture that encourages innovation and risk-taking, even the best thought-out digital transformation strategy will fail.

9. Reeducate your leadership team.

Face the facts. Your organization does not have the skills today to succeed at this effort. You can't just hire consultants to change the DNA of your company. You can't simply hire a systems integration firm, write it a check for $100 million to $500 million, and make this problem go away. You need to infuse your executive team and your employees with new skills and a new mindset to succeed at digital transformation. And then you and your team need to manage the projects in a hands-on manner.

Start with an executive reading list. I recommend that you and your executive team consider the following list to become familiar with how the historical context of this market has developed; how the technology is changing today; the underlying theory of AI and IoT; and how to succeed at applying these technologies.

- *The Information: A History, a Theory, a Flood*, James Gleick. This book takes you back to the beginnings of information theory, putting today's innovations into historical context.

- *The Innovators: How a Group of Hackers, Geniuses, and Geeks Created the Digital Revolution*, Walter Isaacson. Isaacson's history of information technology, from Ada Lovelace and Charles Babbage in the 19th century to the iPhone and the internet, enables you to consider your digital transformation as a natural evolution of a process that has been accelerating for the past 70 years.

- *The Master Algorithm: How the Quest for the Ultimate Learning Machine Will Remake Our World*, Pedro Domingos. If you want to demystify AI, read this book. Domingos provides you an evolution of the underlying theory and promise of AI in the context of the statistics, math, and logic courses that you took in college and high school. Really enlightening.

- *Big Data: A Revolution That Will Transform How We Live, Work, and Think*, Viktor Mayer-Schönberger and Kenneth Cukier. A most pragmatic discussion of a highly misunderstood topic. This book allows you to think about big data in a practical manner devoid of spectacle, extravaganza, and hype.

- *Prediction Machines: The Simple Economics of Artificial Intelligence*, Ajay Agrawal, Joshua Gans, and Avi Goldfarb. A down-to-earth discussion of AI and the problems it can really address.

- *The Second Machine Age: Work, Progress, and Prosperity in a Time of Brilliant Technologies*, Erik Brynjolfsson and Andrew McAfee. This is a visionary work that addresses the art of the possible. Motivating and inspiring.

This may seem a bit daunting, but all of these are highly approachable, good to great books. If you want to play this game, you need to invest some time and energy to acquire domain expertise. It's not magic and it's not mysterious. But you need to learn the language to engage thoughtfully, manage the process, make good decisions, and lead change management. A majority of what you will be told about AI and digital transformation is sheer poppycock delivered by self-proclaimed experts who have accomplished little to nothing in the field. You need to be able to distinguish signal from noise. You should travel with a book in your hand, and you should encourage your management team and key employees to do the same.

10. Continually reeducate your workforce—invest in self-learning.

Again, face the facts—your technical and management personnel currently do not have the skills to succeed at this. Augmenting them with advice from highly paid consultants is not sufficient. It is impractical to think about replacing your workforce with a new qualified team. But you can train them.

At C3.ai, we recruit and hire some of the most highly skilled data scientists and software engineers on the planet. In the past year we had 26,000 applicants for 100 open data science and software engineering positions. We interviewed 1,700 people and hired 120. We will interview as many as 100 candidates to hire one data scientist. And these candidates are trained with PhDs from the world's leading universities. Many have 5 to 10 years of highly relevant work experience. We have an exceptionally talented and well-trained workforce.

But we recognize that even we don't have the skills necessary to excel in this highly dynamic milieu. The field of data science is in an embryonic state—the cell might have divided eight times. The rate of innovation across all these domains—cloud computing, deep learning, neural networks, machine learning, natural language processing, data visualization, the ethics of AI, and related fields—is blistering.

In an effort to keep our employees current at the leading edge of these rapidly changing technologies, we have formalized a program to encourage our workforce to continually refresh and improve their skill sets. I encourage you to consider the same type of program.

The educational resources available today from learning portals like Coursera are simply amazing. Think of the entire curricula of MIT, Stanford, Carnegie Mellon, Harvard, etc. online and immediately available to your workforce. If you are not taking advantage of this 21st century continuing education development, you are missing a big opportunity.

At C3.ai, we incent our employees with both recognition and cash bonuses for successfully completing a curated curriculum to develop additional expertise in the skills necessary for digital transformation.

This has proven an incredibly successful program for skills development. Everyone from the receptionist to our lead data scientist has taken these courses. Each gets a letter of recognition signed by the CEO; his or her name is featured in our headquarters on a Self-Learning Hall of Fame wall; and each gets a bonus check of $1,000 to $1,500 for receiving a certificate of completion.[17]

The courses are listed below:

- Deep Learning:
  https://www.coursera.org/specializations/deep-learning

- Machine Learning:
  https://www.coursera.org/learn/machine-learning

- Programming Foundations with JavaScript, HTML and CSS:
  https://www.coursera.org/learn/duke-programming-web

- Text Mining and Analytics:
  https://www.coursera.org/learn/text-mining

- Secure Software Design:
  https://www.coursera.org/specializations/secure-software-design

- Introduction to Cyber Security:
  https://www.coursera.org/specializations/intro-cyber-security

- Python:
  https://www.coursera.org/specializations/python

- Google Kubernetes Engine:
  https://www.coursera.org/learn/google-kubernetes-engine

- Cloud Computing Applications, Part 1:
  Cloud Systems and Infrastructure:
  https://www.coursera.org/learn/cloud-applications-part1

- Business and Financial Modeling Specialization:
  https://www.coursera.org/specializations/
  wharton-business-financial-modeling

- TensorFlow:
  https://www.coursera.org/specializations/
  machine-learning-tensorflow-gcp

- Advanced Machine Learning Specialization:
  https://www.coursera.org/specializations/aml

- Cloud Computing:
  https://www.coursera.org/specializations/cloud-computing

- IoT and AWS:
  https://www.coursera.org/specializations/internet-of-things

- Functional Programming Principles in Scala:
  https://www.coursera.org/learn/progfun1

You will want to curate a curriculum specific to your company's needs. I offer the above only by example. But you should think about this. The returns are staggering. As you implement a similar self-learning program for your company, it is not sufficient to assign this to your HR department. You, as CXO, need to take ownership, participate, lead by example, recognize participation, and make it central to your ongoing corporate culture.

The Road to Digital Transformation

I hope this book has given you a practical understanding of enterprise digital transformation powered by cloud computing, big data, AI, and IoT. I have described how the evolution of these technologies and their confluence in the early 21st century has produced the current period of mass extinction and mass diversification in the business world.

As in evolutionary biology, the new environment created by the confluence of these technologies poses an existential threat for incumbent organizations, but also creates a massive opportunity for those that take advantage of these new resources. Organizations that recognize the magnitude of the opportunity, and are willing and able to adapt, will be well-positioned to unlock significant economic value. Those resistant to change face a rocky road ahead.

AI- and IoT-driven digital transformations are challenging, but they can unlock tremendous economic value and competitive benefits.

The coming two decades will bring more information technology innovation than that of the past half century. The intersection of artificial intelligence and the internet of things changes everything. This represents an entire replacement market for all enterprise application and consumer software. New business models will emerge. Products and services unimaginable today will be ubiquitous. New opportunities will abound. But the great majority of corporations and institutions that fail to seize this moment will become footnotes in history.

Digital Transformation is the result of a decade of collaboration, discussion, and debate with hundreds of colleagues, customers, co-workers, researchers, and friends.

I first heard the term in board rooms in New York, Shanghai, Rome, and Paris in 2010. In 2011, 2012, and beyond, Digital Transformation was increasingly raised as a strategic corporate mandate by CEOs and executive teams who visited me and my team at C3.ai in Silicon Valley.

I found the term curious. Digital Transformation? As opposed to what? Analog Transformation? What did it mean?

It was clear, as I heard the term bandied about—and with great import—that there was something about this idea that was perceived to be critical. It was also clear there was a lack of common understanding of its meaning. When I probed to find the intended meaning, I found little in common and little of substance.

After hundreds, perhaps thousands, of discussions over the past decade, this book is an attempt to distill the essence of what I have learned from corporate, government, and academic leaders, the core motivation that is driving the mandate, and its social and economic implications in the context of the past 50 years of innovation in the information technology industry.

I have had the great professional privilege to engage with and learn from many of the great corporate and government leaders of the 21st century who are driving innovation at massive scale, including Jacques Attali; Francesco Starace, Livio Gallo, and Fabio Veronese at Enel; Isabelle Kocher and Yves Le Gélard at ENGIE; Jay Crotts and Johan Krebbers at Royal Dutch Shell; Mike Roman and Jon Lindekugel at 3M; Brandon Hootman and Julie Lagacy at Caterpillar; John May at John Deere; Tom Montag at Bank of America; Gil Quiniones at New York Power Authority; Manny Cancel at Con Edison; Lorenzo Simonelli at Baker Hughes; Mark Clare and David Smoley at AstraZeneca; Jim Snabe at Siemens; Heinrich Hiesinger; Secretary Heather Wilson and Assistant Secretary Will Roper at the United States Air Force; Under Secretary of the Army Ryan McCarthy; Mike Kaul and Mike Brown at Defense Innovation Unit; General John Murray at U.S. Army Futures Command; Mark Nehmer at the Defense Security Service; General Gustave Perna at the U.S. Army Materiel Command; and Brien Sheahan, Chairman of the Illinois Commerce Commission.

Many have contributed to this book. Pat House, with whom I co-founded two leading Silicon Valley software companies, was the driving force to organize the completion of this project. Eric Marti served as editor-in-chief with a thankfully heavy editorial hand. Many of my colleagues made significant contributions to this effort, including Ed Abbo, Houman Behzadi, Adi Bhashyam, Rob Jenks, David Khavari, Nikhil Krishnan, Sara Mansur, Nikolai Oudalov, Carlton Reeves, Uma Sandilya, Rahul Venkatraj, Merel Witteveen, Danielle YoungSmith, Lila Fridley, Erica Schroeder, Adrian Rami, and Amy Irvine.

This effort benefited greatly from the generous and active engagement of many leaders in the academy including Condoleezza Rice at Stanford University; Shankar Sastry at UC Berkeley; Andreas Cangellaris and Bill Sanders at the University of Illinois at Urbana-Champaign; Vince Poor and Emily Carter at Princeton University; Anantha Chandrakasan and Ian Waitz at MIT; Jacques Biot at École Polytechnique; Michael Franklin at the University of Chicago; Zico Kolter at Carnegie Mellon University; Pedro Domingos at University of Washington; and Marco Gilli at Politecnico di Torino.

Thank you all.

ABOUT THE AUTHOR

THOMAS M. SIEBEL is the founder, chairman, and chief executive officer of C3.ai, a leading enterprise AI software provider. With a career spanning four decades in technology, he has been at the forefront of several major innovation cycles including relational databases, enterprise application software, internet computing, and AI and IoT.

Following a career at Oracle Corporation beginning in the early 1980s, he pioneered the customer relationship management (CRM) category in 1993 with the founding of Siebel Systems, where he served as chairman and CEO. Siebel Systems rapidly became one of the world's leading enterprise software companies, with more than 8,000 employees, over 4,500 corporate customers, and annual revenue exceeding $2 billion. Siebel Systems merged with Oracle in January 2006.

The Thomas and Stacey Siebel Foundation funds projects supporting energy solutions, educational and research programs, public health, and the homeless and underprivileged. The Foundation supports the Siebel Scholars Foundation (providing grants to graduate students in computer science, engineering, and business); the Siebel Energy Institute (funding research in energy solutions); and the Siebel Stem Cell Institute (supporting research to harness the potential of regenerative medicine), among other philanthropic activities.

Mr. Siebel has authored three previous books: *Virtual Selling* (Free Press, 1996), *Cyber Rules* (Doubleday, 1999), and *Taking Care of eBusiness* (Doubleday, 2001).

He was recognized as one of the top 25 managers in global business by *Businessweek* in 1999, 2000, and 2001. He received the EY Entrepreneur of the year award in 2003, 2017, and 2018, and received the Glassdoor Top CEO Award in 2018.

He is a graduate of the University of Illinois at Urbana-Champaign, where he received a B.A. in History, an M.B.A., and a M.S. in Computer

Science. He is a former trustee of Princeton University, and serves on the boards of advisors for the University of Illinois College of Engineering and the UC–Berkeley College of Engineering. He was elected to the American Academy of Arts and Sciences in 2013.

Data Sources for Figures

1.2 *Cosmos Magazine*, "The Big Five Mass Extinctions," (n.d.): https://cosmosmagazine .com/palaeontology/big-five-extinctions

2.1 World Economic Forum, "Societal Implications: Can Digital Create Value for Industry and Society?" June 2016; PwC, "Sizing the Prize," 2017; McKinsey, "Notes from the AI Frontier: Modeling the Impact of AI on the World Economy," September 2018; McKinsey, "Unlocking the Potential of the Internet of Things," June 2015; *Forbes*, "Gartner Estimates AI Business Value to Reach Nearly $4 Trillion by 2022," April 25, 2018

3.4 Cisco, "Cisco Visual Networking Index, 2018"

6.3 AIIndex.org, "2017 AI Index Report"

7.3 IHS Markit, "IoT platforms: Enabling the Internet of Things," March 2016

7.4 McKinsey, "Unlocking the Potential of the Internet of Things," June 2015

7.5 Boston Consulting Group, "Winning in IoT: It's All About the Business Processes," January 5, 2017

7.6 *The Economist*, March 10, 2016

8.1 OECD, "Science, Technology and Innovation Outlook 2018"

8.2 Congressional Budget Office, "The Cost of Replacing Today's Air Force Fleet," December 2018

10.5 Amazon Web Services

11.2 Bain, "Predator or Prey: Disruption in the Era of Advanced Analytics," November 8, 2017

Preface

1 Tom Forester, *The Microelectronics Revolution: The Complete Guide to the New Technology and Its Impact on Society* (Cambridge: MIT Press, 1981).

2 Daniel Bell, *The Coming of Post-industrial Society* (New York: Basic Books, 1973).

3 Malcolm Waters, *Daniel Bell* (New York: Routledge, 1996), 15.

4 Ibid.

5 Forester, *Microelectronics Revolution*, 500.

6 Bell, *Coming of Post-industrial Society*, 126.

7 Ibid., 358–59.

8   Ibid., 126–27.

9   Waters, *Daniel Bell*, 109.

10 Bell, *Coming of Post-industrial Society*, 359.

11 Ibid., 127.

12 Ibid.

13 Waters, *Daniel Bell*.

14 Bell, *Coming of Post-industrial Society*, 359.

15 A. S. Duff, "Daniel Bell's Theory of the Information Society," *Journal of Information Science* 24, no. 6 (1998): 379.

16 Ibid., 383.

17 Forester, *Microelectronics Revolution*, 505.

18 Ibid., 507.

19 Ibid., 513.

20 Ibid., 513–14.

21 Ibid., 521.

22 "Gartner Says Global IT Spending to Grow 3.2 Percent in 2019," Gartner, October 17, 2018, https://www.gartner.com/en/newsroom/press-releases/2018-10-17-gartner-says-global-it-spending-to-grow-3-2-percent-in-2019

23 Larry Dignan, "Global IT, Telecom Spending to Hit $4 Trillion, but Economic Concerns Loom," ZDnet, June 21, 2018, https://www.zdnet.com/article/global-it-telecom-spending-to-hit-4-trillion-but-economic-concerns-loom/

Chapter 1

1   This alludes to a quote frequently attributed to Mark Twain, but there is no record that he actually said it. See: https://quoteinvestigator.com/2014/01/12/history-rhymes/

2   Charles Darwin, *On the Origin of Species by Means of Natural Selection, or Preservation of Favoured Races in the Struggle for Life* (London: John Murray, 1859).

3   *Dinosaurs in Our Backyard*, Smithsonian Museum of Natural History, Washington, DC.

4   Jeffrey Bennet and Seth Shostak, *Life in the Universe*, 2nd ed. (San Francisco: Pearson Education, 2007).

5   Stephen Jay Gould, *Punctuated Equilibrium* (Cambridge: Harvard University Press, 2007).

6   Stephen Jay Gould and Niles Eldredge, "Punctuated Equilibrium Comes of Age," *Nature* 366 (November 18, 1993): 223–27.

7   NASA, "The Great Dying," Science Mission Directorate, January 28, 2002, https://science.nasa.gov/science-news/science-at-nasa/2002/28jan_extinction

8   Yuval N. Harari, *Sapiens: A Brief History of Humankind* (New York: Harper, 2015).

9   Lynn Margulis and Dorion Sagan, "The Oxygen Holocaust," in *Microcosmos: Four Billion Years of Microbial Evolution* (California: University of California Press, 1986), 99.

10 Bennet and Shostak, *Life in the Universe.*

11 Phil Plait, "Poisoned Planet," *Slate*, July 28, 2014, https://slate.com/technology/2014/07/the-great-oxygenation-event-the-earths-first-mass-extinction.html

12 "50 Years of Moore's Law," Intel, n.d., https://www.intel.sg/content/www/xa/en/silicon-innovations/moores-law-technology.html

13 Harari, *Sapiens.*

14 "Timeline," Telecommunications History Group, 2017, http://www.telcomhistory.org/timeline.shtml

15 "Smartphone Users Worldwide from 2014–2020," Statista, 2017, https://www.statista.com/statistics/330695/number-of-smartphone-users-worldwide/

16 Benjamin Hale, "The History of the Hollywood Movie Industry," History Cooperative, 2014, http://historycooperative.org/the-history-of-the-hollywood-movie-industry/

17 *America on the Move*, National Museum of American History, Washington, DC.

Chapter 2

1 Tanguy Catlin et al., "A Roadmap for a Digital Transformation," McKinsey, March 2017, https://www.mckinsey.com/industries/financial-services/our-insights/a-roadmap-for-a-digital-transformation

2 "Overview," DigitalBCG, n.d., https://www.bcg.com/en-us/digital-bcg/overview.aspx

3 Brian Solis, "The Six Stages of Digital Transformation Maturity," Altimeter Group and Cognizant, 2016, https://www.cognizant.com/whitepapers/the-six-stages-of-digital-transformation-maturity.pdf

4 Frederick Harris et al., "Impact of Computing on the World Economy: A Position Paper," University of Nevada, Reno, 2008, https://www.cse.unr.edu/~fredh/papers/conf/074-iocotweapp/paper.pdf

5 Gil Press, "A Very Short History of Digitization," *Forbes*, December 27, 2015, https://www.forbes.com/sites/gilpress/2015/12/27/a-very-short-history-of-digitization/

6 Tristan Fitzpatrick, "A Brief History of the Internet," *Science Node*, February 9, 2017, https://sciencenode.org/feature/a-brief-history-of-the-internet-.php

7 Larry Carter, "Cisco's Virtual Close," *Harvard Business Review*, April 2001, https://hbr.org/2001/04/ciscos-virtual-close

8 Brian Solis, "Who Owns Digital Transformation? According to a New Survey, It's Not the CIO," *Forbes*, October 17, 2016, https://www.forbes.com/sites/briansolis/2016/10/17/who-owns-digital-transformation-according-to-a-new-survey-its-the-cmo/#55a7327667b5

9 Randy Bean, "Financial Services Disruption: Gradually and Then Suddenly," *Forbes*, October 11, 2017, https://www.forbes.com/sites/ciocentral/2017/10/11/financial-services-disruption-gradually-and-then-suddenly/2/#7f15b6e0392

10 Avery Hartmans, "How to Use Zelle, the Lightning-Fast Payments App That's More Popular Than Venmo in the US," *Business Insider*, June 17, 2018.

11 Galen Gruman, "Anatomy of Failure: Mobile Flops from RIM, Microsoft, and Nokia," Macworld, April 30, 2011, https://www.macworld.com/article/1159578/anatomy_of_failure_rim_microsoft_nokia.html

12 Rajeev Suri, "The Fourth Industrial Revolution Will Bring a Massive Productivity Boom," World Economic Forum, January 15, 2018, https://www.weforum.org/agenda/2018/01/fourth-industrial-revolution-massive-productivity-boom-good/

13 Erik Brynjolfsson and Andrew McAfee, *The Second Machine Age: Work, Progress, and Prosperity in a Time of Brilliant Technologies* (New York: W. W. Norton, 2014).

14 Michael Sheetz, "Technology Killing Off Corporate America: Average Life Span of Companies under 20 Years," CNBC, August 24, 2017, https://www.cnbc.com/2017/08/24/technology-killing-off-corporations-average-lifespan-of-company-under-20-years.html

15 BT, "Digital Transformation Top Priority for CEOs, Says New BT and EIU Research," Cision, September 12, 2017, https://www.prnewswire.com/news-releases/digital-transformation-top-priority-for-ceos-says-new-bt-and-eiu-research-300517891.html

16 "Strategic Update," Ford Motor Company, October 3, 2017, https://s22.q4cdn.com/857684434/files/doc_events/2017/10/ceo-strtegic-update-transcript.pdf

17 Karen Graham, "How Nike Is Taking the Next Step in Digital Transformation," *Digital Journal*, October 26, 2017, http://www.digitaljournal.com/tech-and-science/technology/how-nike-is-taking-the-next-step-in-digital-transformation/article/506051#ixzz5715z4xdC

18 Chris Cornillie, "Trump Embraces Obama's 'Venture Capital Firm' for Pentagon Tech," *Bloomberg Government*, February 21, 2018, https://about.bgov.com/blog/trump-embraces-obamas-venture-capital-firm-pentagon-tech/

19 "The Digital Transformation by ENGIE," ENGIE, n.d., https://www.engie.com/en/group/strategy/digital-transformation/

20 Ibid.

21 "Incumbents Strike Back: Insights from the Global C-Suite Study," IBM Institute for Business Value, February 2018, https://public.dhe.ibm.com/common/ssi/ecm/98/en/98013098usen/incumbents-strike-back_98013098USEN.pdf

22 Ibid.

23 "Letter to Shareholders," JPMorgan Chase, 2014, https://www.jpmorganchase.com/corporate/investor-relations/document/JPMC-AR2014-LetterToShareholders.pdf

24 Julie Bort, "Retiring Cisco CEO Delivers Dire Prediction: 40% of Companies Will Be Dead in 10 Years," *Business Insider*, June 8, 2015, http://www.businessinsider.com/chambers-40-of-companies-are-dying-2015-6

25 "Geoffrey Moore—Core and Context," Stanford Technology Ventures Program, April 6, 2005, https://www.youtube.com/watch?v=emQ2innvuPo

26 Curt Finch, "Interviewing Geoffrey Moore: Core versus Context," Inc., April 26, 2011, https://www.inc.com/tech-blog/interviewing-geoffrey-moore-core-versus-context.html

27 Geoffrey Moore, *Dealing with Darwin: How Great Companies Innovate at Every Phase of Their Evolution* (New York: Penguin, 2005).

28 "Digital Transformation Index II," Dell Technologies, August 2018, https://www.dellemc.com/resources/en-us/asset/briefs-handouts/solutions/dt_index_ii_executive_summary.pdf

29 Paul-Louis Caylar et al., "Digital in Industry: From Buzzword to Value Creation," McKinsey, August 2016, https://www.mckinsey.com/business-functions/digital-mckinsey/our-insights/digital-in-industry-from-buzzword-to-value-creation

30 James Manyika et al., "Digital America: A Tale of the Haves and Have-Mores," McKinsey Global Institute, December 2015, https://www.mckinsey.com/industries/high-tech/our-insights/digital-america-a-tale-of-the-haves-and-have-mores

31 "The Digital Transformation of Industry," Roland Berger Strategy Consultants, March 2015, https://www.rolandberger.com/en/Publications/The-digital-transformation-industry.html

32 Manyika et al., "Digital America."

33 "Digital Transformation Consulting Market Booms to $23 Billion," Consultancy, May 30, 2017, https://www.consultancy.uk/news/13489/digital-transformation-consulting-market-booms-to-23-billion

34 "2018 Revision to World Urbanization Prospects," United Nations, May 16, 2018, https://www.un.org/development/desa/publications/2018-revision-of-world-urbanization-prospects.html

35 Ramez Shehadi et al., "Digital Cities the Answer as Urbanisation Spreads," *National*, February 3, 2014, https://www.thenational.ae/business/digital-cities-the-answer-as-urbanisation-spreads-1.472672

36 "Factsheet," AI Singapore, 2018, https://www.aisingapore.org/media/factsheet/

37 "UAE National Innovation Strategy," United Arab Emirates Ministry of Cabinet Affairs, 2015.

38 Leslie Brokaw, "Six Lessons from Amsterdam's Smart City Initiative," *MIT Sloan Management Review*, May 25, 2016, https://sloanreview.mit.edu/article/six-lessons-from-amsterdams-smart-city-initiative/

39 "The 13th Five-Year Plan," US-China Economic and Security Review Commission, February 14, 2017, https://www.uscc.gov/sites/default/files/Research/The%2013th%20Five-Year%20Plan_Final_2.14.17_Updated%20%28002%29.pdf

40 "Digital Business Leadership," Columbia Business School Executive Education, n.d., https://www8.gsb.columbia.edu/exec ed/program-pages/details/2055/ERUDDBL

41 "Driving Digital Strategy," Harvard Business School Executive Education, n.d., https://www.exed.hbs.edu/programs/digs/Pages/curriculum.aspx

42 "MIT Initiative on the Digital Economy," MIT Sloan School of Management, n.d., http://ide.mit.edu

43 Gerald C. Kane, "'Digital Transformation' Is a Misnomer," *MIT Sloan Management Review*, August 7, 2017, https://sloanreview.mit.edu/article/digital-transformation-is-a-misnomer/

44 "Introducing the Digital Transformation Initiative," World Economic Forum, 2016, http://reports.weforum.org/digital-transformation/unlocking-digital-value-to-society-building-a-digital-future-to-serve-us-all/

45 "Societal Implications: Can Digital Create Value for Industry and Society?," World Economic Forum, June 2016, http://reports.weforum.org/digital-transformation/wp-content/blogs.dir/94/mp/files/pages/files/dti-societal-implications-slideshare.pdf

46 Anthony Stephan and Roger Nanney, "Digital Transformation: The Midmarket Catches Up," *Wall Street Journal*, January 19, 2018, http://deloitte.wsj.com/cmo/2018/01/19/digital-transformation-the-midmarket-catches-up/

47 Anja Steinbuch, "We Don't Measure Productivity Growth Correctly," T-systems, March 2016, https://www.t-systems.com/en/best-practice/03-2016/fokus/vordenker/erik-brynjolfsson-463692

48 David Rotman, "How Technology Is Destroying Jobs," *MIT Technology Review*, June 12, 2013, https://www.technologyreview.com/s/515926/how-technology-is-destroying-jobs/

49 "Digital Transformation of Industries: Societal Implications," World Economic Forum, January 2016, http://reports.weforum.org/digital-transformation/wp-content/blogs.dir/94/mp/files/pages/files/dti-societal-implications-white-paper.pdf

50 Derek Thompson, "Airbnb and the Unintended Consequences of 'Disruption,'" *The Atlantic*, February 17, 2018, https://www.theatlantic.com/business/archive/2018/02/airbnb-hotels-disruption/553556//

Chapter 3

1 Jacques Bughin et al., "Notes from the AI Frontier: Modeling the Impact of AI on the World Economy," McKinsey Global Institute, September 2018, https://www.mckinsey.com/featured-insights/artificial-intelligence/notes-from-the-ai-frontier-modeling-the-impact-of-ai-on-the-world-economy; and James Manyika et al., "Unlocking the Potential of the Internet of Things," McKinsey, June 2015, https://www.mckinsey.com/business-functions/digital-mckinsey/our-insights/the-internet-of-things-the-value-of-digitizing-the-physical-world

2 Louis Columbus, "Roundup of Cloud Computing Forecasts, 2017," *Forbes*, April 29, 2017, https://www.forbes.com/sites/louiscolumbus/2017/04/29/roundup-of-cloud-computing-forecasts-2017

3 Ibid.

4 Dave Cappuccio, "The Data Center Is Dead," Gartner, July 26, 2018, https://blogs.gartner.com/david_cappuccio/2018/07/26/the-data-center-is-dead/

5 "Cisco Global Cloud Index: Forecast and Methodology, 2016–2021," Cisco, November 19, 2018, https://www.cisco.com/c/dam/en/us/solutions/collateral/service-provider/global-cloud-index-gci/white-paper-c11-738085.pdf

6 Brandon Butler, "Deutsche Bank: Nearly a Third of Finance Workloads Could Hit Cloud in 3 Years," *Network World*, June 14, 2016, https://www.networkworld.com/article/3083421/microsoft-subnet/deutsche-bank-nearly-a-third-of-finance-workloads-could-hit-cloud-in-3-years.html

7 "Multicloud," Wikipedia, last updated February 18, 2019, https://en.wikipedia.org/wiki/Multicloud

8 Accuracy is reported as recall—i.e., what percentage of the historic engine failures were identified. Precision is the percentage of the time an engine failure actually occurred.

9 The training process is an optimization problem that often uses an algorithm called "stochastic gradient descent" to minimize the error between the output and the actual training data point.

10 Similar to machine learning, deep learning uses optimization algorithms such as stochastic gradient descent to set weights for each of the layers and nodes of the network. The objective is to minimize the difference between the network output and the actual training data point.

Chapter 4

1 Michael Armbrust et al., "A View of Cloud Computing," *Communications of the ACM* 53, no. 4 (April 2010): 50–58.

2 IBM, *Data Processor* (White Plains, NY: IBM Data Processing Division, 1966).

3 John McCarthy, "Memorandum to P. M. Morse Proposing Time Sharing," Stanford University, January 1, 1959, https://web.stanford.edu/~learnest/jmc/timesharing-memo.pdf

4 Control Program-67 / Cambridge Monitor System (GH20-0857-1), IBM, October 1971.

5 "Connectix Virtual PC to Be Offered by Top Mac CPU Manufacturers," Free Library, August 5, 1997, https://www.thefreelibrary.com/Connectix+Virtual+PC+to+be+Offered+by+Top+Mac+CPU+Manufacturers%3B+Mac...-a019646924

6 VMware, "VMware Lets Systems Operate Side by Side," reproduced from *USA Today Online*, November 3, 1999, https://www.vmware.com/company/news/articles/usatoday_1.html

7 "About Us," Defense Advanced Research Projects Agency, n.d., https://www.darpa.mil/about-us/timeline/arpanet

8 Paul McDonald, "Introducing Google App Engine + Our New Blog," Google Developer Blog, April 7, 2008, https://googleappengine.blogspot.com/2008/04/introducing-google-app-engine-our-new.html

9 "Microsoft Cloud Services Vision Becomes Reality with Launch of Windows Azure Platform," Microsoft, November 17, 2009, https://news.microsoft.com/2009/11/17/microsoft-cloud-services-vision-becomes-reality-with-launch-of-windows-azure-platform/

10 "IBM Acquires SoftLayer: The Marriage of Private and Public Clouds," IBM, 2013, https://www.ibm.com/midmarket/us/en/article_cloud6_1310.html

11 Peter Mell and Tim Grance, *The NIST Definition of Cloud Computing* (Gaithersburg, MD: National Institute of Standards and Technology, 2011).

12 Mark Russinovich, "Inside Microsoft Azure Datacenter Hardware and Software Architecture," Microsoft Ignite, September 29, 2017, https://www.youtube.com/watch?v=Lv8fDiTNHjk

13 "Gartner Forecasts Worldwide Public Cloud Revenue to Grow 17.3 Percent in 2019," Gartner, September 12, 2018, https://www.gartner.com/en/newsroom/press-releases/2018-09-12-gartner-forecasts-worldwide-public-cloud-revenue-to-grow-17-percent-in-2019

14 "Cisco Global Cloud Index: Forecast and Methodology, 2016–2021," Cisco, November 19, 2018, https://www.cisco.com/c/dam/en/us/solutions/collateral/service-provider/global-cloud-index-gci/white-paper-c11-738085.pdf

15 *State of the Internet: Q1 2017 Report*, Akamai, 2017, https://www.akamai.com/fr/fr/multimedia/documents/state-of-the-internet/q1-2017-state-of-the-internet-connectivity-report.pdf

16 "Gartner Forecasts Worldwide Public Cloud Services Revenue to Reach $260 Billion in 2017," Gartner, October 12, 2017, https://www.gartner.com/en/newsroom/press-releases/2017-10-12-gartner-forecasts-worldwide-public-cloud-services-revenue-to-reach-260-billionin-2017; and "Public Cloud Revenue to Grow."

17 Armbrust et al., "View of Cloud Computing."

18 "British Airways IT Outage Caused by Contractor Who Switched off Power: Times," CNBC, June 2, 2017, https://www.cnbc.com/2017/06/02/british-airways-it-outage-caused-by-contractor-who-switched-off-power-times.html

19 "Amazon Compute Service Level Agreement," Amazon, last updated February 12, 2018, https://aws.amazon.com/ec2/sla/

Chapter 5

1 Catherine Armitage, "Optimism Shines through Experts' View of the Future," *Sydney Morning Herald*, March 24, 2012, https://www.smh.com.au/national/optimism-shines-through-experts-view-of-the-future-20120323-1vpas.html

2 Gareth Mitchell, "How Much Data Is on the Internet?," *Science Focus*, n.d., https://www.sciencefocus.com/future-technology/how-much-data-is-on-the-internet/

3 "A History of the World in 100 Objects: Early Writing Tablet," BBC, 2014, http://www.bbc.co.uk/ahistoryoftheworld/objects/TnAQ0B8bQkSJzKZFWo6F-g

4 "Library of Ashurbanipal," British Museum, n.d., http://www.britishmuseum.org/research/research_projects/all_current_projects/ashurbanipal_library_phase_1.aspx

5 Mostafa El-Abbadi, "Library of Alexandria," *Encyclopaedia Britannica*, September 27, 2018, https://www.britannica.com/topic/Library-of-Alexandria

6 Mike Markowitz, "What Were They Worth? The Purchasing Power of Ancient Coins," *CoinWeek*, September 4, 2018, https://coinweek.com/education/worth-purchasing-power-ancient-coins/

7 Christopher F. McDonald, "Lost Generation: The Relay Computers," *Creatures of Thought* (blog), May 10, 2017, https://technicshistory.wordpress.com/2017/05/10/lost-generation-the-relay-computers/

8 "Delay Line Memory," Wikipedia, last updated December 20, 2018, https://en.wikipedia.org/wiki/Delay_line_memory#Mercury_delay_lines

9 "Timeline of Computer History: Memory & Storage," Computer History Museum, n.d., http://www.computerhistory.org/timeline/memory-storage/

10 "Timeline of Computer History: 1980s," Computer History Museum, n.d., http://www.computerhistory.org/timeline/1982/#169ebbe2ad45559efbc6eb357202f39

11 "The History of Computer Data Storage, in Pictures," Royal Blog, April 8, 2008, https://royal.pingdom.com/2008/04/08/the-history-of-computer-data-storage-in-pictures/

12 "Western Digital Breaks Boundaries with World's Highest-Capacity microSD Card," Western Digital, August 31, 2017, https://www.sandisk.com/about/media-center/press-releases/2017/western-digital-breaks-boundaries-with-worlds-highest-capacity-microsd-card

13 Gil Press, "A Very Short History of Big Data," Forbes, May 9, 2013, https://www.forbes.com/sites/gilpress/2013/05/09/a-very-short-history-of-big-data/

14 Doug Laney, "3D Data Management: Controlling Data Volume, Velocity, and Variety," META Group, February 6, 2001, http://blogs.gartner.com/doug-laney/files/2012/01/ad949-3D-Data-Management-Controlling-Data-Volume-Velocity-and-Variety.pdf

15 Seth Grimes, "Unstructured Data and the 80 Percent Rule," Breakthrough Analysis, August 1, 2008, http://breakthroughanalysis.com/2008/08/01/unstructured-data-and-the-80-percent-rule/

16 Steve Norton, "Hadoop Corporate Adoption Remains Low: Gartner," Wall Street Journal, May 13, 2015, https://blogs.wsj.com/cio/2015/05/13/hadoop-corporate-adoption-remains-low-gartner/

Chapter 6

1 Bernard Marr, "The Amazing Ways Google Uses Deep Learning AI," Forbes, August 8, 2017, https://www.forbes.com/sites/bernardmarr/2017/08/08/the-amazing-ways-how-google-uses-deep-learning-ai/#1d9aa5ad3204

2 Cade Metz, "AI Is Transforming Google Search. The Rest of the Web Is Next," Wired, February 4, 2016, https://www.wired.com/2016/02/ai-is-changing-the-technology-behind-google-searches/

3 Steven Levy, "Inside Amazon's Artificial Intelligence Flywheel," Wired, February 1, 2018, https://www.wired.com/story/amazon-artificial-intelligence-flywheel/

4 A. M. Turing, "Computing Machinery and Intelligence," Mind 59, no. 236 (October 1950): 433–60.

5 "Dartmouth Workshop," Wikipedia, last updated January 13, 2019, https://en.wikipedia.org/wiki/Dartmouth_workshop

6 John McCarthy et al., "A Proposal for the Dartmouth Summer Research Project on Artificial Intelligence," JMC History Dartmouth, August 31, 1955, http://www-formal.stanford.edu/jmc/history/dartmouth/dartmouth.html

7 James Pyfer, "Project MAC," Encyclopaedia Britannica, June 24, 2014, https://www.britannica.com/topic/Project-Mac

8 "Project Genie," Wikipedia, last updated February 16, 2019, https://en.wikipedia.org/wiki/Project_Genie

9 John Markoff, "Optimism as Artificial Intelligence Pioneers Reunite," *New York Times*, December 8, 2009, http://www.nytimes.com/2009/12/08/science/08sail.html

10 "USC Viterbi's Information Sciences Institute Turns 40," USC Viterbi, April 2012, https://viterbi.usc.edu/news/news/2012/usc-viterbi-s356337.htm

11 Will Knight, "Marvin Minsky Reflects on a Life in AI," *MIT Technology Review*, October 30, 2015, https://www.technologyreview.com/s/543031/marvin-minsky-reflects-on-a-life-in-ai/

12 Louis Anslow, "Robots Have Been about to Take All the Jobs for More Than 200 Years," Timeline, May 2016, https://timeline.com/robots-have-been-about-to-take-all-the-jobs-for-more-than-200-years-5c9c08a2f41d

13 "Workhorse of Modern Industry: The IBM 650," IBM Archives, n.d., https://www-03.ibm.com/ibm/history/exhibits/650/650_intro.html

14 "iPhone X: Technical Specifications," Apple Support, September 12, 2018, https://support.apple.com/kb/SP770/

15 "Apple iPhone X: Full Technical Specifications," GSM Arena, n.d., https://www.gsmarena.com/apple_iphone_x-8858.php

16 Marvin Minsky and Seymour Papert, *Perceptrons: An Introduction to Computational Geometry* (Cambridge: MIT Press, 1969)

17 Henry J. Kelley, "Gradient Theory of Optimal Flight Paths," *Ars Journal* 30, no. 10 (1960): 947–54.

18 Ian Goodfellow et al., *Deep Learning* (Cambridge: MIT Press, 2016), 196.

19 James Lighthill, "Artificial Intelligence: A General Survey," *Lighthill Report* (blog), survey published July 1972, http://www.chilton-computing.org.uk/inf/literature/reports/lighthill_report/p001.htm

20 Pedro Domingos, *The Master Algorithm: How the Quest for the Ultimate Learning Machine Will Remake Our World* (New York: Basic Books, 2015).

21 Peter Jackson, *Introduction to Expert Systems* (Boston: Addison-Wesley, 1998).

22 Bob Violino, "Machine Learning Proves Its Worth to Business," *InfoWorld*, March 20, 2017, https://www.infoworld.com/article/3180998/application-development/machine-learning-proves-its-worth-to-business.html

23 R. C. Johnson, "Microsoft, Google Beat Humans at Image Recognition," *EE Times*, February 18, 2015, https://www.eetimes.com/document.asp?doc_id=1325712

24 Jacques Bughin et al., "Artificial Intelligence: The Next Digital Frontier," McKinsey Global Institute, June 2017.

25 Michael Porter and James Heppelmann, "How Smart Connected Products Are Transforming Competition," *Harvard Business Review*, November 2014; and Porter and Heppelmann, "How Smart Connected Products Are Transforming Companies," *Harvard Business Review*, October 2015.

26 J. Meister and K. Mulcahy, "How Companies Are Mastering Disruption in the Workplace," McGraw Hill Business Blog, October 2016, https://mcgrawhillprofessional

businessblog.com/2016/10/31/how-companies-are-mastering-disruption-in-the-workplace/

27 Maureen Dowd, "Elon Musk's Billion-Dollar Crusade to Stop the A.I. Apocalypse," *Vanity Fair*, March 2017, https://www.vanityfair.com/news/2017/03/elon-musk-billion-dollar-crusade-to-stop-ai-space-x

28 Dan Dovey, "Stephen Hawking's Six Wildest Predictions from 2017—from a Robot Apocalypse to the Demise of Earth," *Newsweek*, December 26, 2017, http://www.newsweek.com/stephen-hawking-end-year-predictions-2017-755952

29 Richard Socher, "Commentary: Fear of an AI Apocalypse Is Distracting Us from the Real Task at Hand," *Fortune*, January 22, 2018, http://fortune.com/2018/01/22/artificial-intelligence-apocalypse-fear/

30 "Gartner Says by 2020, Artificial Intelligence Will Create More Jobs Than It Eliminates," Gartner, December 13, 2017, https://www.gartner.com/en/newsroom/press-releases/2017-12-13-gartner-says-by-2020-artificial-intelligence-will-create-more-jobs-than-it-eliminates

31 "Artificial Intelligence Will Dominate Human Life in Future: PM Narendra Modi," *Economic Times*, May 10, 2017, https://economictimes.indiatimes.com/news/politics-and-nation/artificial-intelligence-will-dominate-human-life-in-future-pm-narendra-modi/articleshow/58606828.cms

32 Jillian Richardson, "Three Ways Artificial Intelligence Is Good for Society," *iQ by Intel*, May 11, 2017, https://iq.intel.com/artificial-intelligence-is-good-for-society/

33 Gal Almog, "Traditional Recruiting Isn't Enough: How AI Is Changing the Rules in the Human Capital Market," *Forbes*, February 9, 2018, https://www.forbes.com/sites/groupthink/2018/02/09/traditional-recruiting-isnt-enough-how-ai-is-changing-the-rules-in-the-human-capital-market

34 *2017 Annual Report*, AI Index, 2017, http://aiindex.org/2017-report.pdf

35 AI was a major theme at Davos in 2017, 2018, and 2019. See, for example, "Artificial Intelligence," World Economic Forum annual meeting, January 17, 2017, https://www.weforum.org/events/world-economic-forum-annual-meeting-2017/sessions/the-real-impact-of-artificial-intelligence; "AI and Its Impact on Society," *Business Insider*, January 25, 2018, http://www.businessinsider.com/wef-2018-davos-ai-impact-society-henry-blodget-microsoft-artificial-intelligence-2018-1; and "Artificial Intelligence and Robotics," World Economic Forum Archive, n.d., https://www.weforum.org/agenda/archive/artificial-intelligence-and-robotics/

36 Nicolaus Henke et al., "The Age of Analytics: Competing in a Data-Driven World," McKinsey Global Institute, December 2016.

37 "LinkedIn 2018 Emerging Jobs Report," LinkedIn, December 13, 2018, https://economicgraph.linkedin.com/research/linkedin-2018-emerging-jobs-report

38 Will Markow et al., "The Quant Crunch: How the Demand for Data Science Skills Is Disrupting the Job Market," IBM and Burning Glass Technologies, 2017, https://public.dhe.ibm.com/common/ssi/ecm/im/en/iml14576usen/analytics-analytics-platform-im-analyst-paper-or-report-iml14576usen-20171229.pdf

39 Catherine Shu, "Google Acquires Artificial Intelligence Startup DeepMind for More Than $500 Million," *TechCrunch*, January 26, 2014, https://techcrunch .com/2014/01/26/google-deepmind/

40 Richard Evans and Jim Gao, "DeepMind AI Reduces Google Data Centre Cooling Bill by 40%," DeepMind, July 20, 2016, https://deepmind.com/blog/deepmind-ai-reduces-google-data-centre-cooling-bill-40/

41 Tony Peng, "DeepMind AlphaFold Delivers 'Unprecedented Progress' on Protein Folding," *Synced Review*, December 3, 2018, https://syncedreview.com/2018/12/03/ deepmind-alphafold-delivers-unprecedented-progress-on-protein-folding/

42 David Cyranoski, "China Enters the Battle for AI Talent," *Nature* 553 (January 15, 2018): 260–61, http://www.nature.com/articles/d41586-018-00604-6

43 Carolyn Jones, "'Big Data' Classes a Big Hit in California High Schools," *Los Angeles Daily News*, February 22, 2018, https://www.dailynews.com/2018/02/22/big-data-classes-a-big-hit-in-california-high-schools/

44 "Deep Learning Specialization," Coursera, n.d., https://www.coursera.org/ specializations/deep-learning

45 "Insight Data Science Fellows Program," Insight, n.d., https://www.insightdatascience .com/

46 Dorian Pyle and Cristina San José, "An Executive's Guide to Machine Learning," *McKinsey Quarterly*, June 2015, https://www.mckinsey.com/industries/high-tech/ our-insights/an-executives-guide-to-machine-learning

47 Philipp Gerbert et al., "Putting Artificial Intelligence to Work," Boston Consulting Group, September 28, 2017, https://www.bcg.com/publications/2017/technology-digital-strategy-putting-artificial-intelligence-work.aspx

Chapter 7

1 Mik Lamming and Mike Flynn, "'Forget-Me-Not' Intimate Computing in Support of Human Memory," Rank Xerox Research Centre, 1994.

2 Kevin Ashton, "That 'Internet of Things' Thing," *RFID Journal*, June 22, 2009, http:// www.rfidjournal.com/articles/view?4986

3 John Koetsier, "Smart Speaker Users Growing 48% Annually, to Hit 90M in USA This Year," *Forbes*, May 29, 2018, https://www.forbes.com/sites/johnkoetsier/2018/05/29/ smart-speaker-users-growing-48-annually-will-outnumber-wearable-tech-users-this-year

4 Derived from C. Gellings et al., "Estimating the Costs and Benefits of the Smart Grid," EPRI, March 2011.

5 Joe McKendrick, "With Internet of Things and Big Data, 92% of Everything We Do Will Be in the Cloud," *Forbes*, November 13, 2016, https://www.forbes.com/ sites/joemckendrick/2016/11/13/with-internet-of-things-and-big-data-92-of-everything-we-do-will-be-in-the-cloud

6 Jennifer Weeks, "U.S. Electrical Grid Undergoes Massive Transition to Connect to Renewables," *Scientific American*, April 28, 2010, https://www.scientificamerican .com/article/what-is-the-smart-grid/

7   James Manyika et al., "The Internet of Things: Mapping the Value beyond the Hype," McKinsey Global Institute, June 2015, http://bit.ly/2CDJnSL

8   "Metcalfe's Law," Wikipedia, last updated December 28, 2018, https://en.wikipedia .org/wiki/Metcalfe%27s_law

9   Alejandro Tauber, "This Dutch Farmer Is the Elon Musk of Potatoes," Next Web, February 16, 2018, https://thenextweb.com/full-stack/2018/02/16/this-dutch-farmer-is-the-elon-musk-of-potatoes/

10 James Manyika et al., "Unlocking the Potential of the Internet of Things," McKinsey, June 2015, https://www.mckinsey.com/business-functions/digital-mckinsey/our-insights/the-internet-of-things-the-value-of-digitizing-the-physical-world

11 Michael Porter and James Heppelmann, "How Smart Connected Products Are Transforming Competition," *Harvard Business Review*, November 2014; Michael E. Porter and James E. Heppelmann, "How Smart, Connected Products Are Transforming Companies," *Harvard Business Review*, October 2015.

12 "Number of Connected IoT Devices Will Surge to 125 Billion by 2030, IHS Markit Says," IHS Markit, October 24, 2017, http://news.ihsmarkit.com/press-release/number-connected-iot-devices-will-surge-125-billion-2030-ihs-markit-says

13 Manyika et al., "Mapping the Value."

14 "Automation and Anxiety," *The Economist*, June 25, 2016, https://www.economist .com/news/special-report/21700758-will-smarter-machines-cause-mass-unemployment-automation-and-anxiety

15 "Technology Could Help UBS Cut Workforce by 30 Percent: CEO in Magazine," Reuters, October 3, 2017, https://www.reuters.com/article/us-ubs-group-tech-workers/technology-could-help-ubs-cut-workforce-by-30-percent-ceo-in-magazine-idUSKCN1C80RO

16 Abigail Hess, "Deutsche Bank CEO Suggests Robots Could Replace Half the Company's 97,000 Employees," CNBC, November 8, 2017, https://www.cnbc .com/2017/11/08/deutsche-bank-ceo-suggests-robots-could-replace-half-its-employees.html

17 Anita Balakrishnan, "Self-Driving Cars Could Cost America's Professional Drivers up to 25,000 Jobs a Month, Goldman Sachs Says," CNBC, May 22, 2017, https:// www.cnbc.com/2017/05/22/goldman-sachs-analysis-of-autonomous-vehicle-job-loss.html

18 Louis Columbus, "LinkedIn's Fastest-Growing Jobs Today Are in Data Science and Machine Learning," *Forbes*, December 11, 2017, https://www.forbes.com/ sites/louiscolumbus/2017/12/11/linkedins-fastest-growing-jobs-today-are-in-data-science-machine-learning

19 Louis Columbus, "IBM Predicts Demand for Data Scientists Will Soar 28% by 2020," *Forbes*, May 13, 2017, https://www.forbes.com/sites/louiscolumbus/2017/05/13/ibm-predicts-demand-for-data-scientists-will-soar-28-by-2020

20 Nicolas Hunke et al., "Winning in IoT: It's All about the Business Processes," Boston Consulting Group, January 5, 2017, https://www.bcg.com/en-us/publications/2017/ hardware-software-energy-environment-winning-in-iot-all-about-winning-processes.aspx

21 Ibid.
22 Harald Bauer et al., "The Internet of Things: Sizing Up the Opportunity," McKinsey, December 2014, https://www.mckinsey.com/industries/semiconductors/our-insights/the-internet-of-things-sizing-up-the-opportunity
23 Tyler Clifford, "RBC's Mark Mahaney: Amazon Will Compete Directly with FedEx and UPS—'It's Just a Matter of Time,'" CNBC, November 8, 2018, https://www.cnbc.com/2018/11/08/amazon-will-soon-compete-directly-with-fedex-ups-rbcs-mark-mahaney.html
24 Porter and Heppelmann, "Smart, Connected Products."
25 Ibid.

Chapter 8

1 "'Whoever Leads in AI Will Rule the World': Putin to Russian Children on Knowledge Day," RT News, September 1, 2017, https://www.rt.com/news/401731-ai-rule-world-putin/
2 *Worldwide Threat Assessment of the U.S. Intelligence Community*, Office of the Director of National Intelligence, January 29, 2019, 5, https://www.dni.gov/files/ODNI/documents/2019-ATA-SFR-SSCI.pdf
3 Brendan Koerner, "Inside the Cyberattack That Shocked the US Government," *Wired*, October 23, 2016, https://www.wired.com/2016/10/inside-cyberattack-shocked-us-government
4 Devlin Barrett, "U.S. Suspects Hackers in China Breached about Four (4) Million People's Records, Officials Say," *Wall Street Journal*, June 5, 2015.
5 Tim Dutton, "An Overview of National AI Strategies," *Medium*, June 28, 2018, https://medium.com/politics-ai/an-overview-of-national-ai-strategies-2a70ec6edfd
6 *Annual Report to Congress: Military and Security Developments Involving the People's Republic of China*, US Department of Defense, May 16, 2018, https://media.defense.gov/2018/Aug/16/2001955282/-1/-1/1/2018-CHINA-MILITARY-POWER-REPORT.PDF
7 *Report to Congress*, US Department of Defense, May 2018.
8 Bill Gertz, "China in Race to Overtake U.S. Military in AI Warfare," *National Interest*, May 30, 2018, https://nationalinterest.org/blog/the-buzz/china-race-overtake-us-military-ai-warfare-26035
9 Robert Walton, "Report: Malware Traced to Ukraine Grid Attacks Could Be Used to Target US Grid," Utilitydive, June 14, 2017, https://www.utilitydive.com/news/report-malware-traced-to-ukraine-grid-attacks-could-be-used-to-target-us-g/444906/; and Morgan Chalfant, "'Crash Override' Malware Heightens Fears for US Electric Grid," *The Hill*, June 15, 2017, http://thehill.com/policy/cybersecurity/337877-crash-override-malware-heightens-fears-for-us-electric-grid
10 Stephanie Jamison et al., "Outsmarting Grid Security Threats," Accenture Consulting, 2017, https://www.accenture.com/us-en/insight-utilities-outsmart-grid-cybersecurity-threats; and Peter Maloney, "Survey: Most Utility Executives

Say Cybersecurity Is a Top Concern," Utilitydive, October 5, 2017, https://www
.utilitydive.com/news/survey-most-utility-executives-say-cybersecurity-is-a-top-
concern/506509/

11 Rebecca Smith, "U.S. Risks National Blackout from Small-Scale Attack," *Wall Street Journal*, March 12, 2014, https://www.wsj.com/articles/u-s-risks-national-blackout-from-small-scale-attack-1394664965

12 James Woolsey and Peter Vincent Pry, "The Growing Threat from an EMP Attack," *Wall Street Journal*, August 12, 2014, https://www.wsj.com/articles/james-woolsey-and-peter-vincent-pry-the-growing-threat-from-an-emp-attack-1407885281

13 *2008 EMP Commission Report*, Commission to Assess the Threat to the United States from Electromagnetic Pulse (EMP) Attack, April 2008, https://empactamerica.org/our-work/why-is-emp-a-threat/the-emp-commission/commission-reports/

14 "House Subcommittee Hearing: Electromagnetic Pulse (EMP): Threat to Critical Infrastructure, Panel II," US House Committee on Homeland Security, May 8, 2014, https://www.govinfo.gov/content/pkg/CHRG-113hhrg89763/html/CHRG-113hhrg89763.htm

15 Ted Koppel, *Lights Out: A Cyberattack, a Nation Unprepared, Surviving the Aftermath* (New York: Broadway Books, 2015), 15.

16 Rebecca Smith and Rob Barry, "America's Electric Grid Has a Vulnerable Back Door—and Russia Walked through It," *Wall Street Journal*, January 10, 2019, https://www.wsj.com/articles/americas-electric-grid-has-a-vulnerable-back-doorand-russia-walked-through-it-11547137112

17 John R. Allen and Amir Husain, "On Hyperwar," *Proceedings*, US Naval Institute, July 2017, https://www.usni.org/magazines/proceedings/2017-07/hyperwar

18 Kyle Mizokami, "Russia Tests Yet Another Hypersonic Weapon," *Popular Mechanics*, December 27, 2018, https://www.popularmechanics.com/military/weapons/a25694644/avangard-hypersonic-weapon/

19 *Providing for the Common Defense*, US Department of Defense, September 2018, https://media.defense.gov/2018/Oct/03/2002047941/-1/-1/1/PROVIDING-FOR-THe-COMMON-DEFENSE-SEPT-2018.PDF

20 David Axe, "The U.S. Air Force Is Headed for a Crash: Too Many Old Planes, Not Enough Cash," *Daily Beast*, December 25, 2018, https://www.thedailybeast.com/the-us-air-force-is-headed-for-a-crash-too-many-old-planes-not-enough-cash

21 *Summary of the 2018 National Defense Strategy of the United States of America*, US Department of Defense, 2018.

22 Report to Congress.

23 Stephen Losey, "Fewer Planes Are Ready to Fly: Air Force Mission-Capable Rates Decline amid Pilot Crisis," *Air Force Times*, March 5, 2018, https://www.airforcetimes.com/news/your-air-force/2018/03/05/fewer-planes-are-ready-to-fly-air-force-mission-capable-rates-decline-amid-pilot-crisis/

24 Axe, "U.S. Air Force."

25 *The FY 2019 Defense Overview Book*, US Department of Defense, February 13, 2018, https://comptroller.defense.gov/Portals/45/Documents/defbudget/fy2019/FY2019_Budget_Request_Overview_Book.pdf

26 Tajha Chappellet-Lanier, "DIU Chooses Ex-presidential Innovation Fellow to Fill Director Role," *Fedscoop*, September 24, 2018, https://www.fedscoop.com/michael-brown-diu-director/

27 *Providing for the Common Defense.*

28 Sean Kimmons, "After Hitting Milestones, Futures Command Looks Ahead to More," *Army News Service*, October 9, 2018, https://www.army.mil/article/212185/after_hitting_milestones_futures_command_looks_ahead_to_more

29 *Summary of the 2018 National Defense Strategy.*

30 Kris Osborn, "F-35 Combat Missions Now Have Operational 'Threat Library' of Mission Data Files," Fox News, October 24, 2018.

31 *Charting a Course for Success: America's Strategy for STEM Education*, National Science and Technology Council, December 2018, https://www.whitehouse.gov/wp-content/uploads/2018/12/STEM-Education-Strategic-Plan-2018.pdf

32 National Background Investigations Bureau, *Report on Backlog of Personnel Security Clearance Investigations*, Clearance Jobs, September 2018.

33 Lindy Kyzer, "How Long Does It Take to Get a Security Clearance (Q1 2018)?," Clearance Jobs, March 13, 2018, https://news.clearancejobs.com/2018/03/13/long-take-get-security-clearance-q1-2018/

34 Rick Docksai, "Continuous Evaluation System Aims to Streamline Security Clearance Investigations," Clearance Jobs, September 7, 2018, https://news.clearancejobs.com/2018/09/07/continuous-evaluation-system-aims-to-streamline-security-clearance-investigations/

Chapter 9

1 Christopher Harress, "The Sad End of Blockbuster Video: The Onetime $5 Billion Company Is Being Liquidated as Competition from Online Giants Netflix and Hulu Prove All Too Much for the Iconic Brand," *International Business Times*, December 5, 2013, http://www.ibtimes.com/sad-end-blockbuster-video-onetime-5-billion-company-being-liquidated-competition-1496962

2 Greg Satell, "A Look Back at Why Blockbuster Really Failed and Why It Didn't Have To," *Forbes*, September 5, 2014, https://www.forbes.com/sites/gregsatell/2014/09/05/a-look-back-at-why-blockbuster-really-failed-and-why-it-didnt-have-to/#6393286c1d64

3 Celena Chong, "Blockbuster's CEO Once Passed Up a Chance to Buy Netflix for Only $50 Million," *Business Insider*, July 17, 2015, http://www.businessinsider.com/blockbuster-ceo-passed-up-chance-to-buy-netflix-for-50-million-2015-7

4 Jeff Desjardins, "The Rise and Fall of Yahoo!," *Visual Capitalist*, July 29, 2016, http://www.visualcapitalist.com/chart-rise-fall-yahoo/

5 Ibid.

6 Ibid.

7   Associated Press, "Winston-Salem Borders Store to Remain Open despite Bankruptcy," *Winston-Salem Journal*, February 16, 2011, https://archive .is/20110219200836/http://www2.journalnow.com/business/2011/feb/16/3/winston-salem-borders-store-remain-open-despite-ba-ar-788688/

8   Ibid.

9   Ibid.

10 Ibid.

11 "Transformation d'Engie: Les grands chantiers d'Isabelle Kocher," *RSE Magazine*, January 4, 2018, https://www.rse-magazine.com/Transformation-d-ENGIE-les-grands-chantiers-d-Isabelle-Kocher_a2531.html#towZyrIe8xYVK106.99

12 "Isabelle Kocher: 'We Draw Our Inspiration from the Major Players in the Digital World,'" ENGIE, November 3, 2016, https://www.ENGIE.com/en/group/opinions/open-innovation-digital/usine-nouvelle-isabelle-kocher/

13 "Enel Earmarks €5.3bn for Digital Transformation," Smart Energy International, November 28, 2017, https://www.smart-energy.com/news/digital-technologies-enel-2018-2020/

14 Derek du Preez, "Caterpillar CEO—'We Have to Lead Digital. By the Summer Every Machine Will Be Connected,'" *Diginomica*, April 25, 2016, https://diginomica .com/2016/04/25/caterpillar-ceo-we-have-to-lead-digital-by-the-summer-every-machine-will-be-connected/

15 "A Q&A with 3M's New CEO Mike Roman," 3M Company, July 31, 2018, https:// news.3m.com/qa-3m-new-ceo-mike-roman

Chapter 11

1   Michael Sheetz, "Technology Killing Off Corporate America: Average Life Span of Companies under 20 Years," CNBC, August 24, 2017, https://www.cnbc.com/2017/08/24/technology-killing-off-corporations-average-lifespan-of-company-under-20-years.html

2   Thomas M. Siebel, "Why Digital Transformation Is Now on the CEO's Shoulders," *McKinsey Quarterly*, December 2017, https://www.mckinsey.com/business-functions/digital-mckinsey/our-insights/why-digital-transformation-is-now-on-the-ceos-shoulders

3   Dan Marcec, "CEO Tenure Rates," Harvard Law School Forum on Corporate Governance and Financial Regulation, February 12, 2018, https://corpgov.law.harvard .edu/2018/02/12/ceo-tenure-rates/

4   Sheeraz Raza, "Private Equity Assets under Management Approach $2.5 Trillion," *Value Walk*, January 31, 2017, http://www.valuewalk.com/2017/01/private-equity-assets-management-approach-2-5-trillion/

5   Preeti Varathan, "In just Two Hours, Amazon Erased $30 Billion in Market Value for Healthcare's Biggest Companies," *Quartz*, January 30, 2018, https://qz.com/1192731/amazons-push-into-healthcare-just-cost-the-industry-30-billion-in-market-cap/

6 Alison DeNisco Rayome, "Why CEOs Must Partner with IT to Achieve True Digital Transformation," *TechRepublic*, February 21, 2018, https://www.techrepublic.com/article/why-ceos-must-partner-with-it-to-achieve-true-digital-transformation/

7 Claudio Feser, "How Technology Is Changing the Job of the CEO," *McKinsey Quarterly*, August 2017, https://www.mckinsey.com/global-themes/leadership/how-technology-is-changing-the-job-of-the-ceo

8 Rayome, "CEOs Must Partner with IT."

9 Khalid Kark et al., "Stepping Up: The CIO as Digital Leader," *Deloitte Insights*, October 20, 2017, https://www2.deloitte.com/insights/us/en/focus/cio-insider-business-insights/cio-leading-digital-change-transformation.html

10 Ivan Levingston, "Health Stocks Fall after Amazon, JPMorgan, Berkshire Announce Health-Care Deal," *Bloomberg*, January 30, 2018, https://www.bloomberg.com/news/articles/2018-01-30/health-stocks-slump-as-amazon-led-group-unveils-efficiency-plans; and Paul R. LaMonica, "Jeff Bezos and His Two Friends Just Spooked Health Care Stocks," CNN, January 30, 2018, http://money.cnn.com/2018/01/30/investing/health-care-stocks-jpmorgan-chase-amazon-berkshire-hathaway/index.html

11 Levingston, "Health Stocks Fall"; and LaMonica, "Jeff Bezos."

12 Antoine Gourévitch et al., "Data-Driven Transformation: Accelerate at Scale Now," Boston Consulting Group, May 23, 2017, https://www.bcg.com/publications/2017/digital-transformation-transformation-data-driven-transformation.aspx

13 Jacques Bughin, "Digital Success Requires a Digital Culture," McKinsey, May 3, 2017, https://www.mckinsey.com/business-functions/strategy-and-corporate-finance/our-insights/the-strategy-and-corporate-finance-blog/digital-success-requires-a-digital-culture

14 Forrester Consulting, "Realizing CEO-Led Digital Transformations," Thought Leadership paper commissioned by C3.ai, May 2018, https://c3iot.ai/wp-content/uploads/Realizing-CEO-Led-Digital-Transformations.pdf

15 Peter Dahlström et al., "From Disrupted to Disruptor: Reinventing Your Business by Transforming the Core," McKinsey, February 2017, https://www.mckinsey.com/business-functions/digital-mckinsey/our-insights/from-disrupted-to-disruptor-reinventing-your-business-by-transforming-the-core

16 Gerald C. Kane et al., "Aligning the Organization for Its Digital Future," *MIT Sloan Management Review*, July 26, 2016, https://sloanreview.mit.edu/article/one-weird-trick-to-digital-transformation/

17 Adi Gaskell, "The Tech Legend Who Pays Staff to Upskill," *Forbes*, August 17, 2018, https://www.forbes.com/sites/adigaskell/2018/08/17/the-tech-legend-that-pays-staff-to-upskill/